DOING HISTORY

DOING HISTORY

AN INTRODUCTION TO THE HISTORIAN'S CRAFT

with workbook activities

WENDY POJMANN

BARBARA REEVES-ELLINGTON

KAREN WARD MAHAR

NEW YORK   OXFORD
OXFORD UNIVERSITY PRESS

Oxford University Press is a department of the University of Oxford.
It furthers the University's objective of excellence in research,
scholarship, and education by publishing worldwide.

Oxford   New York
Auckland   Cape Town   Dar es Salaam   Hong Kong   Karachi
Kuala Lumpur   Madrid   Melbourne   Mexico City   Nairobi
New Delhi   Shanghai   Taipei   Toronto

With offices in
Argentina   Austria   Brazil   Chile   Czech Republic   France   Greece
Guatemala   Hungary   Italy   Japan   Poland   Portugal   Singapore
South Korea   Switzerland   Thailand   Turkey   Ukraine   Vietnam

To Our Students

TABLE OF CONTENTS

PREFACE

Our project emerged when, after a series of discussions about texts currently in use in methodology and senior thesis courses, Charles Cavaliere, our perceptive editor, asked whether Wendy Pojmann would be interested in writing the sort of book she would want to use in her own courses. She immediately thought that, yes, she would love to have her idea of a single great resource at hand to assign to her students, but she also recognized that alone she did not possess the breadth of experience and knowledge she knew would be necessary to have the book Charles and she envisioned take shape. Wendy turned to her colleagues, Barbara Reeves-Ellington and Karen Ward Mahar, whose proven pedagogical creativity and skills she was sure would complement hers and whose own research and writing were current and being praised by respected peers. Thankfully, they accepted what we all recognized to be both a challenge and a great opportunity.

This two-part, hands-on methodology and research textbook provides a valuable resource for students enrolled in courses similar to Siena College's two-semester proseminar/capstone course sequence and other research-methods courses at the undergraduate and graduate levels. Students in historiography and methodology courses will find the text valuable for its intellectually engaging discussions of the discipline of history, which are enriched by concrete examples of published scholarship. At the same time, students preparing primary source–driven research projects will benefit from straightforward guidelines to the research and writing process that are supplemented by assessment exercises and skill-building assignments.

In this text we offer concrete examples of historical approaches and theories and have developed specific assignments to identify students' weaknesses, build their skills, and provide detailed guidelines to help them complete their work within the constraints of the academic term. We have integrated our efforts into a single, comprehensive narrative written in lively, accessible prose. We use simple, direct language to help students grapple with complex ideas and avoid the pitfalls that commonly entrap them as they learn to think and write as historians.

The text draws directly from our experiences as educators and scholars. It is rooted in classic teaching techniques that have endured for good reasons as well as in some of the latest strategies known to be effective with today's undergraduates, many of whom are now completing research seminars or senior capstone courses as part of the requirements of the major and pursuing graduate study. Our trial and error in the classroom and subsequent successes and shortcomings in working with students have led us to design and redesign a curriculum that works well for them. We are excited to be able to assign this book in our courses and confident that students and faculty across history departments and campuses of all sizes and configurations will find it to be a valuable resource.

ACKNOWLEDGMENTS

We thank the staff at Oxford University Press, especially our enthusiastic and intrepid editor, Charles Cavaliere, and his efficient assistant, Lynn Luecken. The production staff proved especially deft at shaping the layout for the workbook.

Many reviewers commented on the project at various stages and offered much welcome praise. They also challenged us to make the text as comprehensible as possible while maintaining intellectual rigor. We appreciate all their feedback, both positive and negative, and know the book is better for it. In particular, we would like to thank W. Brian Newsome, Elizabethtown College; Connie Shemo, SUNY-Plattsburgh; Kyle Livie, San Francisco State University; Scott K. Taylor, University of Kentucky; Lyn A. Blanchfield, SUNY-Oswego; William Caraher, University of North Dakota; Eric Josef Carlson, Gustavus Adolphus College; Bernard Cooperman, University of Maryland; Adam M. Schor, University of South Carolina; Sherry J. Katz, San Francisco State University; and Christina M. Jimenez, University of Colorado-Colorado Springs. Of course, any errors and omissions remain our own.

At Siena College we benefited from an environment that values great teaching and scholarship and seeks ways for faculty to model best practices for students. We thank James C. Harrison and Bruce W. Eelman for having introduced and developed the capstone course for which our text is intended and Karl Barbir for his leadership in the proseminar course that precedes it. Discussions in our department led to many of the ideas and examples used in this text. We particularly thank Tim Cooper III for sharing a few of his most effective assignments with us. Our close working relationship with the staff of the Standish Library, especially information literacy librarian Catherine Crohan and technology expert Sean Conley, allowed us to explore new ideas for helping students conduct research. We greatly value the contributions of two of our outstanding students, Nick Moscatiello and Francis Butler, who agreed to allow us to use their work but also recognize so many others whose struggles and triumphs have shaped our approach to teaching.

We extend our sincerest appreciation to the colleagues, archivists, librarians, and students we have had the benefit of working with over the years in institutions across the United States and Europe. Finally, we express our gratitude to the numerous friends and family members who supported us in fundamental, human ways.

ABOUT THE AUTHORS

Dr. Wendy Pojmann is Professor of History at Siena College. Her teaching interests include world history surveys, upper-level courses in modern European and women's history, and the methodology and senior thesis courses. Pojmann has spearheaded engagement on capstone learning with the wider academic community (*Perspectives in History*, March 2009; Council of Independent Colleges Conference, March 2011; American Historical Association roundtable on capstone courses, January 2013; Phi Alpha Theta biennial conference panel on the teaching of historiography to undergraduates, January 2014). Also an active scholar, Pojmann is the author of *Italian Women and International Cold War Politics, 1944–1968* (Fordham University Press, 2013) and *Immigrant Women and Feminism in Italy* (Ashgate, 2006). She edited *Migration and Activism in Europe since 1945* (Palgrave Macmillan, 2008) and has published in leading history journals, such as the *Journal of Women's History* and *Gender & History*. She is currently working on a book about the history of espresso in modern Italy.

Dr. Barbara Reeves-Ellington was until recently Associate Professor of History at Siena College. Her teaching interests include U.S. foreign relations, immigration, and globalization studies as well as the global and American history surveys and senior thesis course. An early advocate of information literacy learning and undergraduate research at Siena, she joined the scholarly debate on capstone courses with a co-authored article that appeared in *Perspectives in History* in March 2009. Reeves-Ellington has been a Fulbright scholar (Institute of Balkan Studies, Sofia, Bulgaria, 1999–2000) and fellow of the Leslie Center Humanities Institute, Dartmouth College (2002) and the Rothermere American Institute, University of Oxford (2012–2013). She is the author of *Domestic Frontiers: Gender, Reform, and American Interventions in the Ottoman Balkans and the Near East* (University of Massachusetts Press, 2013) and co-editor of *Competing Kingdoms: Women, Mission, Nation, and the American Protestant Empire, 1812–1960* (Duke University Press, 2010). She is currently writing a book about Anglo-American politics in nineteenth-century Istanbul.

Dr. Karen Ward Mahar is Professor of History at Siena College and the co-director of the American Studies Program. Her teaching interests include world history surveys, U.S. history since 1877, and upper-division courses on public history, women's history, gender, culture, business, and the history of capitalism in the United States. As an American Studies professor, Mahar taught the original capstone requirement in the School of Liberal Arts at Siena College. She was also an early advocate for information literacy and is interested in digital humanities and the role of user-generated data (SUNY Conversations in the Discipline: "Developing Metaliterate Learners: Transforming Literacy across Disciplines," December 2013). Author of *Women Filmmakers in Early Hollywood* (Johns Hopkins University Press, 2006, co-winner of the OAH Lerner-Scott Prize as a dissertation), Mahar is currently examining the masculinized culture of the American corporate elite for a book-length project and is active in several scholarly organizations as well as local museums and historic sites.

PART ONE
THE HISTORIAN'S CRAFT

CHAPTER ONE

What Is the Discipline of History?

"The best history is always informed by art," explained the celebrated historian C. Vann Woodward (1908–1999) in an interview with his former student James M. McPherson, now himself a famous historian of the United States.[1] That history is the study of the past that is *scientific* in method and *artistic* in its conclusions is a common explanation of the discipline of history. Some of the most highly regarded historians of yesterday and today have succeeded in making effective arguments about the past using ample evidence from a variety of sources, such as empirical data, archival documents, and oral histories, while at the same time crafting prose with the finesse of a literary fiction writer. Like biologists working in a laboratory, historians offer hypotheses and set out to support them with a collection of facts. They also lead their readers to think about big questions they have presented through a creative form, writing, much as a skilled painter would do through brushstrokes.

Of course, history is neither pure science nor pure art. It is, in fact, sometimes quite difficult to neatly label and classify. Some college and university administrators have even debated where history should be located within the structure of their institutions. Is history part of the **humanities**? Or is it a **social science**? History departments throughout the United States and England can be found in either grouping. Some people view history's primary role as fostering an understanding about what it means to be human and therefore tie it to the humanities along with literature, philosophy, art history, classics, and religious studies. Other people, however, focus on historical methodology as evidence based and thus categorize history as a social science, seeing it as more similar to political science, sociology, and psychology. Such overlapping classifications underscore the idea that history is both an art and a science. How much of each infuses its way into the writing of history depends very much on the historian and his or her own approach to understanding the past. This chapter addresses the question of what precisely history is as a discipline and examines ways in which history has been told since the advent of the written word. It also explains differences between popular and academic history in an attempt to set apart the methodologies and skills students develop in college and university classrooms.

What historical study is not

Far too frequently, many people tend to view history as a static set of names and dates from the past, as a kind of record that changes little unless someone discovers new pieces

---

[1.] James McPherson, "History: It's Still about Stories," *The New York Times* on the Web, September 19, 1999 (http://www.nytimes.com/books/99/09/19/bookend/bookend.html/).

of information and adds them to the larger picture. Even in the minds of many students of history, only a previously unknown diary of a famous person, a cache of hidden government documents, or the restoration of a damaged artifact are the sorts of items that have the power to alter our understandings of the past. Sometimes this is indeed the case. In *The Pope and Mussolini*, for example, David Kertzer turned to little-studied documents in the Vatican Archives to show the ways in which Italian fascist dictator Benito Mussolini enlisted the support of Pope Pius XI. Kertzer, using sources such as spy records, argues that contrary to the popular view of the Vatican fighting fascism, the two leaders actually closely cooperated for more than a decade until Italy's alliance with Germany turned more virulently anti-Semitic.[2] Tangible, documented facts, such as the ones Kertzer consulted in his study, are important evidence to consider when rewriting history, but reinterpretations do not necessarily depend on them. Some individuals, in fact, are not swayed by new discoveries at all because they see little purpose to historical study. They argue that so little changes over time that it is useless to study what happened before. Pronouncements such as "throughout history people have always" or assertions that rely on notions such as "it is human nature to" are indications of the kind of perspective that holds that although numerous, disparate events may occur, women and men have remained basically unchanged since the beginning of time. According to proponents of this point of view, human motivations, emotions, and desires have been constant and consistent and are at the source of all that has happened in the world, even if the names and details of events have changed. For instance, many people believe that love and marriage have remained largely unchanged throughout the centuries despite ample evidence to the contrary. Historian Stephanie Coontz, for example, has successfully demonstrated that the Western notion of intimate, companionate marriage has not always been prevalent but is instead a product of the Victorian age when ideals of individualism contributed to the search for emotional and sexual satisfaction within the bonds of a lifelong union.[3] Still another camp of historical naysayers recognizes that history does imply change but questions whether anybody is paying attention. The old cliché that history repeats itself is typically followed by a mention that so few of us notice when this happens that it may not be worth looking for patterns. What good is it to alert others to a similar sequence of events taking place now if no one intends to do anything differently this time around anyway? Such arguments are common among people who view warfare as inevitable.

Of course, each of the perspectives above fails to account for dynamism in historical study and points to the fact that few educated people, even within the **academy** itself, really understand what it is that professional historians do. Unfortunately, the misconception that historians are just storytellers who keep alive knowledge about days long gone persists. Some people believe historians are mainly men who have stored hundreds of facts in their heads to rattle off when the opportunity presents itself. Popular culture frequently depicts history teachers and professors as monotonous drones who call on

---

[2.] David Kertzer, *The Pope and Mussolini: The Secret History of Pius XI and the Rise of Fascism in Europe* (New York: Random House, 2014).

[3.] Stephanie Coontz, *Marriage, a History: From Obedience to Intimacy or How Love Conquered Marriage* (New York: Viking, 2005).

unsuspecting students to recite names and dates in front of their classmates before cueing up a long, boring documentary film about wartime experiences. Sometimes history educators appear in television shows and films as the not-so-bright teacher and coach, insulting, of course, to both. After all, if all that is at stake is memorizing a timeline, any average Joe or Jane can do it, right? Even when former students fondly remember a history teacher, they do not always have a correct idea of what comprehensive study of the discipline entails. A common fallacy, for example, is that historians are mainly preoccupied with what might have happened, the "what-ifs?" of history. What would have happened if the South had won the Civil War? What if President Harry Truman had decided not to use the atomic bomb on Japan? Such questions can generate lively discussions and debates but are not really a fundamental part of the academic discipline of history. Instead, historians are preoccupied with alternatives in another sense. That is, they often search for new or other evidence and interpretations of the past to show that there are many differences and variations among people of multiple times and places. The world was not and does not have to be seen in a singular way. As we discuss in detail in Chapter Three, **historiography**, or the history of writing history, allows for the possibility that there are many compelling and ordinary tales to share and evaluate.

Arguably, the ways in which history is taught in many high schools, especially when the focus is on passing state mandated exams, perpetuate the sorts of stereotypes outlined above. In college classrooms, too, students generally spend more time learning content than engaging in historical writing themselves, which contributes to the perpetuation of the view that what is really important to know is what happened, not how or why it did. Instructors may struggle to incorporate methodology and skills development into their courses, particularly when there is so much material they would like to cover over the limited time they have at their disposition. However, in a rigorous course of study, students do begin to develop an awareness of historical debate and historiography, to interpret the use of **primary** and **secondary source evidence**, and to analyze the application of theory to history—all activities professional historians undertake themselves. By moving beyond a timeline of events that occurred in the past, history students come to realize that the discipline is anything but static. Since the time of the Greeks, historians have defined the past through analysis, not just storytelling, and have been aware that history can be approached from multiple vantage points. Historians have long been concerned with interpreting, not just recounting, the meanings of specific events as well as examining big transformations over time. The best historians also succeed in helping their contemporaries to develop a sense of what men and women were like in the past and even to feel empathy for them. After all, without historical actors, change carries little significance.

DOES HISTORY REPEAT ITSELF? UNDERSTANDING HISTORICAL ANALOGIES

The answer is no. We would like to be clear. History does not repeat itself. It simply cannot. No two situations can ever be identical. The historical actors involved are different people with their own experiences. Circumstances are not the same. Context is made up of so many disparate factors that it is just not possible for all of them to line up together and

continued on next page

continued

allow us to reach the same conclusions about two distinct moments. We can, however, look to analogous conditions to help us recognize similarities between past and present. Analogies suggest that certain times are like others, not that they are the same, and therefore they should offer us the opportunity to reach more nuanced or precise considerations of key factors in two events. Analogies also offer historians moments for underscoring the importance of history in understanding how we got to where we are now. Caution should be taken even here, however. How many of us have seen images depicting the hated German dictator Adolf Hitler on one side and any recent U.S. president on the other? This is an example of a terrible analogy. No matter how much someone may despise George W. Bush or Barack Obama, to compare either of them to a man responsible for the mass executions of more than 6 million Jews and 6 million others labeled as undesirables is simply reckless. In contrast, to use knowledge about the horrors of the Holocaust and apply it to the study of other genocides in the hopes of preventing new ones from occurring can be an effective use of history. Unfortunately, this has not been the case, as the genocides in Rwanda, the Sudan, and the former Yugoslavia show us. During the 2008 economic crisis that hit the United States, economic historians turned to the Great Depression for possible insights and solutions but mainly just came to realize that the periods were so distinct that only a few ideas, such as public works projects, seemed relevant. James J. Sheehan, past president of the American Historical Association, has described inaccuracies historical commentators made when comparing the American occupations of Germany in 1945 and Iraq in 2003, noting that primary source evidence indicates that the Germans, unlike the Iraqis, were not opposed to the American presence. Sheehan writes, "Without [the proper tools] what we extract from history will not be grains of wisdom but the fool's gold all too often offered as precious lessons from the past. *What* we learn from history depends entirely on *how* we do it."[4] Students of history should strive to do it with care.

NOTE

[4] James J. Sheehan, "How Do We Learn from History?" *Perspectives on History*, January 2005, http://www.historians.org/publications-and-directories/perspectives-on-history/january-2005/how-do-we-learn-from-history/.

History and context

Perceptions of the ways in which history shifts are key to establishing what history is and how it should be studied, assuming it should be studied at all. The notion that history is **linear** is relatively modern; ancient peoples saw time as **cyclical**. More than two thousand years ago, the Maya created calendars based on the cycles of the moon, stars, and planets. The Maya held that some of these cycles began and ended while others continued and they established a sense of order in a context of instability. By the time of the scientific revolution of the seventeenth century, however, concepts of time had dramatically changed. Modern men and women conceived of time as a line advancing into the future. In other words, people today tend to see history as moving forward in time, whereas the people of early premodern societies did not believe there was a direction to history or held that historical moments recurred. A linear approach to history developed within the Judeo-Christian tradition that accounted for a beginning and an end to history, marked by God's creation of the universe at the start and concluding with the appearance of the Messiah or the return of Christ. Modern historical study, and in particular the creation of a category of professional historians, can be said to date to the work of Leopold von Ranke, a German **Romanticist** of the nineteenth century who developed the concept of *historicism*. According to von Ranke, historicism holds that the past and the present are distinct. We must have some recognition of the autonomy of history to be able to understand the present and not see it as a continuous process. In other words, the past is different from the present. It is not made up of the same values, emotions, or actions. People have not always behaved as they do now. Therefore, we should not make the assumption that humans have always behaved in the same ways because they are human. Instead, the past requires a **context**. We need to know something about the larger picture to understand how people react to situations. Von Ranke suggested applying the scientific method to historical study. Using empirical evidence, such as recorded data, as well as primary source materials, historians could form a clearer idea of why and how events unfolded. Historicism treats history as a process in which there is cause and effect. There is always a reason behind human responses; things do not just "happen." It is the historian's task to discover and share what those reasons are. Historicism lends itself to narrative history; the recounting of the past emerges as a story with a beginning, a middle, and an end. History in this sense follows a timeline of events in which facts take center stage and a sort of truth of history told from an objective standpoint unfolds. The historian's role in this case is to decide where the beginning, middle, and end are situated, which facts are worth emphasizing, and whose vantage point is the objective one. The Oxford History of the United States, for example, is a series especially known for its comprehensive narratives of countries and periods and its ability to reach broader audiences than more analytical texts. As renowned historian and series editor C. Vann Woodward explained in an interview, "'Narrative history is the end product of what historians do. The narrative is where they put it together and make sense of it for the reader. Other types of history—analytical, quantitative, comparative history—as important as they are, are mainly for other historians."[5] Woodward advocated writing for general readers who appreciated strong storytelling.

Metahistorians work within the framework of historicism but search for an underlying meaning to history that can be uncovered by seeking to understand its mechanisms, an ordered set of patterns that can be studied for certain regularities. By examining history through a primary motor of change, such as economics or demographics, metahistorians look to offer a scientific measure of human progress. For example, in his award-winning text *Pathfinders*, Felipe Fernandez-Armesto bases the history of global exploration on the ideas of human cultural divergence and convergence to show that traversing the globe is a distinctly human phenomenon.[6] Metahistorians such as

---

[5.] McPherson, "History: It's Still about Stories."

[6.] Felipe Fernandéz-Armesto, *Pathfinders: A Global History of Exploration* (New York: Norton, 2007).

Alfred Crosby and William McNeill have successfully demonstrated that approaching big historical questions through narrower lenses can open up crisp and exciting interpretations of the past. Both Crosby and McNeill demonstrated that pathogens, as well as people and goods, traveled the world. By examining the impact of some of the living organisms (including animals, plants, and diseases) that crossed the Atlantic during the late fifteenth century, Crosby's 1972 *The Columbian Exchange* became one of the founding works of environmental history. McNeill's 1976 *Plagues and Peoples* introduced readers to the long-term global impact of disease on political, economic, and cultural development.[7]

Of course, not all historians have followed Ranke's characterization of historical study. *Postmodernists*, such as Michel Foucault and Jacques Derrida, for example, whom we will discuss at length in the next chapter, reject the notion of a scientific or objective truth of history. They hold that history is constructed, especially through language, and argue for a discursive study of the past that considers power/knowledge systems as a driving force behind historical change. Followers of the Annales School, too, rejected Ranke's historicism in favor of a problem-based approach to historical inquiry that attempted to be both more empirical and total. Although the Annales historians, most famously the school's founder, French historian Fernand Braudel (1902–1985), were overwhelmingly scientific in their methodologies, some social scientists in disciplines such as anthropology and sociology have seen little relevance for the study of history at all. They argue that cultural differences, kinship structures, linguistic traditions, and other factors may have more bearing in understanding differences among peoples than do actual historical events. In her classic *Coming of Age in Samoa*, for example, anthropologist Margaret Mead (1901–1978) focused on how cultural rather than temporal differences shape adolescence. Mead found that Samoan girls made a smoother transition to adulthood than their American counterparts because Samoans prioritized discussions of matters such as sexuality and death.[8] Working from different methodologies than historians, social scientists may also apply theory to conceptions of society without accounting for particularities or larger processes. Moreover, many individuals simply believe that instincts and emotions drive human actions and argue that they have changed little over time. If love, hate, greed, desire, and compassion have consistently informed human interactions, what is to be gained by knowing the larger context? Historical anachronisms frequently result from this line of thinking, however. We cannot simply apply elements from one period to another without creating large inaccuracies. For instance, historians, such as Philippe Ariès, have shown that the idea of a distinct and protected period labeled childhood emerged in Western Europe in the seventeenth century.[9] To accuse medieval Frenchmen of abusing their children by not sending them to school or letting them play would be erroneous because it would mean placing modern values on people who lived before the values took shape. It is also problematic to suggest

---

[7.] Alfred W. Crosby, *The Columbian Exchange: Biological and Cultural Consequences of 1492* (Westport, CT: Greenwood, 1972); William H. McNeill, *Plagues and Peoples* (Garden City, NY: Anchor Press, 1976).

[8.] Margaret Mead, *Coming of Age in Samoa: A Psychological Study of Primitive Youth for Western Civilization* (New York: Morrow, 1928).

[9.] Philippe Ariès, *Centuries of Childhood: A Social History of Family Life* (New York: Alfred A. Knopf, 1962).

that individuals in the past were "ahead of their time" since doing so ignores the historical context that produced them.

Another form of **ahistoricism** practiced in the academy, even by some historians, comes from *presentists*. These individuals maintain that history is fixed and stable but that our ideas about it change based on what is going on now. They assess progress and decline in the past based on how things have turned out in the present. A couple of big problems result from evaluating history from an exclusively contemporary vantage point. First, presentism can lead to *nostalgia*, or to a decrying of loss of the good old days when everything was better. Common myths disseminated by nostalgists are that life was simpler and easier, that roles were better defined and understood, and that people knew their "place" in the world. Such beliefs tend to be used for political purposes, especially to glorify a past in which women, African Americans, or less desirable "others" had little voice or to uphold the traditional values of a group that feels threatened by perceived change. Second, presentism may lead to apathy. If life is challenging today, it means it can only get better from here. Why bother to try to do anything about it when you can just wait and see what happens? The advantages of evaluating history on its own terms should not be lost behind contemporary preoccupations. To discount the richness of the past and see only thousands of years of sameness is to lose the ability to comprehend how we got to where we are now.

WHAT IF? THE PURPOSES AND PITFALLS OF COUNTERFACTUAL QUESTIONS

In his Pulitzer prize–winning book *Embers of War: The Fall of an Empire and the Making of America's Vietnam* (2013), Fredrik Logevall offers some illuminating examples of how prominent historians engage in counterfactuals. His intention is to demonstrate that nothing in history is preordained. The Vietnam War was not inevitable. Logevall reminds us that, for actors who had responsibility for making decisions in the past, "the future was merely a set of possibilities."[10] In this vivid account of Vietnamese attempts to gain their independence from France through diplomacy and war, French efforts to salvage their empire, and increasing U.S. engagement in southeast Asia in the early years of the Cold War, Logevall shows how key players wrestled with those possibilities and how they succeeded, or failed, to imagine alternative outcomes. They always had choices but the choices were always constrained by context.

Logevall shows us that counterfactuals serve a valid purpose when they are used by players in the past to help make decisions. In early 1947, for example, Viet Minh leader Ho Chi Minh encountered the possibility that the French might succeed in enticing away elements of the Vietnamese population that, until then, had supported him. What if French diplomats made a deal with a rival leader who could undermine his position? Logevall tells us that this kind of question was not merely an entertaining counterfactual; on the contrary, it was "much discussed in the Viet Minh inner councils and among informed analysts elsewhere."[11] French military officers also envisaged different outcomes as they planned battle strategy. In the autumn of 1946, as the French prepared to strike Viet Minh positions in the north of Vietnam, General Jean Étienne Valluy was determined to hold the key port city of Haiphong but nevertheless feared its possible loss: "But what if Haiphong could not be

continued on next page

continued

held?"[12] In 1952, as French politicians became increasingly concerned about the cost of waging war in Vietnam in terms of lives and finances, they also debated the wisdom of relying on material aid from the United States, fearing that American politicians sought to replace France as a colonial power in southeast Asia. What if U.S. advisors became "too meddlesome" and the U.S. administration tried to "tie strings to its aid"?[13] What would the French do? And how would the United States respond? These were real questions that real people had to contend with. Evidence from their deliberations helps us understand the complexities they faced as they imagined different outcomes.

Logevall enters quite different territory when he asks whether things might have turned out differently had people made different decisions. What if Viet Minh General Vo Nguyen Giap had not delayed his attack on French positions at Dien Bien Phu from January 25, 1954, to March 13 of that year?[14] What if French General Henri Navarre had not chosen to make a stand at Dien Bien Phu?[15] Logevall engages in a series of arguments and counterarguments. He nonetheless acknowledges that we can never know how the battle might have developed had Giap and Navarre acted differently. Giap did not attack in January. Navarre did make a stand at Dien Bien Phu. The Viet Minh did win the war. The French did lose Vietnam. Logevall also raises what ifs on the U.S. side but likewise rejects the counterfactuals. What if President Franklin Delano Roosevelt had lived beyond 1945? Logevall argues that it is "not fanciful" to believe that Roosevelt might have changed history by persuading the French to relinquish their colony; but, he counters, "Roosevelt died."[16] Future American administrations might have decided against engagement in Vietnam. Successive presidents and secretaries of state debated the options, and they chose to intervene. Logevall teaches us that we must not allow the distorting influences of hindsight to distract us from the evidence. What we can imagine is merely conjecture.

NOTES

[10] Fredrik Logevall, *Embers of War: The Fall of an Empire and the Making of America's Vietnam* (New York: Random House, 2013), xvii.

[11] Ibid., xviii.

[12] Ibid., 155.

[13] Ibid., 312.

[14] Ibid., 424–25, 445.

[15] Ibid., 543.

[16] Ibid., 710.

Defining history

So what is history? We asserted that it is part art and part science. We challenged the notion that it is a mere recounting of facts. We questioned historical understandings based solely on present-day considerations. But, as professional historians we want to begin to define the discipline. We would like to suggest that history is a form of **collective memory** that is key in the formation of identity. Identity, of course, encompasses many groups of people. One of the challenges historians face is to decide who is "in" or "out" of a particular group at a particular moment and how group identities change over time. Shifts in identity often reveal major historical trends, in fact. Historians writing about traditionally underrepresented groups, for example, such as African Americans or women, have noted that definitions of who exactly is "black" or what makes someone a "woman" have not been consistent. Legal decisions, social customs, and considerations of class, among other variables, have affected perceptions of blackness and womanliness in specific contexts. Nationality, a central marker of collective memory and identity, must also be understood in historical terms. Groups that define themselves based on a national identity and then make claims to actual statehood are at the center of countless historical developments. The breakup of the Austro-Hungarian Empire at the conclusion of World War I, for example, allowed for the later creation of independent states such as Czecho-slovakia and Hungary. Nationality can be tied to traditions, to ethnicity, to what language people speak, which religion they practice, and what they eat for dinner. Many Japanese, for example, claim that eating Japanese food and speaking the Japanese language is what makes them Japanese and contributes to national unity. In Italy, the prevalence of regional dialects and food traditions, pasta versus polenta, for instance, hindered the unification of that country in the late nineteenth century. Part of having a history as a people is therefore based on writing and disseminating it or, as in the case of many Native American tribes, passing it along through oral tradition. For example, scholar Peter Nabokov has written about the importance of the self-transmission and interpretation of history to Native American tribes in their identity formation and survival.[17] His careful study reminds us that professional historians must take care not to flatten identities and assess how they construct or represent historical groups and for what purpose. They must also keep in mind the importance of collective identity. After all, history is not the story of one individual but that of many individuals. Biographers, too, must consider relationships and context when telling the story of a particular person, since they cannot rely solely on the memories of the subject at hand.

The concept of social memory is intrinsically linked to identity formation and thus to the definition of history. Memory is based on the reflection of experiences that have already occurred. It means having a recollection of the past. An awareness of the past is not the same thing as the development of social memory, however. On one hand, participants in the same event may not remember it in the same way. In the famous 1950 Japanese film *Rashomon*, for example, four eyewitnesses to the murder of a samurai and the rape of his wife recount the event in dramatically different ways. The story of one person can add an important dimension to a historical account, but it is generally not sufficient for a professional historian to base an entire argument on that singular tale. We would not expect a peasant, an urban worker, and an aristocrat to have the same experience of the French Revolution. Collective memory, as told through multiple first-hand accounts, is thus much more reliable. On the other hand, historical actors may instead seek to use an event to generate knowledge about shared experiences and construct an identity. In this case, collective memory is different from history because

---

[17.] Peter Nabokov, *A Forest of Time: American Indian Ways of History* (New York: Cambridge University Press, 2002).

individuals use it for their own purposes, especially by selecting certain moments to recount while intentionally ignoring others. For instance, ultranationalist histories, such as Nazi leader Albert Speer's *Inside the Third Reich*, use historical "facts" to recount false glories and distort reality.[18] Recalling the past requires that the historian pay attention to accuracy and to matters that are not necessarily those with which we are preoccupied in the present. Social memory that primarily serves particular political, social, or cultural needs should be discarded in favor of greater accuracy. Clearly, even when we are working from a largely unbiased perspective, we know that memories can be misleading or incomplete and they will always be filtered by a current vantage point. The historian's task is to see the larger picture and attempt to reach an honest conclusion about it based on available evidence.

When and where

One of the greatest values of history as a discipline is its ability to sort and categorize small and large blocks of time to establish periods, which is a useful tool for characterizing common elements and understanding change. Historians have established a vocabulary for discussing particular eras. If we use the term Renaissance, for example, we understand it to encompass the years between roughly the fourteenth and seventeenth centuries, depending on the region of Europe. American history is commonly divided at the Civil War, with the terms antebellum and postbellum used to distinguish the decades before and after the Civil War itself (1861–1865). New historiographical interpretations have also led to modifications of terminology. Referring to the Middle Ages as the Dark Ages is no longer accepted practice since the idea of darkness suggests that no learning or progress took place. Instead, medievalists now make distinctions among the Early, High, and Later Middle Ages to more accurately define periods. Dating conventions have also changed. Archaeologists and historians have moved away from the use of BC, "before Christ," and AD, "*anno Domini,*" meaning in the year of our Lord, in favor of BCE and CE, "before the common era" and "common era," in recognition of the non-universalism of Christianity.

So exactly when and where has history occurred? Although the response to such a question might seem facile or obvious, historians do not universally agree on which eras and places make suitable subjects for historical study. At the edges of what is considered history are the very distant and the very recent past. Most historians look to ancient Mesopotamia as the birthplace of civilization. On the banks of the Tigris and Euphrates rivers, in modern-day Iraq, the hero Gilgamesh ruled his kingdom, a stable agricultural society that developed writing. Of course, civilization is a loaded term. It implies that nonnomadic peoples who kept written records were more advanced than their more mobile counterparts who practiced oral traditions for the passing on of information about their communities. Nevertheless, many Western or world civilization instructors choose Mesopotamia as their starting point. They perhaps make a nod to earlier groupings of humans and the role of cave paintings in understanding how they lived as well.

[18.] Albert Speer, *Inside the Third Reich: Memoirs* (Bronx, NY: Ishi Press International, 2009).

Egypt, Greece, and Rome also fall in the realm of ancient civilizations, but not all history departments have specialists in these fields. Some colleges and universities place studies of the early centuries in other disciplines, such as classics and archeology. Egyptology is even noteworthy for having its own name. Arguably the placement of these fields outside history has to do with the availability and types of sources they utilize. Ruins of ancient cities, such as Pompeii, epic mythological tales, such as the *Iliad*, and the carefully preserved bodies of ancient kings, such as that of Ramses II (1303 BCE–1213 BCE), require special research skills outside the purview of traditional historical study. On the other side of the temporal continuum is the contemporary era. Most historians define contemporary as pertaining to events after World War II or to occurrences in the second half of the twentieth century through today. A few conservative scholars, however, question whether matters of very recent or current interest can really be evaluated as historical. They suggest that the methodologies used in fields such as political science or sociology may be more appropriate for discussing the immediate past. For instance, it may be premature to evaluate the historical significance of the Egyptian Revolution of 2011 while unrest is ongoing there. What such questions about history reveal, in any case, is that the discipline is broad, covering centuries of time, all parts of the world, and multiple facets of human life.

Primary sources

A further distinguishing characteristic of the field of history is primary source research. In Chapter Four, we will discuss locating and evaluating primary sources in greater detail. It is worth pointing out now, however, that historians work from multiple types of original documents to develop and refine their understandings of the past. They utilize primary sources as evidence in their scholarship. They ask students to read and interpret primary sources in class. Primary sources are like windows to the past. They allow us to gain greater access to the lives of the people who came before us. Government documents tell us something about how state bureaucracies function. Diaries and memoirs provide intimate insights into individual experiences. Portrait paintings depict men, women, and children of long ago and provide us with an idea of how they dressed and furnished their homes. Still and moving images have captured battles and revolutions. Letters, whether between leaders or lovers, provide details about events as well as clues about personalities. Church records list full names, birth and death dates, and special moments such as baptisms and marriages. A primary source can be nearly any surviving record that provides a firsthand account of the past. Generally speaking, the closer the record to the time the event occurred the better, but reflections by individuals of one era on another time can also offer valuable insights into their mind-set. Historians tend to privilege the written word but also consider visual and oral sources valid. Of course, the number and quality of original documents historians have at their disposal vary because of limitations on what has survived. Conservation is key, not only in terms of maintaining the integrity of a text but also in terms of decisions made by people in the past as to what was worth holding onto and what they preferred to discard. The natural elements, limitations of space, warfare, and other considerations also factor into what accounts for documentation. For instance, whereas government officials may have realized the importance of keeping archival records, members of the nonelite classes may have considered their family histories of little interest to others and thus threw away information about genealogy when lines came to an end or no one wanted to preserve them. Regardless of their form, quantity, or condition, in any case, primary sources set history apart from the other humanities and social science disciplines.

Historical subfields

Historical study includes numerous subfields, such as Marxist history and postcolonial history, which will be discussed at length in Chapter Two and relies on interdisciplinary approaches to offer more detailed or finely tuned accounts of the past, no matter how distant or recent they may be. It is worth considering here, however, the ways in which historians have advanced the discipline by developing broad approaches through which to recount and interpret earlier times. *Political history*, according to some individuals, is history. It is certainly one of the oldest forms of historical writing, practiced by ancient historians such as Herodotus (Greece), Tacitus (Rome), and Sima Qian (China). Political history is particularly concerned with rulers, whether kings, emperors, or presidents, and focuses especially on the development of the communities they govern, whether fiefdoms, empires, or nation-states. The organization of governing bodies and relations with neighboring or distant lands take center stage in most political histories. Military history is often subsumed under this category as well, especially as it is connected to conflicts and wars generated by breakdowns in internal and external relations. Political history also serves as the guiding timeline of history in general. King Henry VIII ruled England from 1509 to 1547. John Wilkes Booth assassinated President Abraham Lincoln on April 14, 1865. The Berlin Wall fell on November 9, 1989. The politics surrounding each of these moments fills volumes of historical texts. Moreover, important political events delimit particular historical periods, providing starting and ending points for narrative storytelling. Although historical subdisciplines, such as women's history, have offered challenges to the traditional periodizations of political history, for the most part these periodizations persist.

Social and *economic* history, *intellectual* history, and *cultural* history are the other major areas of concentration in traditional historical study. Each has produced many subfields, which we will address in depth in the following chapter. Here we merely wish to offer some parameters of the main themes of these specializations. Social and economic history dates to the time of Karl Marx (1818–1883), whose model of historical materialism based on class conflict served as a way of accounting for major shifts in the social and economic climate that were also directly tied to political upheavals, such as the French Revolution. In the more recent past, however, especially beginning in the 1960s, social and economic history has come to be understood as history from below. Rather than focusing on the elites, historians became more concerned with the experiences of "ordinary" men and women. Daily life attracted their interest. How did people live long ago? What were their homes like? What kinds of work did they do? Did they engage in leisure activities? Did their religious lives determine their social roles in their families or communities? In what ways did men's and women's social consciousness influence changes in private and public life? In history told from below, social and economic structures emerge as more significant than do treaty negotiations or royal successions. Intellectual history examines ideas as a key component of change. Unlike philosophers, who are primarily concerned with the ideas themselves, intellectual historians seek to understand the ways in which ideas become motors of transformation. They analyze great philosophical texts, such as those produced by René Descartes or Friedrich Hegel, but also value what academic philosophers may discount as minor works, such as some of the writings of Montesquieu and Voltaire, **Enlightenment philosophes**, because those sources offer a clearer picture of the relationship between ideas and actions. Cultural historians emphasize artistic, literary, and popular traditions in their work. They seek to explain creative representations of social elements. What do films, photographs, or paintings tell us about the people of particular periods or places? How do folk tales reproduce the values of particular communities? How does culture reflect not only the individuals who make and consume it but also their larger contexts? Such questions about both high and low culture drive much of the work undertaken by cultural historians whose contributions have offered counternarratives to those offered by political or economic historians. Jordan Sand, a cultural historian of modern Japan, for example, has shown that in the early twentieth century, changing patterns in the ways bourgeois intellectual Japanese conceived of the space of their homes contributed to the transformation of the meanings of tradition and modernity and influenced the new leaders of the Meiji state.[19] Of course, few historians remain embedded in just one of these traditions of historical writing, and as we will see in the following chapter, historical methodologies have expanded and deepened, especially since the 1960s. Few professional authors today would define themselves solely in one major field.

Popular versus academic history

History is indeed a broad discipline that attracts many followers. Any visit to a bookstore (admittedly an increasingly infrequent occurrence) will take in customers browsing the history shelves. We might notice that the sections devoted to military history, especially the Civil War and World War II, include numerous books, many of them bestsellers. We would be able to identify titles dealing with highly popular and especially villainous monarchs and other world leaders, such as Adolf Hitler or Joseph Stalin. We might pick up on the recent trend of covering a particular year in history—*Paris 1919*, *Six Months in 1945*, and *1861: The Civil War Awakening* are but a few examples.[20] Many of us, however, might be at a bit of a loss to discern between the popular and academic texts. The vast majority of books available in large bookstore chains are intended for a general reading public. Although many popular history books are frequently based on legitimate scholarship and written in lively, engaging prose, this is not always the case.

[19.] Jordan Sand, *House and Home in Modern Japan: Architecture, Domestic Space and Bourgeois Culture, 1880–1930* (Cambridge, MA: Harvard University Press, 2004).

[20.] Margaret MacMillan, *Paris, 1919: Six Months That Changed the World* (New York: Random House, 2002); Michael Dobbs, *Six Months in 1945: FDR, Stalin, Churchill, and Truman—From World War to Cold War* (New York: Knopf, 2012); Adam Goodheart, *1861: Civil War Awakening* (New York: Knopf, 2011).

WHAT IS A (HISTORICAL) FACT?

Historians are often thought to be adept at memorizing facts about the past and using those facts to tell accurate stories. Good historians add interesting anecdotes but, according to this view, all historians will tell the same basic story about the Battle of Hastings, or the French Revolution, or World War II, because there is one body of facts for each of these events. But is history a collection of facts? In 1961, British historian E. H. Carr famously rejected what he called the "common sense" notion of history that "there are certain basic facts which are the same for all historians and which form, so to speak, the backbone of history." In a lecture entitled "The Historian and His Facts," Carr told his audience that it was just as much a fact that they arrived at the auditorium thirty minutes earlier as it was that the Battle of Hastings was fought in 1066. Carr argued that a fact only becomes "historical" when historians select it and promote it as significant.[21] Historical facts are not born, they are made. It would be irrational to deny that a battle took place in Hastings in 1066, but its significance required the subjective interpretation of historians. Today even the category of "fact" is questioned. Postmodern theories of language and knowledge have destabilized the idea of a fact by questioning how we know what we know and exposing the ways that language and power shape our understanding of reality. Carr anticipated postmodernity when he rejected the concept of one true history based on objective facts (a **metanarrative**). Historical metanarratives smooth out the chaos of the past and present a unified story that appears to be objective and true, but rest on power structures that are invisible because they have naturalized a particular view of history and the facts that underpin it. Consider the ideas about racial differences that were accepted as facts only a few generations ago. One need not read theory to grasp how language and power can order the world. Pull a dollar bill out of your wallet. What makes a piece of paper with green ink work as money? You cannot turn it in for its equivalent in gold or silver. That piece of paper is worth one dollar because the United States says it is, and we believe it. Facts do not speak for themselves, and historians do not just memorize the past. We constantly question it.

NOTE

[21.] Edward Hallett Carr, *What Is History?* (1961; repr. New York: Penguin Books, 1987), 10–11.

The authors of many mass-marketed books base their work almost exclusively on secondary sources, which they reinterpret, rather than on original primary source research. Their frameworks tend to be simple and limited to allow them to veer away from analysis in favor of storytelling for its own sake. Some popular history authors do not really engage in historical writing at all and instead utilize some of the ahistorical approaches mentioned previously, such as writing about what might have happened, rather than what actually did, or making a case for current political perspectives by misrepresenting the past. *Historical myths* are often created and upheld through popular history writing and can be difficult to dismantle. In the history of the United States, for instance, the so-called Founding Fathers are almost untouchable. Historians who attempt to offer critical or at least nuanced interpretations of the ideas, contributions, and lives of the American signatories to the Declaration of Independence may be labeled unpatriotic. Of course, national myths exist around the world and people invoke them especially in times of crisis or great difficulty to help unite a populace. In this sense, they can be seen as a positive, if naive, use of history. However, myths can also perpetuate hatred founded on "history" as defined by a particular group. The myth of Aryan superiority, for example, was central to the development of Nazi Germany's anti-Semitic racial state. Problems emerge when readers are eager to learn about history without having the knowledge or background to be able to recognize solid historical scholarship. It is important to keep in mind that facts can be manipulated or invented to suit the needs of the author and her intended audience. Publication alone is not an indication of validity. Popular titles are a great entry point to cultivate and sustain an interest in history but intellectual rigor is the mark of good work. Over their course of study, history students learn that professional academic historians produce work that is both in depth and vast and that they attempt to advance their specific fields of study as well as the discipline in general. When it is well crafted, academic history can also be popular by appealing to a broad reading public. The achievements of National Book Award winners Peter Gay, a historian of the Enlightenment, and John W. Dower, a historian of modern Japan, offer ample proof that serious history writing can reach a wide audience.

How can students tell the difference between an academic, or scholarly, book and one intended primarily for general readers without having to read all of it? Is it necessary to analyze the author's approach and major themes before deciding whether a text meets certain markers of good scholarship? A quick examination of a book is generally sufficient to determine whether it is scholarly or not. A good place to start is with the publisher. Many academic presses are housed within universities and thus identify with their standards and principles. Oxford University Press, Duke University Press, and Indiana University Press, for example, all enjoy close relationships with their parent institutions and their profits go back into the universities that support them. They operate as nonprofit organizations. A number of highly regarded scholarly presses, however, such as Brill, Ashgate, and Berghahn, are not affiliated with a university. There are also a few presses that include the word university in their names but are not affiliated with an academic institution and are not generally esteemed by scholars. So "University Press" should not be the only tool used for evaluating whether a book is scholarly. The author's credentials, especially if they are provided on the dust jacket of the book or on a page inside the text, can offer some additional assessment material. Does the author hold the highest degree in her field, for history the Ph.D., and currently work at a college or university? Has he published other articles or books or delivered papers or talks at academic conferences? Of course, professional journalists also produce excellent historical work but because their audiences are usually larger, they may aim for impact rather than analysis. A final place to turn for a rapid examination of the level of scholarship is the sources, namely the notes and bibliography. Has the author consulted a number of primary sources as well as secondary materials? If the subject matter of the book focuses on a non–English speaking part of the world, has the author also utilized texts in the related languages? If the author of a book on the French Revolution had not consulted any or few French language sources, we would be suspicious of her command of the field. Greater mastery of a language opens resources and offers the sort of cultural understanding that is difficult to acquire without access to such sources or through translated works and thus indicates a higher level of scholarship. Ideally, all of the considerations mentioned here should be taken into account when evaluating whether a text is scholarly or popular and therefore how history students might best use it. If still in doubt, consulting your instructor or college librarian is a good idea.

Becoming a professional historian

Not all students of history become professional historians, but they can all carry their love for the past as well as their finely tuned skills into careers in business, the legal profession, the nonprofit sector, or most any other area of their choosing. Professional historians instead engage in a variety of activities that may not always seem evident to everyone outside, or even inside, the academy. Most historians teach at the college or postgraduate level and write and make presentations regarding their specialized fields. The specific demands of particular colleges, universities, and other academic institutions often determine how much of each activity professors perform, but generally speaking, they keep up with the latest developments in their main teaching and research fields. They also attempt to impart their knowledge to students as they guide and encourage them to become competent historians themselves. As we have explained in this chapter, becoming a historian means recognizing that history is part art and part science; good history incorporates both. Historians seek to understand something meaningful about people who lived in the past—how they governed, what they produced, what their daily lives were like, etc.—sometimes in an attempt to help us understand a little bit more about how we arrived at where we are and sometimes just to show us that things were not always as they are now. Historians make it possible to decode meanings from long ago and to sort out the major characteristics of large and small changes that have unfolded over delimited periods of time. They consult evidence in the form of primary sources and use it to build arguments about the men and women who preceded us or who may still be among us. Historians work from a multiple array of methodologies and vantage points. They strive to achieve high standards and maintain integrity in their work. The best historians also show us that history is worthwhile because it is so often complex, challenging, disheartening, or encouraging. It can also be great fun.

CHAPTER TWO

The Development of the Discipline of History

At the beginning of each semester, freshmen history majors at our college meet with the department's faculty to discuss which areas of history most interest them and what they hope to study. A majority of students identify a part of the world or a historical era as the reason that first attracted them to the discipline. They often express an overwhelming fascination with American history and with the history of warfare. Some new students specifically state that they hope to learn more about the history of the Civil War because they visited the historic battlefield site in Gettysburg, Pennsylvania, where some of the bloodiest fighting of the conflict took place in July of 1863. Other students declare an interest in Renaissance Italy or the contemporary Middle East. Significantly, few students say that they have studied or would like to study areas such as social history or popular culture. Rarely do any students mention any sort of comparative focus, such as relations between the United States and Latin America.

Such introductory meetings reveal some of the limitations of students' experiences of history in high school but also the ways in which popular and public history tend to be presented. A burgeoning passion for history is certainly an important aspect of students' success in their studies, but it is telling that few students know anything about the development of the discipline. And seldom are they aware that their professors are also researchers who work on specialized topics. One faculty member may be an expert in early modern French religious history, another in women and empire in sub-Saharan Africa, and another in Japanese culture since the Meiji Restoration. These same faculty members might offer courses on the Enlightenment, modern world history, and the history of Southeast Asia, respectively, since teaching fields tend to be broader than research specializations. Undergraduate students are not always likely to know much about the approaches their professors take until they have worked with them and begun to develop their own understandings of what history is.

Although arguably fewer professional historians today than twenty years ago would define themselves within narrow parameters and declare themselves exclusively to be a certain type of historian, most do tend to work with subject matters, primary sources, and theoretical backgrounds that characterize them as practitioners of a specified field. Whether through their own writing or in class preparations, history professors will usually favor a particular vantage point, even when introducing others. In terms of research, *total history*, or an attempt by one person to cover everything about a topic, is rarely possible and it is not necessarily desirable. However, there are benefits to examining even the same event from multiple perspectives, which is what often happens in a classroom setting. When a student signs up for a course simply titled The Civil War, she might not be aware that her professor has likely designed the course to incorporate multiple historical vantage points. For instance, the story of the battle of Gettysburg looks quite different if told by a military historian who focuses on such matters as troop movements, the layout of the terrain, the impact of multiple forms of artillery, and the skills of battlefield commanders than one written by a social historian who perhaps considers instead where the soldiers lived, their class backgrounds, the impact of their service on their families and communities, and so on. An intellectual historian working from the framework of discourse analysis might examine Gettysburg in terms of its cultural production, especially written texts, to see how the battle was presented and represented in accounts by leaders, soldiers, and observers alike to create particular narratives and meanings of what transpired there, depending on the power relationships that existed among its participants. In each case, it is clear that every historical methodology makes valuable contributions to understanding the past. This chapter aims to make students aware of how and why different fields of history have developed and to think about the ways in which different approaches to the telling of history allow us to interpret any historical event, person, place, or time from multiple vantage points.

Politics, economics, and society

As we discussed in the previous chapter, *political history* is the oldest form of history and remains essential to the discipline to this day. The study of the formation and dissolution of fiefdoms, kingdoms, empires, and nation-states and the rulers who governed them has driven much about our knowledge of how human societies were organized in the past. How centralized were ruling bodies? Was there one leader or rule by many? How was citizenship defined and practiced? Why did neighbors enter into conflicts with each other? What led some leaders to seek territories elsewhere and what happened because of their exchanges with other peoples? These are just a few of the questions political historians have been asking for centuries. From the old classic *Decline and Fall of the Roman Empire* published by Edward Gibbon in 1776 to Paul Kennedy's 1987 classic *The Rise and Fall of the Great Powers*, political historians have been looking to uncover the reasons behind the successes and failures of particular states and empires.[1] Gibbon, for example, accounted for the fall of Rome by pointing to the rise of Christianity and its new values and the waning willingness of its citizens to sacrifice all for the good of the empire. Gibbon argued that a loss of "civic virtue" weakened unity in Rome and allowed the "barbarian kingdoms" to encroach on its territories and structures until it finally collapsed. Ideas and values are ultimately what upset established political structures, according to Gibbon's account. In contrast, Kennedy has argued that technology and economics are the keys to political success and primacy. Through an examination of major world powers, such as Japan, China, the United States, the Soviet Union, and the Western European states, Kennedy posited that relationships among states in terms of economic growth and stability as well as their military prowess in peace and war determine their place in the chain of power. In other words, even if all the powers are experiencing economic challenges, what matters most is which states are better off in relation to the others. Both Gibbon and Kennedy did much more than recount the story of

---

[1] Edward Gibbon, *The Decline and Fall of the Roman Empire: The Modern Library Collection* (New York: Modern Library, 2013); Paul M. Kennedy, *The Rise and Fall of the Great Powers: Economic Change and Military Conflict from 1500 to 2000* (New York: Random House, 1987).

ancient Rome or relations among the great powers; they provided arguments and interpretations of the workings of politics and diplomacy. Importantly, they considered factors other than high politics alone in accounting for shifts in power.

Political history has become increasingly global and interdisciplinary in recent years, even if the nation-state remains a central focus. Historians of nationalism, for example, often look to outside forces to explain how states influence each other and how certain ideas about government and citizenship enter into the collective consciousness. Lucy Riall has shown that during the mid-nineteenth century as Italy was unifying its many diverse, independent regions into a single nation-state, the United States was experiencing tensions between the interests of its strong single states and the central government.[2] The Italians, although accustomed to deep-seated regional traditions, viewed American federalism with suspicion since it appeared to be failing and looked instead to models of centralized parliamentary democracies led by a monarch, such as in France and Great Britain, when devising a new government. Diplomatic historians, long interested of course in state relations, foreign policy, and alliances, also study international governing bodies such as the United Nations (since 1945) or regional cooperative groups such as the pan-African Congress (1900–1945) to reach conclusions about their reach and efficacy. Military historians preoccupied with the weapons, strategies, and skills of volunteer and conscripted national armies also look at the roles and influence of nonnationals, such as mercenaries in the Spanish civil war. The influence of fields such as women's history is also apparent in an international approach to political history. Charlotte Bunch, for example, has examined the relationship of the advancement of a human and women's rights agenda in the history of nongovernmental organizations and their influence in policy revisions in state governments and at the United Nations level.[3]

Political historians have the advantage and disadvantage of being able to draw from ample primary sources, especially government documents. When researchers have access to plentiful sources that are deposited in a centralized location, such as the Library of Congress in the United States, it means they do not have to spend a lot of time determining where to find materials. However, having an abundance of documents to examine can be quite overwhelming and time-consuming. Historians working with these types of sources, particularly in the modern era, must make careful decisions about what to include and exclude from their studies. In fact, not all government documents are readily available. Classified materials usually require a lengthy waiting period before they can be consulted and many governments around the world are not open democracies. They do not allow outsiders or even their own citizens to access most records. The significance of limiting entry into archives can be enormous. For example, once the former Soviet Union allowed researchers into its once highly protected storage facilities, historians such as Vladislav Zubok were able to use declassified documents, such as those held by the Politburo, to offer crucial new insights into the inner workings of the

---

[2.] Lucy Riall, *Risorgimento: A History of Italy from Napoleon to Nation-State* (New York: Palgrave Macmillan, 2009).

[3.] See, for instance, Charlotte Bunch, *Passionate Politics: Essays 1968–1986* (New York: St. Martin's Press, 1987), and Charlotte Bunch and Niamh Reilly, *Demanding Accountability: The Global Campaign and Vienna Tribunal for Women's Human Rights* (New York: United Nations Development Fund for Women, 1994).

Soviet government and its Communist Party.[4] Political history, although often thought of as a traditional and even conservative field, is clearly anything but static and stale and it continues to fascinate popular and scholarly readers of all levels.

Biography is a historical field that derived from political history, especially from an interest in the lives of loved and hated leaders of the past. Political biographies have an ancient lineage and writings on some of history's most famous figures from antiquity, such as Alexander the Great (356–323 BCE), continue to proliferate. Roman historian Quintus Curtius Rufus captured Alexander's legacy in his Latin biography written in the first decades after the birth of Christ. Peter Green's 1991 *Alexander of Macedon* remains among the top sellers in historical biography.[5] In modern history, the lives and leadership styles of American presidents attract broad readership and the attentions of both popular and academic historians. Historian Jules Tygiel's *Ronald Reagan and the Triumph of American Conservatism* (2004), for example, accounts for Reagan's personal success in becoming the fortieth president of the United States but also succeeds in explaining how Reagan was able to usher in a new spirit of conservatism at a critical moment in American history by appealing to such values as personal responsibility and self-determination.[6] Political biographers have also introduced readers to impressive women rulers such as Catherine the Great of Russia, whose transformation into an "enlightened despot" in the eighteenth century was brilliantly captured by John T. Alexander.[7] Of course, the "big names" of political history remain among those most studied and written about, but biographers have also turned to lesser-known figures, particularly to identify them with an age or to mark an important transformation. Like Alexander's book, Amy Kelly's *Eleanor of Aquitaine and the Four Kings* shows the difficulties women faced in navigating the inner workings of high politics and examines how they commanded and retained respect among their advisors, armies, and subjects.[8]

Biographers write broadly about all sorts of nonpolitical figures as well, such as entertainers, business leaders, athletes, and even college presidents. In fact, some professional academic historians have dismissed the genre of biography because of what they see as a lack of attention to "serious" subjects. Others question the use of sources based on conjecture, as might be the case in a sensationalized biography. Professional historians know, however, that a true historical framework is based on the sources the biographer uses and his or her attention to the larger context of the period. Government documents are often central to understanding individual political figures but personal papers, diaries, photos or other images, interviews, and many other sorts of records can offer important insights as well. Original research and new ways of thinking about an individual's influence inform the biographer's process. As we mentioned in the previous chapter, since we are always approaching the past from our current place in history, the

---

[4.] Vladislav Zubok, *A Failed Empire: The Soviet Union in the Cold War from Stalin to Gorbachev* (Chapel Hill: University of North Carolina Press, 2007).

[5.] Peter Green, *Alexander of Macedon 356–323 B.C.: A Historical Biography* (Berkeley: University of California Press, 1991).

[6.] Jules Tygiel, *Ronald Reagan and the Triumph of American Conservatism* (New York: Longman, 2004).

[7.] John T. Alexander, *Catherine the Great: Life and Legend* (New York: Oxford University Press, 1989).

[8.] Amy Kelly, *Eleanor of Aquitaine and the Four Kings* (Cambridge, MA: Harvard University Press, 1991).

kinds of questions we may ask about a man or woman who lived before us will change with the concerns of our day. That explains why new texts of much studied individuals continue to be published. There is never a definitive work that ends all further discussion. Moreover, the successful historical biographer will shed light on his subject's relevance to his own era as well as to those who followed. Although many exceptional figures appear to be just that, exceptional, they rarely truly are. In fact, it is anachronistic to suggest that even someone as brilliant as Leonardo da Vinci was "ahead of his time." He may have been much more intelligent and creative than the average Florentine of his day, but he was also the product of his surroundings. A good historical biographer such as Charles Nicholl knows he must understand da Vinci's influences and inspirations to represent him as the quintessential "Renaissance man."[9] Sources and interpretative frameworks take historical biographers beyond the individual and place them in the collective, a defining aspect of history (see Chapter One).

Economic history is another, if more recent, traditional historical field. Economic historians view productive forces as the primary motor of history, accounting for even the most significant political developments primarily in economic terms. Paul Kennedy's work mentioned above, for example, highlights the ways in which economics and politics influence each other. Military historians have often pointed to the ability of states to successfully mobilize a wartime economy as indicative of how they will perform during a conflict. Economic history as a distinct field, however, emerged with Jean-Baptiste Say (1767–1832) and David Ricardo (1772–1823) and became especially known through the work of theorist Karl Marx (1818–1883), who was interested in how class consciousness led to social and political revolts. According to Marx in his *Communist Manifesto* (1848), all history was the history of class struggle. What he meant was that once an oppressed class developed an understanding of the injustices committed against it, its leaders began to organize to overthrow the class in power. Marx insisted that this had happened during the French Revolution (1789–1799) when the bourgeoisie, which by then had recognized its exclusion from the powers and privileges enjoyed by the aristocracy, rose up and claimed its right to rule. In the modern, industrial age, Marx argued that the bourgeoisie had taken control of productive forces and then excluded the working class, or proletariat, from the direct benefits of its labor. In time, and as capitalism imploded on itself, the workers, too, would revolt against their oppressors. Since Marx firmly believed in the progressive force of history, he saw a future in which all men and women would be realized through their productive activity and class would no longer exist. Marx, of course, had the political objective of coming to the aid of mid-nineteenth-century urban workers who were suffering from an uneven process of industrial growth. He was not strictly a professional historian.

Many historians, however, have found Marx's economic concepts to be extremely valuable in interpreting the past. The **dialectical** process laid out in Marx's analysis of class conflict, his emphasis on material conditions as fundamental to human existence and experience, and his attention to labor as a central organizing principle of communities have led historical research in many exciting directions. It is not necessary to be a

---

[9]. Charles Nicholl, *Leonardo da Vinci: Flights of the Mind* (New York: Viking Penguin, 2004).

red flag–waving communist revolutionary to appreciate the far-reaching impact of economic conditions across time and place. For instance, an emphasis on class led Marxist historians away from the circles of elite rulers to studies of ordinary men and women who shared an identity based on their working conditions. Historian Georges Lefebvre, like Marx, looked to the tumultuous time of the French Revolution to understand the roles peasants played in the transformation out of feudal agricultural systems. His 1924 *The Peasants of the North during the French Revolution* was pivotal in the coining of the term **history from below**, which means beginning with the lower classes rather than the upper classes when studying the past.[10] E. P. Thompson's 1963 *The Making of the English Working Class* also followed in the Marxist tradition by emphasizing how material conditions contributed to identity formation in the working classes, whose values differed from those of other classes.[11] Thompson did not take a deterministic approach in his work, however, and in fact argued that the working class very much made itself. That is, workers acted as a group aware of their own economic conditions, as can be seen in the example of the Luddites, a group of English laborers who destroyed the machines that were threatening their livelihoods. Historians today are perhaps less likely to embrace the Marxist label than in Lefebvre's or Thompson's day, but the influence of Marxist economic history continues. Few historians would now ignore the role of class in determining individual and collective identity and most historians recognize the importance of economics in historical change even if they stress other factors more. They also turn more often to economic data, such as production and wages, as primary sources.

Another specialized field in economic history is *business history*, which refers to the development and influence of particular businesses or industries and the individuals who run and work for them. Some business historians may emphasize how a company influenced growth in a certain region or part of the world or examine the political reach and power of specific corporations. During Japan's peak of economic productivity in the 1980s, for example, historians published widely on the country's rapid growth seeking explanations in its past. William Wray's *Mitsubishi and the N.Y.K., 1870–1914* was among numerous texts on the *zaibatsu*, or family businesses that formed the basis of the Japanese economy and led to its post–World War II successes.[12] Once Japan fell victim to a housing bubble and economic decline in the early 2000s, historians again looked for answers in the way Japanese business practices emerged, suggesting that perhaps there was something ethereal about the Japanese character. In addition to companies, influential business leaders such as Walt Disney and Steve Jobs have fascinated biographers and led them to uncover illuminating facts about how companies are run under these sorts of visionaries but also how large companies infiltrate daily life and popular culture. Business historians have also turned their attention to the very development of corporate culture itself. Who is in and who is out as companies expand and shape their images? What is the relationship between corporations and legislation in such areas as the

---

[10] Georges Lefebvre, *Les Paysans du Nord pendant la Révolution française* (Lille: O. Marquant, 1924).

[11] E. P. Thompson, *The Making of the English Working Class* (New York: Pantheon Books, 1964).

[12] William D. Wray, *Mitsubishi and the N.Y.K., 1870–1914: Business Strategy in the Japanese Shipping Industry* (Cambridge, MA: Harvard University Press, 1984).

environment and civil rights? How are business and politics intertwined and what have been some of the results of their interactions? Historians asking these sorts of questions look to the records of the actual companies to answer them as well as to sources such as trade publications, advertising, and government documents. And because so much of what happens in business extends beyond the confines of the nation-state, business historians may also examine international trade documents and seek information in multiple countries. Geoffrey Jones's *Beauty Imagined: A History of the Global Beauty Industry* is an example of an international business history.[13] In fact, "business" encompasses so much human activity that business historians often apply the methodologies of other fields, such as gender studies, management theory, or even labor history. Wendy Gamber's *The Female Economy: The Millinery and Dressmaking Trades, 1860–1930* is a social and cultural study classified as labor history, women's studies, and business history.[14] And Louis Hyman's numbers-heavy *Debtor Nation: The History of America in Red Ink* is considered both economic and business history.[15] The interconnectedness between economic, business, and labor history has inspired a new category of inquiry: the *History of Capitalism*.

The study of economic history led also to the study of *social history*. The "history from below" of Lefebvre's and other historians' work contributed to a desire to know more about the material conditions and hence the daily lives of the lower classes. Social history is not limited to studies of particular classes, however, and takes into consideration a variety of social relations. Members of the Annales School, named for its journal *Annales: économies, sociétés, civilisations* and founded by French historians Lucien Febvre (1878–1956) and Marc Bloch (1886–1944), sought to expand historical inquiry from its limited focus on politics and the elite and began to gather data on most everything about past societies in an attempt to practice a sort of "total history." Emmanuel Le Roy Ladurie's classic *Montaillou* (1975), for example, offered a compelling look at life in a medieval French village.[16] Ladurie was interested not only in how men and women lived on a day-to-day basis, that is, knowing what they ate, wore, and used to furnish their homes, as well as how they farmed, conducted trade, and governed their village, but also in what the Annales historians termed **mentalité**, a frame of mind or outlook shared among a group of individuals. Using records from the Inquisition trials conducted in the small village, Ladurie was able to learn a great deal about such matters as how the villagers practiced their religion and demonstrated spirituality, their sanctioned and illicit sexual lives, their opinions about each other and neighboring villagers, and how they passed their limited free time.

Social historians such as Ladurie certainly expanded the scope of historical study. Perhaps more importantly, however, they took an array of traditional sources, such as

---

[13.] Geoffrey Jones, *Beauty Imagined: A History of the Global Beauty Industry* (New York: Oxford University Press, 2010).

[14.] Wendy Gamber, *The Female Economy: The Millinery and Dressmaking Trades, 1860–1930* (Bloomington, IL: University of Illinois Press, 1997).

[15.] Louis Hyman, *Debtor Nation: The History of America in Red Ink* (Princeton, NJ: Princeton University Press, 2011).

[16.] Emmanuel Le Roy Ladurie, *Montaillou, village occitan de 1294 à 1324* (Paris: Gallimard, 1975).

church records, and approached them in new ways. Demographic data on births, deaths, and marriages as well as detailed interviews by the Inquisitors granted access to aspects of daily life that had escaped the attention of conservative political historians. Social historians continue to rely on empirical data, archaeological evidence, and topography as well as more traditional sources. They also approach old questions in new ways. In his highly influential *Red, White, and Black*, which was first published in 1975 and is still being used in an updated edition in American history courses today, U.S. social historian Gary B. Nash skillfully interweaves the histories of Native Americans, African Americans, and Euroamericans to recount a more complex view of the history of the colonial and revolutionary eras than many of his predecessors.[17] Nash explores the lives of Native Americans and slaves from their own perspectives rather than pushing them into a framework based solely on their victimization. In other words, he makes them the subjects rather than the objects of historical inquiry. The study of underrepresented groups has advanced because of the subfield of social history.

SPOTLIGHT   **Alfred D. Chandler Jr., *The Visible Hand: The Managerial Revolution in American Business* (Cambridge, MA: Harvard University Press, 1977).**

Before Alfred D. Chandler Jr.'s *The Visible Hand* appeared in 1977, American business history was mired in a moralistic battle between robber barons and industrial statesmen. Matthew Josephson's *The Robber Barons: The Great American Capitalists, 1861–1901* (1934) depicted men with names like Vanderbilt, Rockefeller, and Morgan as ruthless tyrants, whereas Allan Nevins countered this view with *John D. Rockefeller: The Heroic Age of American Enterprise* (1940). Receiving his Ph.D. in 1952, Alfred D. Chandler Jr. asked a neutral question: how can we explain the emergence of large corporations? In *The Visible Hand*, Chandler argues against the reigning idea that the invisible hand of the free market allowed for the economic success of large enterprises. Instead, he finds that productivity was created through deliberate, rational resource allocation by a new business class of salaried managers who leveraged technological advances and new organizational forms in the interest of efficiency. *The Visible Hand* won the Pulitzer Prize and the Bancroft Prize, and Chandler became the lead historian in a new paradigm that historian Louis Galambos called the organizational synthesis.[18] Chandler's influence was so profound that earlier business histories seemed almost quaint (or B.C.: Before Chandler).[19] Chandler's insights impacted many disciplines but, for non–business historians, it was difficult to integrate his bloodless and implicitly positive analysis of the rise of powerful companies with the social history of the relatively powerless that was then in ascendance.[20] Still, decades passed before a new framework appeared. Recently, in the early twenty-first century, "the history of capitalism" has emerged as a frame to describe business histories that question any approach that makes an institutional outcome appear natural. Slavery, politics, workers, gender, race, and the vagaries of capitalism that are absent from Chandler's clean, linear analysis are open for investigation.[21]

[17.] Gary B. Nash, *Red, White and Black: The Peoples of Early America*, 6th ed. (New York: Pearson, 2010).

Although this new scholarship questions Chandler's perspective and arguments, Chandler's brilliant insights and discipline-altering reputation remain intact.

NOTES

18. Louis Galambos, "Technology, Political Economy, and Professionalization: Central Themes of the Organizational Synthesis," *Business History Review* 57, no. 4 (Winter 1983): 471–93.

19. Richard R. John, "Elaborations, Revisions, Dissents: Alfred D. Chandler, Jr.'s, 'The Visible Hand' after Twenty Years," *Business History Review* 71, no. 2 (Summer 1997), 167.

20. Ibid., 175.

21. Sven Beckert, "History of American Capitalism," in *American History Now*, eds. Eric Foner and Lisa McGirr (Philadelphia: Temple University Press, 2011), 314–35.

Cultural and intellectual history and the "postmodern turn"

Cultural historians have borrowed from their social history colleagues, especially in terms of analyzing *mentalités* but from a slightly different framework than that of daily life and material conditions, namely, by looking at the role of culture in historical development and change. In his highly influential 1978 book *Popular Culture in Early Modern Europe*, historian Peter Burke defined culture as "a system of shared meanings, attitudes, and values and the symbolic forms [performances, artifacts] in which they are expressed or embodied."[22] By looking at cultural practices across much of western Europe, Burke noted that men and women formed common identities less on the basis of nation or region than on divisions such as rural versus urban or those created through traditions in certain trades, for example, sheepherding versus shoemaking. His work allowed historians to think about social organization as disconnected from political affiliation. It also suggested that the study of culture was not limited to the high arts but could also reflect folk traditions. Today's cultural historians discuss a broad range of cultural expressions—from opera and fine painting to cinema and graffiti art. Even reality television has gained a foothold in cultural historical studies. What cultural historians share regardless of the level of culture they study is the idea that although it reflects and shapes history, it also has its own history. In other words, culture does not have to be a product of something else and can and should be studied in its own right. Cultural historians agree that cultural production is imbued with ample ways of understanding change over time and argue that it follows its own trajectory, which it may or may not share with other historical events, and maintain that it can usher in change that is independent of politics or economics. At the same time, however, the relationship among politics, economics, and culture can be better understood by asking who makes it, who buys it, who

22. Peter Burke, *Popular Culture in Early Modern Europe* (New York: Harper & Row, 1978), xiii.

uses it, who does or does not have access to it, who builds identities around it, and so on. At the high political level, cultural historians may examine the creation and circulation of propaganda posters selling war bonds. To understand the formation of a national cultural identity, they may analyze paintings such as "I vespri siciliani ["The Sicilian Vespers"] for messages about kinship and honor.[23] Or they may trace a cultural phenomenon such as the New Wave cinema movement in the 1950s and 1960s that vividly illustrated discontent among French youth. Some of the special sources cultural historians use include the actual works of art and information about how they were created, distributed, and received.

The *history of science* is rooted in social and cultural history but has emerged as a distinct subfield. Historians of science are especially interested in tracing the development of scientific thought through the ages. They generally focus on areas such as the hard sciences, medicine, technology, and the environment to explore how science interacts with and informs human relations. Both the natural world and human societies are thus at the center of the work of historians of science. Their innovative methodologies that bring together scientific study and the social sciences have decreased the distance between these disciplines. David Gooding, a former president of the History of Science section of the British Science Association, explained in a popular forum, "Historians no longer take the cognitive or moral priority of science for granted, or the existence of nature as an objective source of information. If scientists' learning about nature is not as distinct from other, more familiar forms of learning, invention and expression as we used to think, then we may be close to writing a history of science which explains why science has been so successful as a way of learning about nature and so powerful an influence upon the way we live and think."[24] In addition to compiling histories of great scientific thinkers, such as Galileo Galilei (1564–1642) or Sir Isaac Newton (1643–1727), and particular periods of great scientific advances, such as the Second Industrial Revolution (1870–1914), historians of science seek to explain the ways in which science shapes economic development, state-building, and relations of power. For example, Donald Worster's award-winning 1979 *Dust Bowl* is a cautionary tale that helped to define environmental history.[25] Worster linked the economic principles that contributed to the Great Depression to the ecological mishandling of lands in the American Midwest that caused the dust bowl of the 1930s. Unfettered capitalism, in Worster's estimation, wreaked havoc on the land as much as it did on financial institutions. The history of science recognizes the impact of humans on the natural world as much as the natural world on us.

Similarly to cultural historians who view artistic production as worthy of stand-alone analysis, *intellectual historians* grant principal authority to written texts. The subfield originally developed as the history of ideas and was therefore based especially on

---

23. Francesco Hayez, *I vespri siciliani (1846)*, Galleria d'Arte Moderna e Contemporanea, Rome, Italy.

24. David Gooding quoted in Richard Tomlinson, "What Is the History of Science, Part I," *History Today* 35, no. 4 (1985), http://www.historytoday.com/richard-tomlinson/what-history-science-part-i/.

25. Donald Worster, *Dust Bowl: The Southern Plains in the 1930s*, 25th anniversary ed. (New York: Oxford University Press, 2004).

philosophical writings, but it has expanded to include a broader conception of what intellectual production and circulation mean. Historian Peter Gordon has defined current intellectual history as "the study of intellectuals, ideas, and intellectual patterns over time" and he distinguishes it from the history of ideas, arguing that intellectual history "tends to regard ideas as historically conditioned features of the world which are best understood in some larger context."[26] In other words, early practitioners of intellectual history worked on specific concepts, tracing their development over time and looking for ways in which they did or did not evolve. According to these historians, the Western intellectual tradition from the time of Plato on could be understood as a set of ideas on which the rest of human society had been founded. Some historians, however, have argued that separating the idea from its context is ultimately ahistorical and is indicative of an approach that remains more rooted in the realm of philosophy than history. Instead, what they claim intellectual historians should do is look at ideas in relation to their settings, for example, in the creation of intellectual or social movements. For example, Herbert Marcuse's 1969 *An Essay on Liberation* is important in understanding both the development of critical thought in the German social theory group known as the Frankfurt School, of which Marcuse was a member, and the mobilization of students' and workers' movements in France.[27] Marcuse's essay moreover marks a transition away from rigid Marxist interpretations of economics and society and the entrance of the new Left, that is, a group of intellectuals who stood for tolerance, fulfillment, and equality but without necessarily embracing the idea that worker control of the means of production would result in a less oppressive society. An intellectual biography of Marcuse himself, a collective biography of the Frankfurt School, or a history of the rise of new Left from the social movements of the late 1960s would all prove of interest to intellectual historians.

In the late 1960s and into the 1970s intellectual history took an important new direction that was greatly influenced by the disciplines of literary criticism and European continental philosophy. It is often referred to as "the linguistic turn" and categorized as part of the *deconstructionist* and *postmodernist* movements. Postmodernists emphasize language as key to constructing the world, but they moved away from the work of linguistic structuralists, such as J. L. Austin, who saw language as determinant of human existence. Philosophers such as Jacques Derrida developed a theory of poststructuralism, which seeks to uncover "holes" in language and therefore looks for meaning in the deconstruction of terms or even the entire linguistic order. The work of philosopher and historian Michel Foucault has been especially influential both in broadening the scope of intellectual history and in suggesting new methodologies for its study based on deconstruction. In 1964, Foucault published *Madness and Civilization*, which is a fascinating account of the history of the definition and treatment of mental illness from the

---

[26.] Peter E. Gordon, "What Is Intellectual History? A Frankly Partisan Introduction to a Frequently Misunderstood Field," Paper for Harvard University [Revised Spring 2012]. http://history.fas.harvard.edu/people/faculty/documents/pgordon-whatisintellhist.pdf/

[27.] Herbert Marcuse, *An Essay on Liberation* (Boston: Beacon Press, 1969).

Renaissance through the modern age.[28] Foucault decentered the human subject to look at how ideas of madness were constructed through a complex system of power and knowledge. In his subsequent work and, in particular, in his highly celebrated 1976 book *The History of Sexuality*, Foucault emphasized the role of discourse in the creation of modern subjectivity and pointed out the linguistic holes through which the subject was destabilized.[29] By questioning the notion of full human agency, Foucault was able to show that the historical subject is mutable and contextual. Since textual analysis is always open to interpretation and there is no way to constitute the self outside language, Foucault and his followers have questioned the very notion of getting at a permanent set of truths in history.

For postmodernists, there is no historical advance toward anything in particular and therefore teleological approaches to history serve no real purpose. Critics of postmodernism argue that nothing is left of history when it enters the realm of relativism. However, rigorous historians who use postmodernism in their work do not necessarily completely reject the standards and practices of the discipline. Instead, they seek to understand how dominant narratives became dominant or to offer counternarratives to them, that is, to suggest alternatives to what we think we know. Postmodernism's influence is far reaching in *postcolonial studies*, for instance. Historians of colonialism and empire have analyzed how the creation of a **subaltern** "other" contributed to the notions of European superiority that were fundamental to the imperial project. In other words, by seeing difference as in need of correction or assistance, colonizers were able to justify their control over otherwise sovereign people. Europeans dominated colonial subjects not only through political and economic relations but also through cultural exchanges that depended on imbalances of power and knowledge and were linguistically created. In her *Specters of Mother India: The Global Restructuring of an Empire*, Mrinalini Sinha utilizes a postcolonial approach to examine how an American woman journalist's negative depictions of Hindu culture ultimately fueled reforms of the colonial system although they actually suggested that Indians could not be changed.[30] Postmodernism and postcolonialism often succeed, in fact, in focusing on the ambiguities of human societies by uprooting long-held truths or absolutes about them.

SPOTLIGHT   **Michel Foucault, *The History of Sexuality: An Introduction*, Vol. 1 (originally published in 1976).**

Foucault's approach to his study of the history of sexuality is as significant as his findings. In this crucial postmodernist text, Foucault distanced himself from the economic interpretations of the development of sexuality that were prevalent among leftist thinkers in

---

[28.] Michel Foucault, *Madness and Civilization: A History of Insanity in the Age of Reason* (London: Routledge, 2001).

[29.] Michel Foucault, *The History of Sexuality* (London: Penguin, 1990).

[30.] Mrinalini Sinha, *Specters of Mother India: The Global Restructuring of an Empire* (Durham, NC: Duke University Press, 2006).

the 1970s and instead put discourse analysis into practice within a historical framework. Foucault disputes the claims of historians and other theorists who argue that nineteenth-century bourgeois productive culture created a climate of sexual repression—what he calls the repressive hypothesis. Moreover, Foucault refuses a teleological, or forward-moving, understanding of the history of sexuality between the eighteenth and late twentieth century that suggested sex had been repressed but was now entering a liberatory phase. Far from being hidden and then slowly seen again, Foucault argues, sex could scarcely have been discussed more. Western societies produced multiple ways of studying and talking about sex, whether through the confessional, medicine, or psychology, all of which concerned themselves with arriving at its underlying meaning. An objective truth of sex interests Foucault far less than the "regime of power-knowledge-pleasure" its search generated. Foucault, in fact, displaces the idea of an agency of sex, or the notion that it is a fixed historical subject we can come to know, in favor of a history of sexuality, or the idea that "'sex' is historically subordinate to sexuality," which means its meanings shift over time and inside relations of power.[31] To show how such shifts occur, Foucault looks at how who is speaking about sex and controlling knowledge about it permeates relations among individuals as well as between individuals and institutions. Discourses, not data, shape the ways in which sex and desire come to be understood and regulated. For example, in the modern age, new sciences such as psychology hystericized women's bodies, problematized childhood sexuality, and stigmatized gay and lesbian relationships as perversities. Although all of these examples do point to forms of the repression of sex, Foucault says they more importantly indicate a deployment of sexuality concerned with its own proliferation, which he concludes has ironically led us to believe our own liberation is at stake.

NOTE

[31.] Foucault, *The History of Sexuality*, 157.

The challenge of women's history

Sinha's work is an example not only of postcolonial studies but also of *women's history*. Like several of the other subfields we have discussed here, women's history grew out of social history. And, as is the case for labor history, women's history is closely tied to social movements, specifically the feminist movements of the late 1960s and 1970s that challenged the notion that women's subordination to men was somehow inevitable. Women's history is usually still linked to the struggle for political, economic, social, and cultural equality for women but it is not always explicitly feminist in tone, in part because a single definition of feminism would be difficult to spell out today. As we have seen, early forms of traditional history often focused on the lives of the elite, mostly great men and a few exceptional women. Students of history learned about Elizabeth I of England or Cleopatra of Egypt, but most women remained hidden to history. Some historians with an interest in women's stories looked to uncover at least something about the women behind the important men of the past and began to offer biographical sketches of intriguing figures such as Joan of Arc and Marie Antoinette. With the advent of social history came the idea of looking at the family as valuable to historical understanding. As historians asked questions about the organization of public and private life, they uncovered important details about changes in women's roles over time, noting, however, that most women have always worked or made some sort of economic contribution to their families, even if those contributions were not always regarded as of equal value to those of men. Historians of women found, for example, that the normative myth of the middle-class housewife can be traced to developments in post–World War II America even if the idea of "separate spheres" for women and men dates to the nineteenth century and appears in some earlier periods as well. Historian Glenna Matthews argued in *Just a Housewife* that the "cult of domesticity" that gave women high status in the American middle-class home in the nineteenth century had mostly disappeared by the 1920s with the spread of consumerism and professionalism.[32]

As historians of women began to publish new work on the lives of women around the world and in most historical eras, theorists began to ask whether they were perhaps just, to paraphrase Joan W. Scott in her famous essay "Gender: A Useful Category of Historical Analysis," adding women and stirring.[33] In other words, although knowing more about women and their lives was certainly valuable, was not the point of women's history to challenge the dominant narratives? What if women's history were told from a new timeline, one that focused on changes in women's roles and statuses rather than on big political events? Other historians emphasized the need to look at gender relations, not exclusively at women, to uncover how ideals of masculinity and femininity were created and expressed. How did women and men operate in specific contexts and under certain conditions? How did the sexes interact with one another and act on their own? As more work on sex and gender began to circulate in academic circles, historians began to recognize that it could not stand completely on its own. Since women's roles have been shaped also by economic conditions and racial considerations, historians acknowledged the need to look at the ways in which class and race intersect with gender. As Sojourner Truth asked in an 1851 speech, later named "Ain't I a Woman?" by a white abolitionist, so newer generations of women of color began to question whether their stories had received adequate attention in historical writing and found that they had not. Women's and gender historians realized that collective identities sometimes require that historical subjects prioritize certain aspects of their experiences. In some cases, women may see race as more critical than sex or view their class interests as more fundamental to how they have faced specific situations. Historian Evelyn Brooks Higginbotham, for example, has examined how African American Baptist women positioned gender, race, and religious identity in helping the poor and building a women's movement in the black community.[34] She and many other historians of women and gender have been especially

---

[32] Glenna Matthews, *Just a Housewife: The Rise and Fall of Domesticity in America* (New York: Oxford University Press, 1987).

[33] Joan Wallach Scott, "Gender: A Useful Category of Historical Analysis," *The American Historical Review* 91, no. 5 (December 1986): 1053–75. It should be noted, however, that Scott later critiqued the use of "gender" in historical writing. See her *The Fantasy of Feminist History* (Durham, NC: Duke University Press, 2011).

[34] Evelyn Brooks Higginbotham, *Righteous Discontent: The Women's Movement in the Black Baptist Church, 1880–1920* (Cambridge, MA: Harvard University Press, 1993).

important in discussions of the complexity of individual and collective experience. Arguably some of the most sophisticated historical studies over the past few decades have appeared in journals, such as the *Journal of Women's History* and *Gender & History*, in which gender theory frames interpretations of key moments and changes in the past.

National and international approaches to historical questions

In this chapter, we have discussed many subfields that make up the discipline of history. It is worth pointing out that historical studies are taking other directions as well. Traditionally, whether a historian declared himself a political or a cultural historian, he would also limit his area of study to a nation-state or region. The websites of history departments across the United States often list specializations first by place, for example, American, European, Asian, Middle Eastern, and African history, and then perhaps by subfield or era (e.g., American Revolution, Material Culture, women and gender). Increasingly, however, historians are bridging geographical divides and emphasizing transnational, international, or global relationships. For instance, migration scholars take a transnational perspective because they are usually considering what happens to migrants in both the home and the host countries, even if they may emphasize one side of the migration pattern. In her *Italy's Many Diasporas*, for instance, historian and migration scholar Donna Gabaccia analyzed the ways in which the migration of Italians transformed Italy as well as more than a dozen countries around the globe.[35] In the wake of political and economic hardship in Italy, she found that migration served as a "safety valve" for a struggling Italian government and at the same time contributed to growth in the Americas and Australia.

In fact, many historians today are specialized not by period or nation-state but by lands linked by a major body of water. The subfields of the *Atlantic World*, the *Mediterranean Basin*, and *Indian Ocean* studies developed in recognition of the complex economic, social, and cultural networks of peoples who interact across territories, often first through trade relations, and influence each other with far-reaching and long-lasting consequences. To understand how individuals fit into historical patterns, historians in these subfields consider a multitude of factors including, but not limited to, economics, politics, culture, society, and ideas. Historians of the Atlantic World, for example, study developments on the four continents connected by the Atlantic Ocean between the late fifteenth century, following Columbus's voyages to the "new world," and the late nineteenth century, when slavery in the Americas came to an end. They work from the concept that this vast region was one of constant change in which ideas, items, and people continually interacted with one another without a clear center of exchange or well-defined borders. For example, in *The Atlantic in World History*, Karen Ordahl Kupperman explains that the North African sailing technologies that made Columbus's voyages possible contributed to numerous related dramatic changes, such as the

---

[35.] Donna Gabaccia, *Italy's Many Diasporas* (Seattle: University of Washington Press, 2000).

transformation of the European diets and consumption of luxury goods, the organization of the transatlantic slave trade, and the spread of both technology and disease
among native peoples in the Americas.[36] Historians of the Mediterranean focus especially on the interplay among the populations of North Africa, Anatolia (Turkey), the
Balkans, the Levant, and Southern Europe and reflect on historical events and trends
that have characterized the region, such as the impact of the rise and fall of the Ottoman
Empire (1299–1922), the spread of Muslim and Christian religious traditions, and cooperation and conflict over natural resources. Historians of the Indian Ocean have challenged Eurocentric definitions of historical periods in their histories of the areas that
now comprise the countries of India, Pakistan, Sri Lanka, Nepal, the Maldives, Bhutan,
and Bangladesh. Historians of this region, moreover, refer to the Indian Ocean as the
"cradle of globalization," thereby displacing Europe as the birthplace of the system of
exchanges that typifies our world today. Each of these subfields has contributed to more
complete understandings of how individuals and groups that are not close neighbors
nevertheless effect change on each other.

Globalization studies is another burgeoning field that requires expertise in multiple
parts of the world as well as a solid base in economic and cultural history. The work of
historian Jerry Bentley (1949–2012) is especially influential in opening up the fields of
world and globalization history. Bentley's *Old World Encounters* highlights the fact that
while the term "globalization" has been popularized since the 1990s, the processes it
describes originated in the ancient world.[37] Bentley's careful analysis of key turning
points that altered global relationships has influenced the development of the subfield of
world history. The historical profession is also changing because of increased attention
to larger themes over the course of much longer periods of historical inquiry. Increasingly, graduate programs are offering specializations in global history and encouraging
students to develop a subfield in a part of the world outside their major concentration or
to emphasize the **transnational** aspects of the major field. A student of early modern
Spain, for example, could focus in detail on the New World while exploring changes
taking place in Europe. Rarely can today's historians remain fully enmeshed in the
details of their nation-state or region of choice without making comparative analyses or
considering far-reaching networks. As Immanuel Wallerstein's world system theory
makes clear, historians should rely on analytical frameworks that allow us to better comprehend how different parts of the world are connected but also why some become more
powerful. Wallerstein's *The Modern World System* seeks to make sense of the processes
of modernization that developed between the fifteenth and seventeenth centuries and
made the Europeans economically dominant and capitalism relevant across the globe.[38]
The relatively new field of "Big History" is claiming to offer more comprehensive approaches to historical study.[39] It has already made inroads into high schools and is likely

---

[36.] Karen Ordahl Kupperman, *The Atlantic in World History* (New York: Oxford University Press, 2012).

[37.] Jerry Bentley, *Old World Encounters: Cross-Cultural Exchanges in Pre-modern Times* (New York: Oxford
University Press, 1993).

[38.] Immanuel Wallerstein, *The Modern World System: Capitalist Agriculture and the Origins of the European
World Economy in the Sixteenth Century* (New York: Academic Press, 1974).

[39.] See, for instance, the Big History Project at https://www.bighistoryproject.com/home/.

to have an impact at the undergraduate and graduate levels in coming years. Proponents of Big History emphasize the connections among the past, present, and future and feature science and technology in more prominent ways than do traditional historians, who prefer to focus on the relationship between past and present and study humans.

SPOTLIGHT **Andrew Zimmerman, *Alabama in Africa: Booker T. Washington, the German Empire, and the Globalization of the New South* (Princeton, NJ: Princeton University Press, 2010).**

Andrew Zimmerman combines the approaches of cultural, social, and economic history and works across geographical divides to provide new historical insights into imperial connections in the modern Atlantic World. Beginning with an analysis of imperial German efforts to develop a cotton economy in late-nineteenth-century Togo using African American expertise, Zimmerman skillfully connects German, African, and American histories in a complex transnational account of the ideas that shaped global economic, race, and labor relations in the twentieth century. Zimmerman argues that the political, social, and economic structures that emerged after Reconstruction in the American South provided a model that allowed the inequalities of colonial modernization projects and "civilizing missions" to continue in the global South. The German government, which already had experience of colonizing Eastern Europe and using free Polish labor to develop a staple beet crop, looked to the American South for expertise in developing a cotton crop in colonial Togo. Ironically, by working with German agricultural experts to provide the technical and social know-how of cotton production, graduates of Booker T. Washington's Tuskegee Institute collaborated in a German imperial venture to exploit the labor of free (but coerced) Togolese peasants before World War I. Expertise also flowed from Europe to the United States. W. E. B. Du Bois was among several Americans who defended their Ph.D. theses in Germany in the late nineteenth century and brought back to the United States German ideas about the new science of sociology. German academic traditions, European colonial modernizing projects, and African American insights all influenced the founding of the Chicago School of Sociology after World War I. By examining the origins of the Tuskegee Institute, the political economy of beet production in Eastern Europe, the development of cotton production in Togo, the transatlantic development of sociology, and the experiences of the individuals involved in the cross-continental travel of ideas, Zimmerman transcends the narrow focus of national histories to clarify global connections and show how the history of any given country is linked to the histories of others.

🔬 Applying subfields

As we have seen in this chapter, the discipline of history is itself rich with history. The field has developed and grown from a relatively narrow focus on the stories of the elites, warfare, and politics to now include a fuller consideration of the multiple aspects of the lives of women and men of all experiences and backgrounds. By approaching historical studies from specialized standpoints, whether ideas or economics or culture, historians have devised important methodologies to help us understand change over time. What happened in the past is, of course, good to know, but without interpretative frameworks to make sense of narratives, history remains just a curiosity. The attention historians pay to particular groups or motors of change as well as to place tells us something about the key questions of our own time as well as in the past. The advent of new fields of history and the continued rethinking of the longest practiced ones have also allowed for the introduction of primary sources that had previously been overlooked. Today's professional historians are more well rounded than ever before and prepared to teach and research subject matters that require an astute awareness of the complexities of human life. This means, however, that when students ask their professors what their areas of specialization are, the response may not always be as clear-cut as they might expect. It also means, however, that undergraduate students have an opportunity to think more broadly about history than they were able to in high school and that they can fuel their own interests by learning more about approaches to history that can help them to ask and answer compelling research questions. Precisely how to do so is the subject of the following chapters.

CHAPTER THREE

Historiography

Our reflections on methodologies and the development of individual schools of historical writing often influence our own approaches to the study of history. They may even lead us to take sides in key debates over interpretation, especially when they appear to have great relevance to current events. As we learned in Chapter Two, historiography expands and changes because of contemporary concerns. Historians also participate in the historiographical process by becoming experts in a particular field and seeking to shed light on the significance of new materials that suggest new ways of writing about the past.

What is historiography?

Historiography is an examination of the way history has been written about a particular topic. As we saw in Chapter Two, historians utilize many theories and methodologies, such as Marxism or postmodernism, in their analysis of what something means and why it may be historically significant. For example, since the Great Recession of 2008, a new school of history has vigorously emerged in the United States: the History of Capitalism.[1] Like many schools of history, the practitioners of this school identify themselves as a generation, one that academically came of age in the 1990s and afterward. According to this generation, the triumph of capitalism over communism occurred long ago and new questions needed to be asked about capitalism, but they were difficult to formulate within the contemporary historiographic landscape. In the 1990s, business history was still dominated by an organizational framework that focused on the development of the firm and appeared to celebrate the corporation in a way that made some historians uncomfortable (see Chapter Two on Alfred D. Chandler Jr.). Social histories emphasizing human agency abounded but were split into women's history, labor history, African American history, and myriad other categories that did not seem to speak to each other. Studies based on quantitative data had been discredited decades before, and the cultural and linguistic turns, including, for example, the theories of Michel Foucault, illustrated the rich possibilities of attention to language and subjectivity, but capitalism was still treated as a force of nature rather than a human creation.

Practitioners of the new History of Capitalism denaturalize capitalism by treating it as a human creation with a history that can be investigated and analyzed. Louis Hyman of Cornell University, one of the spokespersons of this new field, writes, "When capitalist institutions such as banks and corporations are treated as real places with real people, the stories begin to change . . . though important, profit becomes only one factor among many

---

[1.] The History of Capitalism is also current in Europe and Australia, but this discussion is only focused on its development in the United States.

guiding the choices of executives, whose decisions matter more than perhaps anyone in determining our everyday lives, especially those on the bottom."[2] "History from below" defined the previous generation of social and labor historians who emerged in the 1970s and 1980s and in turn defined themselves against earlier generations of historians who wrote about the "top," the winners of history that included presidents, generals, and captains of industry. Historians of capitalism share with social and labor historians a left-wing critique but, in Hyman's words, engage in "history from below, all the way to the top."[3] Since 2000, centers for the study of the history of capitalism have appeared at leading universities such as Harvard, the University of California at Los Angeles, the New School for Social Research, and Cornell University, and the subject has become the focus of conferences, workshops, seminars, and blogs. Scholars are still debating its origins and parameters but, like most schools of history, it emerged in multiple places at about the same time to fill a historiographical gap: to demonstrate that capitalism is not a force of nature and that it can, and should, be historicized and explained.[4]

It can be said then that historiography looks at the ways in which historical events, topics, and even specific documents have been interpreted differently by different historians. Historiography as a field concerns the ways in which historians as individuals and groups have defined a specific field or subject matter. Entire books are devoted to the ways historians have treated a particular topic.[5] Most often you will encounter historiography in the form of an essay published in an academic journal. What historiographical writing has in common is this: the focus is not on informing the reader about the topic itself, but rather informing the reader about the various *approaches* taken by historians *to* that topic. In this chapter, we will explain why historiography is such an important part of what professional historians do, discuss its relevance to student research, and guide you through the process of writing a complete historiographical essay and a historiography section within a major research paper.[6]

WENDY POJMANN: PERSONAL REFLECTION

Much of my own research and writing has been concerned with filling gaps in the historical record. I was trained in the social, cultural, and intellectual history of Europe from the eighteenth to the twentieth century and generally approached my graduate school papers

[2] Louis Hyman, "Why Write the History of Capitalism?" *Symposium Magazine*, July 18, 2013, http://www.symposium-magazine.com/why-write-the-history-of-capitalism-louis-hyman/; Sven Beckert, "History of American Capitalism," in eds. Eric Foner and Lisa McGirr, *American History Now* (Philadelphia: Temple University Press, 2011), 314–35.

[3] Jennifer Schuessler, "In History Departments, It's Up with Capitalism," *New York Times*, April 6, 2013, http://www.nytimes.com/2013/04/07/education/in-history-departments-its-up-with-capitalism.html/.

[4] "Interchange: The History of Capitalism," *Journal of American History* 101, no. 2 (September 2014): 503–36.

[5] See for example, John Marincola, ed., *Greek and Roman Historiography* (New York: Oxford University Press, 2011), and Dhruv Raina, *Images and Contexts: The Historiography of Science and Modernity in India* (New York: Oxford University Press, 2010).

[6] See the assignment guidelines in the companion workbook.

from a perspective that was informed by both postmodernism and feminism. Rather than directly engage in some of the discussions taking place among historians over these theoretical frameworks, however, I have attempted to answer questions about women's lack of access to full political and cultural participation. While living in Italy after I completed my Ph.D., I began to ask some questions about the relationship between the Italian women's movements I had written about for my dissertation and the arrival of large numbers of women from countries outside Europe, about whom I knew very little. Did Italian women, especially women who called themselves feminists, assist migrant women in any way? Did migrant women seek help from Italian women? What were some of the first interactions among such disparate groups of women like? Before me, no scholars had undertaken a systematic study of the history of the connection between feminism and migration in Italy or even asked whether there was a relationship between them, which meant that I would have to find the answers to these sorts of questions on my own. In fact, my first book, *Immigrant Women and Feminism in Italy* (2005), resulted from my desire to know more. Undertaking this new line of research, however, meant having to become familiar with historical writing about immigration and migration to, from, and within Italy, update my knowledge about interpretations of women's movements in Italy, and acquire greater expertise in fields outside history, especially sociology and political science. If I wanted to contribute something I believed was new, I needed to know much more about what other scholars had already done. I had to learn more about how they were interpreting shifts in the population of women living in Italy, women who no longer were always native-born Italians.

Historical debate and revisionism

As readers of history, many of us fall in love with great storytelling. We enjoy learning about "what happened" as well as all the causes and effects surrounding events of interest to us. Many celebrated historians, such as John Dower, Simon Schama, and Michael Beschloss, are skilled in the art of historical **narrative** and draw us into the intrigue and mystery of the past using the techniques of writers of literary fiction. History students at all levels of their education sometimes mistake storytelling for history. As a result, when they write papers for their history courses, students often attempt to follow the models established by their favorite authors but find themselves buried in description, mainly rewriting the same stories that attracted their attention in the first place, albeit after having learned a little more about them through additional research and writing.

In reality, professional historians do much more than tell stories. They evaluate and interpret the past. Since the work of historians reflects both larger and more subtle changes over time, historical writing is itself historical. As we saw in Chapter Two, historiography encompasses a wide range of approaches that historians have developed through dialogue and debate with each other over hundreds of years. They have grappled with large questions concerning the human past and advanced the discipline by asking questions of concern to themselves and their contemporaries. Historiography does not have to be limited to the big controversies of history or defined only by major schools of thought, however. Historians evaluate the state of the field in which they have developed expertise to seek answers to subtle questions, understand nuances of interpretation, and broaden knowledge about the past. They introduce new avenues of research and maintain an acute awareness of their own original contributions. Historians do not just keep stories alive by memorizing and repeating them to others. They seek to enhance knowledge from the vantage point of the present.

Historiography frequently moves forward through what has been coined **revisionism**, which, simply put, means a challenge to the standard interpretation of a particular historical topic. Often a dominant narrative, or **metanarrative**, about a particular event or moment in history is challenged by a new group of historians who have uncovered new evidence and/or have developed alternate ways of asking questions about the existing evidence. They discuss and debate the metanarrative until their challenge to it gains momentum and perhaps eventually even replaces it. Often times, however, a classic narrative remains intact and new interpretations coexist with it. The historiography of the French Revolution is one such example. Building on the work of Karl Marx, historians such as George Lefebvre established the metanarrative of the Revolution as a social class war of the bourgeoisie, or upper middle classes, against the aristocracy. Early revisionist historians such as Alfred Cobban and François Furet viewed the Marxist approach as too limited. More recent scholarship by Lynn Hunt also challenges a class-based interpretation and looks at French political culture and democracy to understand changes in late-eighteenth-century France. Conservative scholars such as William Doyle, in contrast, have represented the Revolution as a violent disruption that affected political life more than social or economic structure. No single viewpoint has dominated the field.

Although the term "revisionist history" has acquired a negative connotation in some political circles, properly understood, it is really an essential part of the discipline of history, one that makes it relevant and consequential both to serious students of history and to its casual consumers. According to James McPherson, former president of the American Historical Association,

> History is a continuing dialogue between the present and the past. Interpretations of the past are subject to change in response to new evidence, new questions asked of the evidence, new perspectives gained by the passage of time. There is no single, eternal and immutable "truth" about the past events and their meaning. The unending quest of historians for understanding the past—that is, "revisionism," is what makes history vital and meaningful.[7]

Participating in the revisionist process can be one of the most interesting and rewarding parts of a historian's career, especially when it is embedded in contemporary concerns and thus connected to bigger questions posed by the humanities and social sciences. For instance, as we learned in Chapter Two, the development of the subfields of African American and women's history is connected to the advance of the Civil Rights and women's movements in the United States. Understanding the different experiences and perspectives of groups not typically recognized in the standard narratives of history

---

[7] James McPherson, "Revisionist Historians," *Perspectives in History*, September 2003 (available at http://www.historians.org/perspectives/issues/2003/0309/0309pre1.cfm/).

required that historians ask new questions, seek new evidence, and find new contexts in which to write about them. Some conservative U.S. historians, for example, may prefer to focus on a heroic tale of the consistent progress of white men, but the social movements of the 1960s and 1970s succeeded in opening additional avenues of scholarly pursuit. Revisionist historians have contributed to a much larger body of historical knowledge by being critical of those historians who preceded them.

The politics of revisionism can have disquieting consequences as well. Two such examples are the Nanking Massacre of 1937 and the Italian Resistance of 1943–1945. Nationalist and revisionist debates over the precise circumstances surrounding events in Nanking (Nanjing) in 1937 continue to surface and have had a negative impact on Sino–Japanese relations. Japanese historians and the government have routinely minimized the number of casualties that occurred during the six-week period that followed the Japanese capture of the former Chinese capital; estimates range from 40,000 to 300,000 noncombatant deaths. Controversy over what happened in Nanking can also be seen in the writing of Japanese middle and high school history textbooks. The publication of the *New History Textbook*, approved by the Japanese Ministry of Education in 2001, was met with protests in Japan, China, and Korea because of its conservative revisionist narrative that downplayed Japanese actions in Nanking as well as several other controversial subjects, such as the use of Korean "comfort women" by Japanese soldiers and the economic impact of the Greater East Asia Co-prosperity Sphere. The extent of Japanese aggression and militarism in the 1930s and 1940s remains a source of contention in educational and political circles. Professional historians persist in defending their versions of what happened during this particularly turbulent period of East Asian history and their claims reverberate inside the government and across the region.[8]

A similarly intense revisionist debate still rages on among historians of Italy over the participation of partisan civilians in the liberation of the Italian state from Nazi-Fascism during the final years of World War II.[9] Histories of the violent period between 1943, when Allied troops landed in Sicily, and 1945, when the war came to end, generally have emphasized either the heroism or the disruption of the partisans. Liberal historians, such as Denis Mack Smith, claim the partisans acquired too much power and influence for the Italian Communist Party and led the country into a civil war, whereas Marxist historians, such as Giuliano Procacci, argue that communist partisans were the only ones ready to analyze the roots of Italian fascism and purge the country of its legacy. A more recent group of historians led by Paul Ginsborg have instead insisted that there has been a tendency to "mythologize" the Resistance when the reality is that it did not produce revolutionary change or eradicate fascist tendencies. As in Japan, public school textbooks in Italy have tended to be one sided on the Resistance, although in this case dominated by a procommunist slant. In both examples, revisionism has produced new scholarship, demonstrated how history is a living, changing discipline, and shown the ways in which historical work influences the larger political and social context.

---

[8] Peter J. Brown, "China, Japan Still Fighting over History," *Asia Times Online*, February 11, 2010 (available at http://www.atimes.com/atimes/China/LB11Ad01.html/).

[9] Michael Kelly, "The Italian Resistance in Historical Transition: Class War, Patriotic War or Civil War?" *Eras* no. 4 (available at http://arts.monash.edu.au/publications/eras/edition-4/kelly.php/).

KAREN WARD MAHAR: PERSONAL REFLECTION

Serendipity shaped my research agenda. I began my graduate work on the east coast with an M.A. thesis on U.S. immigration history, but thanks to a historian I met as an undergraduate, I was offered a full fellowship to complete the Ph.D. on the west coast. Accepting it required switching not only coasts but also research agendas because this program's U.S. strengths were in gender studies, labor history, and business history. To make ends meet, I took a part-time job writing short biographies of women in the American film industry for an organization conducting oral histories. It was while sitting in the library earning just above minimum wage that I discovered some of the first female stars produced and directed their own movies. Given how notoriously masculine the role of producer and director became in the American film industry, this seemed odd. Older descriptive narratives and popular histories told the stories of these women, but I could not find more recent historical scholarship to explain this anomaly. Feminist film scholarship, a field that emerged in the 1970s, was producing a great deal of fascinating work informed by semiotics and strains of Marxism and psychoanalysis, but this literature focused on image and spectatorship and did not address my historical question: how did these women end up behind the camera and why did they disappear? I was not the only budding scholar to discover my topic when I did, as we all ride rising historiographical currents that draw us to similar questions at similar times but, as it also happens, no two scholars have precisely the same training. I positioned my work within business history: how did the gendering of work change as the film industry morphed from an amalgam of small businesses to an oligopoly? I needed to be familiar with the history of the film industry, the sociology of gender, work, and organizations, and the history of the rise of big business, which at the time was dominated by the work of Alfred D. Chandler Jr. and emphasized organizational change. My first book, *Women Filmmakers in Early Hollywood* (2006), tied changing gender ideology to changes in the "strategy and structure" of the early film industry as it grew from a small, decentralized industry anxious for middle-class acceptance to an oligopoly tied to Wall Street investors.[10] I found that the ideology brought by Wall Street bankers to Hollywood in the 1920s held that the expensive feature films generated by the large studios were too risky to be entrusted to women. Since some of these women filmmakers had been quite financially successful thus far, the near-universal exclusion of women filmmakers on the basis of gender was irrational. And it raised another question: what was the connection between masculinity and financial risk? This too has a history, which is now being explored within a vigorous if unwieldy new school of history that came to light at about the same time as the Great Recession: the History of Capitalism.

NOTE

10. Alfred D. Chandler Jr., *Strategy and Structure: Chapters in the History of the Industrial Enterprise* (Cambridge, MA: Massachusetts Institute of Technology Press, 1962).

The importance of historiography to the student research paper

Good student research papers demonstrate familiarity with historiography, whereas poor student research papers ignore the important work historians have already done. Not only is a paper that simply retells well-known stories uninteresting to read, but also it serves little academic purpose. Students must have a good understanding of historiography for several reasons. First, knowing how particular topics have already been interpreted and written about by historians helps students to develop their own *research questions*, especially because knowing the literature gives students the opportunity to pose questions about where the field currently stands, recognize gaps in interpretation and/or documentation, and engage with current scholars who are developing new directions in their work. In other words, a strong historiographical context offers a clear framework from which to begin a project and helps the student see how her or his interests fit into larger historical questions being discussed in the profession. Second, historiography aids in defining and delimiting the exact scope of the research paper. If the student recognizes that one aspect of her topic has already received adequate coverage and is not a source of much debate, she can mention it in passing and move on to less explored or more controversial areas. She may even be able to devise a working *thesis*, or line of argument, she will support in the paper. Students baffled by how big or small their topic should be (who hasn't been told that his or her topic was "too big"?) can use historiography to figure out what they are going to write about and how much information they will need. Finally, to be able to effectively interpret primary source materials, students must have a good understanding of what is already known about the period in which they were produced. Without historiography students cannot really "do" history.

BARBARA REEVES-ELLINGTON: PERSONAL REFLECTION

All historians are located in time, space, and historiography and shaped by their personal and professional trajectories. Just as they live in different eras and locations, enjoy varied experiences, and develop dissimilar standpoints, so, too, they create distinct historiographies. The transnational turn in U.S. History has urged historians to become acquainted with diverse national historiographies; and debates about "positionality" (that is, how scholars are positioned geographically and intellectually) by historians who write in academic cultures outside the United States have highlighted the significance of histories written from without.[11]

My decision to study the transfer of American culture to the Ottoman Balkans was influenced by personal factors and shaped by dynamic new approaches to the study of U.S. history. My experiences working at the American University in Bulgaria at Blagoevgrad, just after the collapse of communism in Eastern Europe in the early 1990s, led me to raise questions about earlier American engagement in the region, and my reading of Jane Hunter's *Gospel of Gentility* in the late 1990s introduced me to the idea of women missionaries as exporters of American culture.[12] Missionaries were no longer the purview of

continued on next page

continued

theologians, missiologists (scholars of mission), and historians of religion but had moved into the sights of social historians and historians of American foreign relations. My research project crossed multiple boundaries during a period when the field of American foreign relations was in a state of flux, moving away from a focus on diplomacy and war to embrace a much broader understanding of foreign relations that included nonstate actors.[13] At the same time, scholarly debates about the strongly contested concept of cultural imperialism, through which missionaries imposed their views on others, began to give way to new discussions about exchanges where local actors had the option to accept, reject, or modify the ideas they came across through their meetings with missionaries.[14] These debates were shaped in turn by the movement to internationalize U.S. history, that is, to see U.S. history within a global context, and by historians whose use of transnational approaches has revealed the connections Americans forged across the world and through which they worked.[15] Scholars who take up the challenge of the new transnational history seek out the foreign environments, scholarship, and sources that reveal new perspectives on Americans abroad. Working on American missionaries among Bulgarian Orthodox Christians in the Ottoman Empire, I became acquainted with Turkish and Bulgarian historiographies and discovered a remarkable divergence of interpretations. Historians argued diversely that American missionaries were benevolent peace-makers and zealous imperialists, that although they worked hard they achieved little, and that although they may have had good intentions, their work among Ottoman Christians was a threat to the Islamic Ottoman state.[16] My questions about the work of women in the missionary endeavor led me to Bulgarian and Ottoman sources that revealed the significance of gender at the nexus of American–Ottoman–Bulgarian encounters and allowed me to reconcile the earlier divergent interpretations.

NOTES

[11.] Thomas Bender, *Rethinking American History in a Global Age* (Berkeley: University of California Press, 2002); Ian Tyrrell, *Transnational Nation: United States History in Global Perspectives since 1789* (London: Palgrave Macmillan, 2007); Nicolas Barreyre, Michael Heale, Stephen Tuck, and Cécile Vidal, *Historians across Borders: Writing American History in a Global Age* (Berkeley: University of California Press, 2014).

[12.] Jane Hunter, *The Gospel of Gentility: American Women Missionaries in Turn-of-the Century China* (New Haven, CT: Yale University Press, 1984).

[13.] Thomas W. Zeiler, "The Diplomatic History Bandwagon: A State of the Field," *Journal of American History* 95, no. 4 (2009): 1053–78.

[14.] Arthur Schlesinger Jr., "The Missionary Enterprise and Theories of Imperialism," in *The Missionary Enterprise in China and America*, ed. John K. Fairbank, 336–73 (Cambridge, MA: Harvard University Press, 1974); Ryan Dunch, "Beyond Cultural Imperialism: Cultural Theory, Christian Missions, and Global Modernity," *History and Theory* 41, no. 3 (2002): 301–25.

[15.] Ian Tyrrell, *Reforming the World: The Creation of America's Moral Empire* (Princeton, NJ: Princeton University Press, 2010).

[16.] James F. Clarke, *The Pen and the Sword: Studies in Bulgarian History*, ed. Dennis Hupchick. (Boulder, CO: East European Monographs, 1998); Andrev Pantev, *Istoricheski pregled kum bulgaristika v Angliya i Sasht, 1856–1919* (Sofia: Nauka i izkustvo, 1986); Tatyana Nestorova, *American Missionaries among the Bulgarians (1858–1912)* (Boulder, CO: East European Monographs, 1987); Selim Deringil, *The Well-Protected Domains: Ideology and the Legitimation of Power in the Ottoman Empire, 1876–1909* (London: Tauris, 1998).

How to research and write historiography

In this final section we will guide you through the research and writing of historiography. Although there are a few important differences between the long and short historiography assignments we have provided in the workbook, much of the process is fundamentally similar. Please keep in mind that we are not suggesting a linear approach to the methods discussed below. Ideas will continue to evolve as you make new discoveries along the way. It is critical to be able to adapt or change strategies when necessary. However, the main guiding principle that must inform your work is that you are evaluating how historians have written about the topic you are investigating. You are not using secondary sources to glean factual information, although you may learn more about your topic along the way. Rather, you are looking for how that particular historian interpreted your topic. What did she or he say was significant about it? Is this different from what another historian argued? How so?

It is likely that you will return to many of the same sources later as you continue your research, but at that point you will be approaching the sources in a new way (covered in Chapter Five). For a typical capstone or senior thesis project, students should expect to write an article-length paper. Academic journal articles usually range between six thousand and ten thousand words, with eight thousand being average. Assuming you are working within these parameters, the historiography section of your final twenty-five to thirty-page paper is likely to be approximately three pages. Of course, your instructor may assign a separate, much lengthier, historiographical essay that you can later use to write the shorter section for your research paper. Assignments and examples are available in the workbook.

 # Research

Ideally, you should begin your research with a topic idea that you will be broadening or narrowing as needed. Your historiographical inquiries will eventually help you to work toward the development of a research question. In the process, you will acquire an understanding of how your investigation will fit in with what historians and other scholars have been writing about the field. It is generally best to develop a topic idea in consultation with your instructor and based on his or her guidelines. However, it is good practice to come up with a few general ideas before you show up in your instructor's office and begin to discuss your interests. Most instructors will allow a fair amount of flexibility for large research undertakings, so use that freedom to your advantage. You should consider whether there is a particular historical methodology or approach, such as those discussed in Chapter Two, that appeals to you. Are you drawn to cultural history, women's history, or diplomatic history? Do you tend to see history as driven by economic factors or sociopolitical ones? Next, consider the historical era that most interests you as well as whether you prefer to focus on developments over a longer or shorter period of time. Consider place. Do you want to examine a limited area, perhaps even undertake a local history, or are you more interested in connections across national borders or time periods? Do you have foreign language skills that could help you read and evaluate both secondary and primary sources? Ask yourself what sorts of historical actors most compel you—the famous, the infamous, the common folk? Finally, you should consider whether you wish to research and write about popular topics that are subject to constant revisionism, such as the Lincoln assassination, America's use of atomic weapons in Japan, or the causes of the French Revolution, or if you would prefer to pursue lesser studied areas where you might be able to offer new perspectives, for example, women's roles in Western European trade unionism, the role of political cartoons in nineteenth-century state building, or the cultural significance of the geisha in early modern Japan. Both "big" and "small" historical topics offer many opportunities for intellectual growth. The big topics are easily recognizable and allow students to easily access an abundance of secondary sources and jump into contentious debates. The main drawbacks, however, are that there may be too many sources to sift through in a short period of time and that it can be challenging to contribute something original to long-standing discussions. Smaller topics, in contrast, usually require a little more effort at the outset to find appropriate materials but can be more manageable and enable students to easily develop their own arguments.

Once you have a general topic idea, or better yet, a fairly narrow one, you can begin to locate appropriate secondary sources for the historiography assignment. You will want to locate an assortment of **monographs**, **scholarly journal** articles, and essays from **edited book volumes**. Your sources should be peer reviewed, that is, read by qualified scholars who are chosen by academic presses to assess the work of their colleagues. Unless your assignment guidelines specify otherwise, ideally you will want to seek the most influential, the most controversial, and the most recent secondary sources in the field. How, you might wonder, can you be expected to find these if you are not an expert in the field already? First, you should simply ask your professor or your college or university librarian for help getting started. They may be able to point you in the direction of notable books recently published by a university press. This, of course, you can also do on your own. Search your library using keywords specific enough to return relevant titles. Be certain to confine your choices to university presses or other academic presses. That is, look for the word "university" in the name of the publishing house (e.g., Oxford University Press or Duke University Press) or consult a librarian or your instructor about other respected publishers (e.g., Routledge, Ashgate, Brill). This is important because it means the book was not only written by a scholar and approved by other scholars (**peer review**), but also it will have the coverage you need for your historiography. Nearly every historical study published by a university press will include some kind of historiographical discussion, often in the introduction. This is where the author will describe the previous scholarship on the topic and where her or his research fits in, perhaps filling holes by revealing new sources, offering a new interpretation of the topic, or asking and answering a new research question. Either directly in the text or almost certainly in the endnotes, the author will refer to the most important books about that particular topic. In some instances, the author will explain in some detail the interpretations or arguments put forward by other scholars who have discussed this topic. In other instances, there simply are endnotes listing titles, but you still have information you did not have before.

Once you get started on this research you may soon find that you can recognize the most influential works since they are the ones most often referred to by other scholars and are likely to have been printed in multiple editions. The most controversial studies will also appear with some frequency in the scholarship of other authors. You will learn to be able to recognize when an argument seems to differ significantly from the standard narrative and therefore may be controversial. The other studies should mainly be recently published texts. One good rule of thumb for the traditional-age college student is that if the book or article is older than you are and does not fall into the category of classic or controversial, it is probably too old to be of value in your historiography. A **textbook** or a monograph from a history course is another useful resource for locating secondary sources. Look carefully through the endnotes or footnotes and the **bibliography** to see which texts the author used most frequently in his or her work. If you are fortunate, there may even be a section with suggestions for further reading or an **annotated bibliography**, which briefly identifies and describes key studies the author has utilized (see companion workbook chapter).

Once you have pinpointed several books that appear relevant to your own topic, you can often find more information about them by locating book reviews and/or review essays in scholarly journals. A great place to begin because of the large number of high-quality reviews it features is the *American Historical Review*, which is available in the widely used JSTOR database (http://www.jstor.org/) to which most libraries subscribe. Most academic journals include at least a few book reviews or a review essay. Reviews not only provide an overview of books but also assess their value to the field. This means that many book reviews include a brief historiographical discussion that indicates where the book they are discussing fits into the overall study of that topic to date. Moreover, the majority of book reviews are brief; you can judge whether they will be useful to you after reading just two or three pages instead of having to read large sections of the book. Review essays tend to be longer pieces that consider several recently published books together. Here, too, you may be led to new sources and acquire a nice overview of the current state of a field by reading a short essay by an area specialist. If you have chosen a topic in American history, for example, the journal *Reviews in American History* is made up entirely of lengthy review essays that will offer significant historiographical information should a review appear on your topic.

In addition to asking experts and looking for reviews, you will want to perform searches for books and journal articles using the resources available to you in your library. Library catalogs vary from institution to institution, but most search functions are quite similar and require you to make choices about the materials you are seeking. If you already have an author's name or a book title, use it to help you get started. An individual catalog entry contains valuable information to help you expand your search. For example, if your instructor recommended the 2008 Oxford University Press book *The Fall of Mussolini* by Philip Morgan, you could easily use the Library of Congress subject headings listed in the catalog entry to locate other books about Mussolini, Italy in World War II, and Italian history and politics. You could also take the call number of the book, in this case beginning with DG572, to physically go into your library's stacks and see what other books are shelved nearby. Some books might not have appeared in your catalog searches because of various database limitations. Once in the stacks, you can pull other books off the shelves and begin to examine them for suitability before even checking them out of the library. With the book in hand, look to see whether the author's credentials are listed, examine the copyright page for the publication date and to see whether the publisher is an academic or university press, and browse quickly through the notes and bibliography to see whether they seem comprehensive, that is, that they refer to a number of both secondary and primary sources in the languages of the research. It would be problematic, for instance, if the author of a book about Mussolini had not consulted any sources in the Italian language. A few minutes in the stacks early in the research process can save you time and effort later. Of course, your library may have limited resources. In this case, you may need to go beyond its walls and seek books from other institutions. Since most academic libraries participate in some sort of consortium with other libraries or in an interlibrary loan program, you have access to thousands of books not available at your college. In fact, today's instructors have little patience for the words "but I couldn't find anything on my topic" because they know that with a little bit of lead time, it is possible to locate a copy of nearly every book published. Your own librarians or instructor can explain the exact procedures for completing requests to retrieve books from outside institutions.

Academic journal articles are the other major type of secondary source you will want to consult for your historiography. Academic libraries usually subscribe to several databases that consolidate multiple journals. Some of the most popular databases used by historians are JSTOR, EBSCOhost (includes America: History & Life and Historical Abstracts), Project Muse, and Oxford Bibliographies Online. Consult your instructor or librarian or your college library website to verify which databases and journals your institution carries. When searching for articles, it is helpful to have an author's name; it is often the case that authors of books have also published articles in the same or related areas of their research. Detailed keyword searches will generate effective results as well. If you are not generating enough results using the main terms associated with your topic, rethink and modify them. Keep in mind that many databases give you the opportunity to weed out materials that will not be useful in putting together your historiographical sources. Always select the "peer reviewed" box when it is given as an option. To find articles, you will want to exclude book reviews from your search. Most databases allow you to do so. To help you find the highest quality articles in a reasonable amount of time, use some of the same strategies you applied to identify appropriate books. Choose recently published texts written by scholars that include extensive documentation. As mentioned previously, most scholarly articles are at least six thousand words; if an article is just a few pages, it may be too cursory for your purposes. Academic journals usually feature brief abstracts for each of the major articles. Before taking the time to save and print a large stack of articles that will be of no use to you, be sure the topic is actually relevant to your research. It takes just a few minutes to read and digest an abstract for its suitability.

Now that you have identified an appropriate number of secondary sources that appear to meet the criteria for your assignment, you can begin to go through them individually and pull out the information you will need to frame your historiography. It is not necessary to read the full texts word by word. A great deal can be understood by reading the table of contents, the introduction and conclusions, the notes and bibliography, and a few selected sections of the chapters and/or article. Of course, if you have the time and inclination, it is advisable to read as much as possible.

The following questions will help you become familiar with your sources:

- What is the story being told in the text? What is it about?
- What is the author's overall argument? Some authors will offer exact statements, such as directly telling you, "I want to argue" or "This book seeks to explain," whereas others require you to search for buried declarative statements. This is often the only place where you will find the word "I" used.
- Is the author's goal to reinterpret existing understandings of the topic, to contribute new material to reinforce previous accounts, or to offer a completely new perspective? She should tell you so through a historiographical section of her own.
- What is the author's overall approach to the topic? Does he identify as a cultural historian, refer to specific theoretical underpinnings (e.g., Marxism), or claim to take a feminist approach, for example? Look for key words such as gender, class, race, and/or ethnicity and refer to the discussions of theories and methodologies in Chapter Two to help you recognize different approaches.
- What kind of primary source evidence does the author use? Does he mention anything about why certain sources were selected or excluded and where they are located?
- Does the evidence seem to support the author's claims? Are most arguments supported by examples drawn from secondary or primary sources?
- Do the endnotes/bibliography seem to represent both relevant secondary and primary sources on the topic?
- How is the study structured? For books, do the chapters appear to be organized in a logical fashion? For articles, do the points flow clearly and support the author's thesis?
- Are there any aspects of the text you would identify as especially important? What appears to be the author's main contribution?
- Are there any flaws you can identify in the study?

Once you have completed your analysis of each source, you can begin to approach the sources together as a group. The following questions will help you to better understand how to compare your texts from a historiographical standpoint:

- How do the texts together contribute to advancing your understanding of the topic? What do you know now that you did not know before?
- How did these texts help you learn more about how historians are writing about this topic? What changes in approach do you see? How and why have these changes developed over time?
- What advantages/disadvantages are there to each of the authors' approaches?
- Do the authors directly mention each other's work? Do the same authors' names appear in several sources?
- Do one or more of the texts seem stronger than the others? How so?
- Which texts seem to be most closely related to what you intend to research for your paper?
- In what ways will your research be influenced by the work of these other scholars? Will your work uphold or challenge their ideas?
- Is there a new angle you hope to pursue in your paper that these authors have not yet covered?

🖎 **Writing**

You can now use your notes on the individual and collective secondary sources to begin to structure the historiographical section or essay. Longer essays are often organized chronologically since the historian's main objective generally is to discuss changes over time in how scholars have written about their fields. A chronological approach facilitates the author's ability to communicate the ways in which external factors, such as politics or social issues, may have factored into how particular topics have been covered in the past and it allows for an unforced progression toward present-day trends in the field. A thematic approach may be preferable in a shorter historiographical section within a research paper, however. In this case, the author's goal is to offer a brief overview of the current state of the field and place her/his work in relation to it. Although the author may refer to bigger changes over a long period of time or to older studies, he/she will usually be more focused on current trends and explaining the significance of his/her research in advancing the field. Of course, you may decide that some combination of chronology and theme works best for your historiographical essay or section. Use your detailed notes to help you arrange the structure by printing and ordering them or by moving them around in your word processing program; sometimes seeing ideas physically next to each other helps you to visualize how your writing will work best.

Whatever your overall organizing principle, you will need to structure your essay or section around a thesis, which, in the case of historiography, means offering an argument about the state of the field you are researching. What is the overall conclusion you have reached about how historians have written about your area of interest? How will you demonstrate your assessment of the field in your discussion of the secondary sources? You will want to keep in mind that your purpose is to evaluate how individual historians and historians as a group have written about their areas of expertise. At the same time, you will need to offer enough historical context about your topic to make it understandable to a general educated reader. It can be challenging to strike a balance between providing background information and understanding the key debates and discussions historians have undertaken. In other words, you need to avoid recounting the full history of your topic as you now know it, but at the same time you want to be sure your reader understands the event, person, or period under consideration. For example, the article sample by Sarah Kinkel should be used to provide an account of how historians have written about eighteenth-century British naval reforms rather than to provide a comprehensive history of them.[17] Use your introduction therefore both to place your topic in a historical framework and to establish what your essay or section will illustrate about the current literature in the field.

The body of your essay or section should be interpretive and analytical. You should consider your sources in relation to each other rather than individually as you would in an annotated bibliography. It is possible to discuss multiple authors together by connecting the ways in which their work overlaps. For example, you can begin by noting that "Historians Smith, Johnson, and Peterson have all argued that X led to Y while Fitzpatrick and Jones instead view Y as a separate case." Transitions between your analyses of the

---

[17.] See Chapter Three in the workbook.

different authors can also help you show how their work is related. In this case, you could use a structure such as "Like historian Philips, historian and women's studies scholar Fredericks has examined Z, but she has also consulted the archives in Little Visited Village where she had access to important never-before-seen documents that dramatically altered her arguments about A and B, the two most contentious areas of debate among today's scholars." A collective treatment of the authors' main arguments, methodologies, and evidence used will allow you to focus on the central tenets of their contributions to the field and to reach conclusions about the strengths and weaknesses in your sources. At this point, you should be able to make suggestions as to which areas are worth further scrutiny. More importantly, however, you should now be ready to explain how your research will fit with the larger literature. Will your paper seek to clarify ambiguities, open new debates, or something else? Ideally, you should now be able to ask a research question, which is the main query you will be pursuing in your research paper, or even to state a working thesis, which is the argument you plan to support through your research.

Historiographical writing can seem daunting, particularly if you have not been required to do much of it during your time in school. It can also be intellectually stimulating and rewarding, however. Thinking like a professional historian will enable you to reach new insights and move beyond the idea that history is just a hodgepodge of facts to be strung together in stories. You will be able to act as a scholar and contribute to the advance of knowledge and interpretation. As one of our students has remarked, by "doing the historiography you know where the gaps are that still need to be filled. Only then can your own voice be heard."

CHAPTER FOUR

Primary Sources

Historiographical papers, such as those discussed in Chapter Three, are a useful starting point for a major research project. They will not, however, interpret primary sources since the purpose of such papers is to trace the arguments made by historians on a particular subject. A primary source is a record that was created during the historical moment under examination, such as a birth certificate, a letter, or a photograph, or evidence created after the event that records the experience of someone who lived through it, such as a diary, oral history, or memoir. A primary source can be as simple as a train ticket issued in 1919 to a delegate to the Paris Peace Conference or as elaborate as a three-hundred-page memoir written by that same delegate published thirty years later. A well-written history thesis without primary sources is like a car without an engine. It might be beautiful on the outside, but it isn't going anywhere. This chapter aims to demystify primary research: it will discuss how to find, evaluate, and use primary sources in your thesis or another assignment. Like many of your history professors, you are likely to find primary research the most energizing and enjoyable part of your thesis experience.

Most professional historians cannot wait to get into the archives, and we hope many of you will feel the same way. But unless you are writing a Ph.D. dissertation, it is unlikely that you will be able to travel to distant archives or learn how to read Old English in time to finish your research on Anglo-Saxon history. A successful research question allows you to find and use relevant primary sources in a timely manner. This is the difference between a student who sails along and finishes on time and the student in a panic as the deadline draws near. Do not put off primary research. You should locate potential primary sources *before* you finalize your research question. You may need to modify what you are asking based on the availability of primary source material. Locate more primary sources than you need, and locate them early. If you are required to use a certain number of primary sources—say, seven—double that number and find fourteen likely sources. A source might look perfect according to its title and description in a library search, but turn out to be unhelpful once you actually read it. The author of this chapter was excited to find an early General Electric publication for executives entitled *Manual for Dictators*. Was it written to help vice presidents become the Stalins of Schenectady (the location of the main GE plant)? No. It was a humorless how-to guide to help businessmen dictate letters to secretaries.[1] Some students locate interesting primary sources and *then* devise a research question to use them. But please read them first!

The most efficient place to begin looking for primary sources is your secondary sources. Read the citations closely. What primary sources did those authors use? Do not assume that an author has squeezed every drop of meaning out of the primary sources and there is nothing left to say. Think of all the different scholars who have written about

---

[1] *Manual for Dictators* (Schenectady, NY: General Electric Co., 1920). Many thanks to Bert Spector of Northeastern University for checking this source, which is only available at Harvard University.

Christopher Columbus, or the D-Day invasion of World War II, or the Black Death, each using roughly the same body of evidence but drawing different conclusions. Each author brings new questions to the primary sources. You have your own research questions, and you will also draw new conclusions. (If your conclusions are similar to that of another author, then you must cite that article or book as a secondary source.) If you find a promising primary source in a citation, request it and review it in its entirety. The quotes or images used by your secondary authors may look rather different viewed in their original context, suggesting new questions or interpretations. And you may discover that a different section of the source is more useful to you. The workbook section on primary sources demonstrates how one author used several different types of primary sources in a single scholarly article, and along the way you will learn how to read the "address" of cited sources so that you can find them for your own research. First, it may be useful to become familiar with the most common types of primary sources.

Finding and using documents

A document is a piece of written evidence that is typically no longer readily available, such as a hymn from the seventeenth century, or something never meant to be widely published in the first place, such as a letter, a list, a memo, a diary, a schedule, a stock certificate, a diploma, a bill of sale, etc. Documents are found in several locations.

Collected Documents. Collected documents, such as the many versions and volumes of the letters of Thomas Jefferson, made primary sources readily available to historians long before the Internet. They are bound together in book form and typically offer an informative introduction to the collection, which you should read. The documents themselves may be annotated, meaning that there are endnotes or footnotes explaining a word or a passage. In fact, you may find translations in printed collections that will allow you to conduct significant research using documents not originally written in English. (At the Ph.D. level, you will be expected to read documents in their original language.) If your library's system does not offer relevant collections of primary printed documents, try WorldCat (http://www.worldcat.org/), which allows you to search in more than ten thousand domestic and international libraries. WorldCat will list all the libraries that have that item, starting with the closest library to you, and the location of free digital copies if they exist. If the only copy is residing on a different continent (e.g., you are in the United States, and the source is in Australia), you may be out of luck. But typically this is not the case, and WorldCat provides enough information to request the item via interlibrary loan. You should be able to pick it up from your library in a few days. Register with WorldCat (it is free), so that you can sort and tag your finds, make notes, and create a bibliography for yourself. WorldCat even offers a mobile app. But there is a caveat with collected documents: they are often edited. That is, you will sometimes see only the part of a document that the editor believed was most important, not the entire document.

Digitized Documents. Every day more primary sources are scanned and made available on the Internet. But be forewarned: *do not depend on the Internet to serve up all of the relevant primary sources you need.* It is difficult to recover from a primary source deficit as your deadline approaches. Nevertheless, there are so many places to find online primary documents that the student can become paralyzed. The Reference and User Services Association provides a brief guide to the interpretation and citation of primary sources and then lists many useful digital collections (http://www.ala.org/rusa/sections/history/resources/pubs/usingprimarysources/). More specifically, there are gigantic collections for Americanists, such as the American Memory project at the Library of Congress (http://memory.loc.gov/ammem/index.html/), which has digitized more than 9 million items thus far, and the Digital Public Library of America (http://dp.la/) with more than 7 million. Historians of Europe might start with EuroDocs (http://eudocs.lib.byu.edu/index.php/Main_Page/), and for documents in English, Fordham University's "Internet History Sourcebooks Project" offers a global reach and several thematic collections (Lesbian/Gay, Jewish, Women) (http://www.fordham.edu/Halsall/index.asp/). More directed searches become possible as you narrow your focus, although many are by library subscription only, such as Women and Social Movements (U.S.), or for British history, Early English Books Online, Eighteenth Century Collections Online, and British State Papers, some are not, such as British History Online (http://www.british-history.ac.uk/Default.aspx/). Finally, there are excellent but widely scattered digitized collections made available by hundreds if not thousands of universities, public libraries, and historic sites. Digitized and downloadable archival material represents only a fraction of what is available and may or may not offer the documents you need for your assignment.

The difficulty with guides to digital sources is that the Internet changes so rapidly that any list of specific sites is outdated on the day that it appears. So how can you discover digitized primary sources that may be useful to you? Use a three-pronged approach:

1. *Your librarian.* Most college and university libraries have one or more individuals dedicated to keeping up with online sources. Your library's site will probably list a number of these sources, but as always, you will get better and faster results by sitting down with your librarian and discussing your research questions. Remember that librarians working in higher education are skilled professionals who often hold advanced degrees in library science and an additional subject.

2. *Your professor.* Although librarians are charged with keeping up with sources, your professor will be more familiar with the techniques of historical inquiry, as well as changes in language, which will help you search more efficiently. And it is quite likely that your professor will be familiar with several relevant online sources.

3. *You.* WorldCat, discussed above, allows you to search for downloadable primary sources using keywords, titles, and names. After you enter your search term and hit return, you will see options on the left-side of the screen under "Format." Choose "downloadable archival material." If you are looking for inspiration, try Serendip-o-Matic (http://serendip-o-matic.org/). You can paste in any text and see what sources it generates. It includes secondary as well as primary sources and is more suggestive than exhaustive, but it is better than a Google search because the results are drawn from libraries, museums, and archives. Want to just Google your topic and see what comes up? Go ahead. You may well find something useful, especially if you use Google Scholar (http://scholar.google.com/), a specialized Google engine designed to return results from scholarly websites.

How can you tell whether what you found online is acceptable? You know that you can trust the Library of Congress to post authentic sources with correct dates and descriptions. But a Google search will likely produce tempting but less verifiable sources. Perhaps a blogger posted a quote about World War II that looks perfect for your thesis, and she claims that it came from a letter that her great-grandfather wrote, but does not post or cite the letter itself. Or you find a graph with just the numbers you need, only it is from the website of an obviously political organization. For example, both the British Gun Control Network (http://www.gun-control-network.org/GCN02.htm/) and the British Campaign for Armed Self-Defence (http://armbritain.com/media.html/) provide historical statistics and graphs about gun violence in the United Kingdom to support their respective views. Politicized sites arrange information to further their interests, but it does not necessarily follow that the data sets are falsified. If the source of the data is identified, you may be able to trace it to a relatively neutral source. Look for official sites from well-known institutions such as universities, governments, national and international news organizations, and established bodies like the United Nations. But what if all you have is a dubious blog or website? If you have been unable to find a substitute in more reliable sources, discuss it with your professor. If you get permission to use it, be sure to describe the nature of your source either in the paper itself or in the citation. The reader must trust your evaluation of the sources or your work will be thrown into question. This can be as simple as introducing the quote with conditional language: "according to the blog of Mary Smith of Chicago, her great-grandfather Captain John Smith said . . ." If your professor allows you to use such sources, use them only sparingly, frame them accordingly, and avoid making them the centerpiece of your primary evidence.

As always, there is an exception. Depending on your research question, a politicized or commercial website may be a central primary source. For example, if you are asking a research question about the history of gun control in early twenty-first-century Britain, you would be interested not only in the most relatively objective data on gun violence, but also in the ways in which pro– and anti–gun control groups presented evidence. Likewise, you would not go to a tourism site to discover what life was like in post-Soviet Russia, unless your research question concerned the history of Russian tourism during that period or efforts by Russia to construct its post-Soviet image. As always in history, everything depends on the context. Remember that you will be expected to analyze these sites as a historian. Whether or not you are an advocate or an opponent of gun control and whether or not you spent your semester abroad in Moscow, you must put your own views to the side and unpack the values, arguments, and meanings of these sites. Your own argument, of course, is subjective. But if you let your own point of view obstruct your ability to analyze your sources, you will lose your credibility with the reader.

Documents Available on Microform. Some collections, and some rare books, might be available only on microfilm (a reel of images) or microfiche (a small sheet of images). Sometimes you can request these materials through interlibrary loan. Before the Internet, this was how scholars could access primary materials that were unavailable in hard copy. If you see the words "microform," "microfilm," or "microfiche," check to make sure that your library has the required reader, and then once the materials arrive, ask for brief instructions regarding its use (Figure 4.1). Some readers allow you to make a copy of the image, but often for a fee.

FIGURE 4.1. Microform machine. Photo by Sergio Sericolo, Siena College.

Documents Located in Archives, Manuscript Collections, and Records. Although we realize that not every student will be able to visit primary collections because of geographical or other restrictions, if you can, you should. Depending on the kind of repository, sometimes the term "manuscript" is used, sometimes "rare books and manuscripts," (Figure 4.2) and government offices that keep deeds, birth certificates, property information, criminal records, and maps use the term "records." Despite the millions of primary sources available on the Internet, there are many more in collections; only a fraction of extant primary sources are digitized. Furthermore, primary source collections typically come with finding aids that include a brief essay about the importance of the person, place, event, or thing that the collection is about and an inventory of what is inside all of those boxes and files. Some of these essays are scholarly and can be cited as secondary sources. And the best part is that primary collections are staffed by archivists who can literally lead you to the best sources and convey information that may cause you to rethink your project in unforeseen and valuable ways. This kind of direct assistance will shorten the time it takes for you to settle on a research question, find useful evidence, and figure out what it all means. However, even enthusiastic students balk at walking into an archive for the first time. Many students falsely assume that archives are just for advanced graduate students or professional scholars. Archives are not self-service, and many of us do not like asking for help. But there is nothing like holding an original primary document in your own hands to make you realize that you *are* a historian. And you

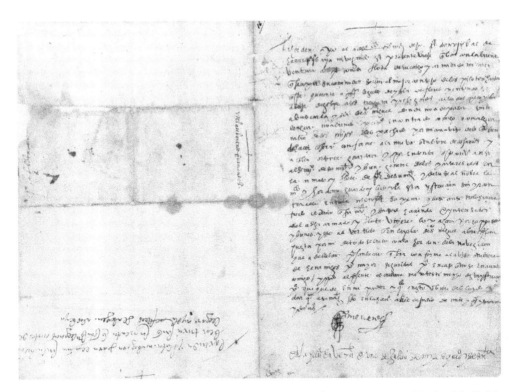

FIGURE 4.2. Pedro Menéndez de Avilés, first governor of Spanish Florida, "Sailing Order to Spain" for Don Cristóbal de Eraso's fleet dated July 3, 1572, Library of Congress Rare Book and Special Collections Division Jay I. Kislak Collection dcu (Acc. 1996.031.00.0002).

will discover that archives are not just for professional historians. You may find yourself working alongside someone researching their family history or someone conducting research for a business. But archives are not generally advertised. So where does one find an archive, and how does one find out whether there is anything useful inside?

If you are free to choose any topic, you might start at home. Finding local primary sources and then creating an argument based on them is a fine way to create a manageable thesis project. Ask whether your college or university has an archive. Most of them do, and they may have much more than just historic papers associated with the institution. Ask your public library. Local institutions that typically keep unpublicized archives include public and private libraries, town halls, museums, and historic sites. Contact them directly and ask. They may be thrilled that someone is going to use their materials.

More commonly, students choose topics based on their interests and then find relevant primary sources. There are two ways to start. First, choose your most interesting secondary sources and comb the citations to see what primary sources the authors used. This will help you understand how primary sources are used to build an argument (the focus of the workbook section), and you may be able to find them for yourself if they are available digitally or locally. Second, find collections by topic and geographic location by using ArchiveGrid (http://beta.worldcat.org/archivegrid/). This powerful tool is a boon to historians, but it can only use what is already online; thus it misses the collections of smaller museums and historic sites.

Once you have found a likely collection, look for the finding aid. This is an overview of the collection that will tell you what it contains, sometimes down to the contents of each file folder. As is true for digitized primary sources, not all finding aids are available online, and not all collections are organized the same way. But most keep their collections in sequential boxes of manila folders, and once you figure out their system it is usually straightforward. Let's say you are interested in the history of advertising and your ArchiveGrid search reveals a collection within driving distance: the Ernst Dichter papers at the Hagley Museum and Library in Wilmington, Delaware. The online description tells you that he was a German-born psychologist who created the field of motivational research to help businesses create more effective advertising and that there are 215 linear feet of records. This is telling you that the boxes of manila folders take up 215 feet of shelf space. This is a large collection, too large to see it all. You want to drill down using the finding aid to unearth the most useful material for your research. The online finding aid for the Ernest Dichter papers includes an extensive biographical "note" about Dichter, as well as general information about the collection, such as beginning and ending dates. The primary source documents and materials are listed in the inventory, which is organized by series, box, and file. For example, Figure 4.3 shows part of the inventory of Box 164. Each entry is a separate file within the box:[2]

164	Canada, Tourism—How to Win Over American Tourists to A Holiday in Canada—*The Globe and Mail*, May 13, 1972
164	Canada Study, undated
164	Candidates—How People Really Feel About the Candidate—an Emotional Barometer, undated
164	Candy - Candy Industry, undated
164	Candy - Consumer Attitudes Towards, 1960
164	Candy - Candy Marketer, July 1965
164	Candy - Miscellaneous, 1970
164	Candy - Proposal for Cadbury, Ltd., Confectionary Group, October 1973
164	Candy - Publicity, 1954
164	Candy - The Stepchild of the Pleasure Society, June 23, 1972
164	Candy - X-Raying the Candy Customer, April 29, 1965
164	Candy Industry, 1965
164	Canning—The Changing Psychology of Canning at Home, November 18, 1965

FIGURE 4.3. Ernest Dichter Papers, 1936–1991, Hagley Museum and Library, Wilmington, DE.

When you find a collection that you would like to see in person, send an email using the name and title of the contact person from the website. In your email, clarify (1) who you are (graduate/undergraduate, your major and institution), (2) what kind of assignment you are working on (undergraduate thesis/M.A. thesis/Ph.D. dissertation), (3) your

---

[2.] "Ernest Dichter Papers," Hagley Museum and Library, Wilmington, DE.

research questions, and, (4) briefly, why you think a particular collection will be useful to you. Archivists want to match their collections to your research questions, and the more they know about your needs, the better they can do their job. You may wish to ask your professor or college librarian to follow up with an email explaining your project and requesting the archivist grant you permission to consult the materials. If you are granted permission, check the hours that the archive is open (most are limited) and make an appointment with the archivist. You may be able to request in advance specific boxes that will be pulled for you when you arrive. In an email confirming your appointment, include all the information for boxes that interest you: the name of the collection, the call number, the series number, and the box number. It is rare, but you may be advised that all or part of a collection is under a time seal, meaning that the donor has asked that the materials not be released before a certain date.

Some archives are large and well organized. Some archives are tiny, cluttered, one-person operations run by a volunteer. Make no judgments based on appearance. On the contrary, make friends with the archivist. The archivist is your research partner. You already know that most documents are not digitized; now you will discover that most finding aids are not online, and your archivist can direct you to collections that you could not have discovered on your own. Be sure to bring your notes regarding which collections and boxes you would like to see. If you are trying to find a particular document that was mentioned in a citation in your secondary research, bring a copy of the citation or the entire book or article to help the archivist locate the file. Although you may have requested certain boxes via email, you may need to repeat your request, only this time using an internal system. Larger archives have lockers to store all of your belongings except for pencil, paper, laptop, phone, and camera. You may not use a pen. There may not be an outlet, so be sure that your computer is fully charged. They may not have an internet connection for users, so make sure that any research notes you have made in preparation for your visit are on your hard drive or on a hard copy. Mute your laptop, camera, and phone so that you do not disturb other researchers. Typically, the archivist will bring a cart with your requested boxes right to you within a few minutes. There will be a limit regarding the number of boxes you may request at one time, so please ask. Once your boxes arrive, you may be asked to wear cotton gloves to handle delicate materials. You may be given a piece of cardboard to use as a bookmark between files. You may see skinny beanbags on the table to use as weights to keep rare books open or a v-shaped foam bookrest to prevent damage to delicate bindings. Whatever they give you, they want you to use it to protect the collection. Pull out one file at a time and keep the files and the papers in precisely the same order that you found them, even if the order seems nonsensical. When you find something useful, make a note of exactly where you found it: page number, title, author, and date of document, file name or number where you found it, box number, series number, name and access number of the collection, and the name of the archive: in other words, all the information you needed to request and find that document. Remember, your citation will be a trail of bread crumbs allowing the interested reader to retrace your steps and find the same document.

What if you want a copy of a document? Most archives prefer that you take photos of materials rather than photocopy them because it is easier on the materials, but some archives prohibit photography. Archives charge for photocopies, so come prepared. If you take photos, take an initial photo of the box and file information, so that when you look at your photos later you will have a visual record of their origin. In addition, take notes for each photo that include a detailed description and the reason why you took the photo (how you thought it would help your thesis), plus its origin—archive, collection, box, file, page number. There is nothing worse than wanting to use a primary source but being unable to locate the information you need to cite it. *If you cannot cite the origin of a primary source, you cannot use it.*

FIGURE 4.4. Student examining a manuscript. Photo by Sergio Sericolo, Siena College.

There will often be an archivist in the reading area; this person is there not only to answer questions and retrieve materials, but also to ensure that the materials are being handled properly. This can be intimidating at first, but you are not an intruder (Figure 4.4). The point of an archive is to make sure that these materials are available to researchers like you, both now and in the future. Once again, make friends with the archivist, who will be as excited as you are when you find useful evidence. Take a few moments to read the acknowledgments of one of your secondary sources. You will typically see several archivists cited by name as persons the author could not have done without.

🔊 Finding and using other primary sources

Primary Books and Pamphlets. A published book, pamphlet, or article may be used as a primary source if it was created and published during the period under investigation and was concerned with contemporary issues. For example, many American students are familiar with Thomas Paine's pamphlet "Common Sense" (1776), a widely circulated treatise that listed the reasons why the American colonies should separate from England. Scholarship on nineteenth- and twentieth-century topics often use published sources. To use the examples above, if you are writing about the history of gun control, you would look not only for books about gun control, but also for books about firearms and their use that were published during the period you are examining. It is a mistake to search too narrowly. A book about guns in general may offer insight into ideas about guns and their use that will prove helpful. Second, before the early 1960s, the phrase "gun control" often applied to the physical control of weapons, for example, on warships. Librarians and professors are knowledgeable about changes in language and thus keywords, so before you conclude that you "can't find anything," ask for assistance. To locate primary books, start with your own library's system, and if possible, choose to restrict the years of publication to your time frame. You may do this using WorldCat's advanced search. A quick search on WorldCat, for example, found Paul Allen Curtis's *Guns and Gunning* (1934), which is described as a book about firearms, shooting, and hunting. If your library system does not have this book, you may request it via interlibrary loan. You may also have luck searching in Google Books (http://books.google.com/), and the Internet Archive (http://archive.org/), both of which offer full or partial books online. If you cannot get the entire book online, you will see enough information to request it via interlibrary loan. Sometimes it is not clear whether a printed source is primary or secondary. What about Winston Churchill's six-volume *The Second World War,* published between 1948 and 1953? Churchill was the prime minister of the United Kingdom for most of the war, thus he was an eyewitness not only to the war but also to top-secret intelligence and decision making. Is it a primary source? It would probably take the skills of an advanced graduate student to tease out the "primary" qualities of these volumes from the "secondary" qualities. Often the context in which a document is used defines it as a primary or a secondary source. History professors typically disallow the use of textbooks as secondary sources. Yet if you wanted to answer the research question "How did the presentation of slavery change in the American educational system during the 20th century?", history textbooks from the period 1900–2000 would function as primary sources.

   Government and Legal Documents. Testimony before Congress, parliamentary debates, court cases, and census records are all excellent primary sources, but because of the unique organization of government and legal publications, finding them often requires the assistance of a librarian. But it is well worth it. For U.S. government documents, a good place to start is the Library of Congress page on "Congressional Committee Hearings" (http://www.loc.gov/rr/main/govdocsguide/Hearings.html/), which lists subscription-only and free online sources of digitized data. There is also the *Congressional Quarterly* (http://www.cq.com/). For state government documents, look up the archive of the state in question. Most have online research tools. Again, many government documents are available in hard copy right in your own library, but getting started will require the help of a librarian. This is also true of legal documents. The Law Library of Congress offers a useful guide to orient the student of legal history (http://www.loc.gov/law/). The University of Minnesota Law Library provides a research guide that includes links to guides to Roman law, Ancient law, Medieval law, Islamic and Middle Eastern law, and American and

European law (http://libguides.law.umn.edu/legalhistoryresearch/). Given its importance to American law, some U.S. law schools provide extensive research guides to British law and legal history: see Duke University (https://law.duke.edu/lib/researchguides/englishlegal/) and Georgetown University (http://www.law.georgetown.edu/library/research/guides/english-legal-history.cfm/).

Newspapers, Magazines, and Popular Journals. Some scholars do not consider these "true" primary sources, but a glimpse at the citations in respected history journals indicates how often they are used. First, popular news items and magazine articles published during the time period typically concern contemporary issues. Sometimes the author experienced the event directly, such as a newspaper reporter on the scene describing a war zone. But even if the reporter is not writing as an eyewitness to a specific event, the historian can glean a sense of the ideology of the period through these sources. For example, even respected American news sources freely used the derogatory term "jap" when referring to the Japanese during World War II, which tells you something significant about the cultural climate of the period. The researcher must also understand that newspapers are made up of several kinds of sources. First, there are reports of "breaking news" written by journalists, such as the description of a war zone. There are also feature stories, which are longer, based on extensive research, and often fall into the category of "investigative reporting." Sources are often confidential, so you may not be able to trace a quote to a specific individual. You—and your reader—will have to trust the newspaper, and some newspapers are more trusted than others. Although every newspaper has a reputation for being "conservative" or "liberal," some have stood the test of time: *The Guardian* (London, UK), *The New York Times*, *The Wall Street Journal*, *The Washington Post*, *Le Monde* (Paris). This list is far from exhaustive; ask your librarian and your professor for more titles. But not every apparent "article" is written by a journalist. Look to see whether the item is an "editorial," meaning that it reflects the political views of the editor of the newspaper (the rest of a newspaper is supposed to be objective). Look to see whether it is a "letter to the editor." These are letters from readers typically praising or protesting the newspaper's coverage or bringing attention to a neglected topic. Look carefully at the name and credentials of the author; it may be a renowned expert in the field. Or it may be a regular reader. Beware of advertisements disguised as articles. Depending on your topic, political cartoons and even advertisements may be useful to you. There is something to be gained by viewing the entire page of a newspaper. What news was deemed worthy of the front page? What sorts of advertisements appeared in the first section of the newspaper, where the "hard" news was reported, what advertisements appeared in the "style" section, and what assumptions were made about who read which section? If you try to find older articles by going directly to the newspaper online (http://www.nytimes.com/), you are likely to hit a pay wall, that is, you will be asked to pay a fee to see the entire article. Do not pay. Your college or university library probably subscribes to a database (ProQuest Central or New York Times Historical, for example) that will allow you to find full-text newspaper and periodical sources for free.

Like newspapers, some magazines are more notable than others for their quality. In the case of the United States, *Time* magazine is probably more reliable if you are looking for information about a famous murder than *True Crime*, but popular detective magazines might offer cultural insight into how some Americans viewed crime in the mid-twentieth century. For American history, the *Reader's Guide to Periodical Literature* has indexed articles since 1901, and your library may subscribe to the online version. Google Books offers full access to many popular magazines, and many more have been preserved on microfilm. If a WorldCat search reveals that your title is available on microform, ask whether it can be borrowed via interlibrary loan.

Quantitative Sources. Census information, consumer surveys, polls, and data sets can be profitably used by the history student even without the benefit of formal statistical training. Students of American history will find the "Historical Statistics of the United States" (http://hsus.cambridge.org/HSUSWeb/HSUSEntryServlet/) potentially helpful because it includes information on labor, crime, housing, standard of living, diet, etc., and makes it easy to customize graphs and charts. Although not quite as user-friendly, U.S. census materials for all extant years can be retrieved through the National Historical Geographic Information System (https://www.nhgis.org/). Similar resources exist for other countries, such as Insee in France (http://www.insee.fr/en/) and ISTAT in Italy (http://en.istat.it/). The Economic and Social Council of the United Nations offers reports on many parts of the world, particularly developing nations (http://www.un.org/en/ecosoc/). Again, your best course of action is to begin by sitting down with your librarian. Interpreting quantitative sources is not as straightforward as one might assume. Although government data are generally more trustworthy than numbers generated by lesser-known private sources, simply the act of choosing what to count is a value judgment, and the same data can be interpreted in contradictory ways. There are several manuals in print to help the historian evaluate quantitative data,[3] but a student could begin online with "Making Sense of Numbers" (http://historymatters.gmu.edu/mse/numbers/). If you want to try your hand at analyzing numbers you have found in your research, the basic tool is a spreadsheet program such as Excel. Data can be compared and viewed as tables and graphs, making it easier to identify trends. Free training videos exist online, but check to see whether your institution offers training or statistical consulting to researchers. "Big Data" production is beyond the scope of this guide, but the work of historians using it may prove helpful. "Big Data" refers to immense "bits of information," scientific, social, financial, and otherwise, captured by twenty-first century technological advances.[4] *Freedom on the Move* (http://freedomonthemove.org/), for example, is an American academic website soliciting information from online users who may have access to some of the estimated 100,000 advertisements that existed for runaway slaves or who can help input data from PDFs of advertisements already collected. Since each advertisement included a physical description of the fugitive slave as well as clues to conditions and geographical information, a database of these advertisements would provide the richest source yet for historians of American slavery. Crowdsourcing

---

[3.] Charles H. Feinstein and Mark Thomas, *Making History Count: A Primer in Quantitative Methods for Historians* (New York: Cambridge University Press, 2002); Pat Hudson, *History by Numbers: An Introduction to Quantitative Approaches*, (New York: Bloomsbury USA, 2000); and Konrad Jaraush and Kenneth A. Hardy, *Quantitative Methods for Historians: A Guide to Research, Data, and Statistics (Baker Library Reference)* (Chapel Hill: University of North Carolina Press, 1991).

[4.] James Grossman, "'Big Data': An Opportunity for Historians?," *Perspectives on History* (March 2012), http://www.historians.org/publications-and-directories/perspectives-on-history/march-2012/big-data-an-opportunity-for-historians/.

introduces its own issues, such as quality control, but it is using technology in ways that were impossible even a generation ago.

Documentary Photographs and Maps. Photographs date from the mid-nineteenth century. Photographs or maps should be used as evidence to support your thesis, not just as window dressing. Documentary photographs were taken to capture a scene for posterity such as a sporting achievement, a gathering of famous politicians, or the conditions suffered by refugees. They may be considered art, but that was not their original purpose. Documentary photographs can be found in archives and online, but like any online primary source, stay with reputable libraries and historic sites. You do not want to analyze an image found through a Google search that seems original but has been altered. Like numbers, photographs seem to tell an objective truth, but the historian must consider their origins and use. Any image, photographic or not, needs thorough analysis. Why was it created? By whom? For whom? The famous photograph (Figure 4.5) taken by Associated Press photographer Joe Rosenthal, "American Marines: Raising the American Flag on Mount Suribachi on Iwo Jima," (http://www.loc.gov/exhibits/treasures/trm023 .html/) appears to document the moment when American Marines successfully captured a strategic island during World War II. It was actually the second flag-raising, and the battle was not yet over. The origins of the photograph led to much debate concerning its significance. This debate may or may not influence a student's use of the photograph, but the student using this photograph should be aware of the story behind it.

FIGURE 4.5. Joe Rosenthal, "American Marines: Raising the American Flag on Mount Suribachi on Iwo Jima," AP Photo/Joe Rosenthal, File.

As with photographs, when you use maps you must trust your source and pay strict attention to the date because borders, place names, and even geographical features may change over time (Figure 4.6). The reference section of your library most likely holds

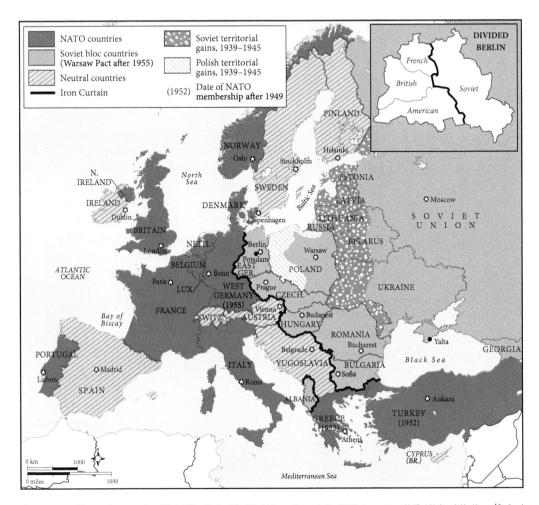

FIGURE 4.6. Map of Europe after World War II, in *The World Transformed: World History since 1945*, Michael H. Hunt (Oxford University Press, 2016). Note that many of the countries here have changed dramatically again since the fall of communism in 1989–1990.

many excellent sources of maps, and the University of Texas, famed for its historical map collection, provides links to more than six hundred historical map collections online (http://www.lib.utexas.edu/maps/map_sites/hist_sites.html/). Students of American history can look for Sanborn maps, which were created for fire insurance purposes and represent many American cities between 1867 and 1970 in great detail. They have been digitized on a subscription basis, and local archives often have hard copies. Maps are no longer just illustrative, but can also be used to [cut as] inform your research question, your evidence, and your argument. For example, see Stanford's Spatial History Project to examine how Richard White, author of *Railroaded: The Transcontinentals and the Making of*

Modern America, uses maps to understand how railroads shaped the American West (http://web.stanford.edu/group/spatialhistory/cgi-bin/site/project.php?id=997/).[5] Some historians speak of a "spatial turn" in history, particularly noting the use of Geographical Information Systems, or GIS, because it allows for the layering of information in three dimensions. Historians can use it to recreate an urban street, for example, if they have enough data. The University of California at Los Angeles (http://guides .library.ucla.edu/gis/) and Tufts University (http://sites.tufts.edu/gis/) offer many guides and links to help students of the humanities understand how to use GIS in their work and find sources. More international sources and maps can be found at the Historical GIS Clearinghouse and Forum (http://www.aag.org/cs/projects_and_ programs/historical_gis_clearinghouse/hgis_databases/). State, county, and local governments may also give students the opportunity to work with GIS maps and historical images. In New York State, for example, the Schenectady County Internet Mapping System (http://www.simsgis.org/sims_lite/default.htm/) provides an open-access database students can use to compare maps at various times between 1941 and the present.

Students wishing to create their own maps but unable to learn GIS can try Google Maps Engine for free (https://mapsengine.google.com/map/). For example, if you are trying to determine distances between ports in the seventeenth century, you can type in the locations, use the tools to determine distance, and save your map. If you have a number of locations or you want to see what census data looks like visually, you can import a CSV file or spreadsheet and the information will automatically appear as points on your map. You can create layers of information, add images and videos, and visually adjust the map to suit your explanatory needs.

Oral History and Memoirs. Oral histories are interviews with historical actors who reflect on the past. They may appear as typescripts in archives, collected documents in published works, or interviews in documentary films. In the past two decades, the oral histories of war veterans have been a particularly popular area. You may begin with the holdings of the Library of Congress (http://www.loc.gov/vets/), but the popularity of oral history programs concentrating on veterans means that such materials are often much closer to home. Ask your college librarian and the surrounding libraries and high schools whether they have such a program. Alternatively, you may know someone that you would like to interview for your own research. The website of the Oral History Association (http://www.oralhistory.org/) offers excellent advice, particularly the section entitled "Principles and Best Practices." *Important*: any interview for your thesis, even with a member of your family, might require approval by your institution's institutional review board, which is charged with screening projects involving human subjects. This is to ensure that the rights of subjects are protected. It is a good idea to check your college or university's policies before embarking on your field work. If you would like to create your own oral histories, you must plan well in advance. It may take weeks or even months before you are cleared to conduct your interviews. One important caveat regarding oral histories and memoirs: both are remembrances of things past, and sometimes long past.

[5.] Richard White, *Railroaded: The Transcontinentals and the Making of Modern America* (New York: Norton, 2011).

All of us tend to edit and embellish our memories over time, and thus the "facts" may or may not have happened the way a person recalls them. In one sense, this is an unfortunate distortion of the past. In another sense, what has been edited and embellished—if you can tell—says something valuable about the individual and the culture he or she represents.

Film, Television, Radio. Media studies are housed in separate disciplines from history, but thesis writers working on twentieth-century topics may find primary sources within modern forms of media. Three types of popular media that are often useful to the historian include:

1. *Documentary films, television, and radio programs.* Documentary films that include interviews with those who experienced or witnessed the event or period are similar to oral histories. Newsreels, which were exhibited in movie theaters in the mid-twentieth century, are similar to newspapers, as are taped news programs. The Internet Archive, referenced above, has made Universal Newsreels (1929–1967) available online, and many non-American newsreels are available from The Newsreel Archive (http://www .newsreelarchive.com/). The Vanderbilt Television News Archive has been archiving U.S. news programs since 1968 and will loan DVDs (http://tvnews.vanderbilt.edu/). Assume that all of these sources are heavily edited and interpreted, but the way they were interpreted may offer great insight into the period in which they were produced.

2. *Fictional and creative media based on contemporary issues* refers to cultural production intended for consumption by popular audiences. These media may deal with current events or trends or historical ones that resonate in the present. An example of this is *Casablanca* (1942), a Hollywood film that is both a love story and a propaganda film meant to stir Americans to support the war against the Axis powers. Graphic novels, such as *Maus* (1980–1991) and *Persepolis* (2000–2003), may offer a contemporary popular perspective of historical events. *Maus* is based on author Art Spiegelman's interviews with his father, a Polish Jew and Holocaust survivor. In *Persepolis*, Marjane Satrapi explores her experiences of the Islamic Revolution in Iran (1979). Moreover, the sudden popularity of a type of media, such as comic books in the mid-twentieth century, could signify some particular cultural need or response, just as the current popularity of reality shows, social media, or the political divisiveness of television news networks will reveal something about our current period to future historians.[6]

3. *Fictional media that captures a prevailing ideology.* In the category of popular media, the story being portrayed may take place long in the past or far in the future, but its themes speak to contemporary issues. For example, in the 1984 film *Red Dawn*, American teenagers living in a Midwestern town take up arms against invading Soviet forces. The American teens are depicted as innocent and heroic, whereas the Russian and Cuban soldiers are caricatured to appear evil and cold, a prevailing image held by many Americans at that time. The television series *24* (2001–2010) played into the widespread fears of many Americans after the terrorist

---

[6.] An excellent discussion of the historical interpretation of popular culture can be found in the December 1992 issue of the *American Historical Review*, which published a "Forum" on the question. The essay by Lawrence W. Levine, "The Folklore of Industrial Society," combined with the essay by T. J. Jackson Lears, "Making Fun of Popular Culture," offers a guide to the historian wondering how to analyze popular culture. Stable URL: http://www.jstor.org/stable/i337849/.

attacks of September 11, 2001, but some critics questioned the series' overuse of the stereotype of Muslims as terrorists and of showing Americans using torture as a valid method for obtaining information.

There are several published guides to help the student use moving images and other media to consider historical questions.[7] It is increasingly easy to find even rare moving images and audio online through free and commercial sources, but again, be aware of adulterated sources. We recommend you begin with trusted sources, such as the Library of Congress (http://www.loc.gov/index.html/) or the British Film Institute (http://www.bfi.org.uk/archive-collections/searching-access-collections/archive-resources-online/). Museums of modern art and media often post sources online. The eclectic Internet Archive offers moving images as well as radio for students of American history (http://archive.org/). We do not rule out YouTube as a potential source, but it is often difficult to know what is original, what has been added, and what is missing. As always, consult your professor if you wish to use a questionable source. Finally, you should consult with your professor before including fictional evidence, such as theatrical films, because you will be doing interdisciplinary work that may not fulfill the assignment.

Material Culture, Architecture, Art, Fashion, Fiction. Like media studies, the studies of art, architecture, material culture, and fictional literature are separate disciplines apart from history, each with their own programs, skills, journals, and scholarly associations. The writer of a history thesis would be well advised to avoid making any of these sources the central body of primary evidence because that would require a different academic paradigm. Yet knowing something about the cultural production and consumption of your historical actors might enrich your analysis. The themes of popular treatises, sermons, novels, plays, or even jokes and parlor games might offer insight. If the question is about literature, find a literature professor to consult with. If your question is about "things" like fashion or farm equipment, you may wish to consult with a local museum. Even if your object is not local, curators know how to interpret material culture. Military historians studying a particular battle may wish to know the accuracy of a particular weapon or the weight and size of cannons. The floor plan of a particular dwelling or commercial structure might shed light on how humans interacted within it. The consumption of fine art by the elite, as well as other symbols of their status—fashions, furnishings, food, etc.—can become sources for the historian, as can evidence of the tastes and living standards of the middle and lower classes. Trends in fashion might be inspired by the wealthy or they might be inspired by the lower classes. The sources of cultural trends are often telling for the historian, but they require some sophisticated analysis and perhaps a conversation with someone from a local museum.

Taking notes from primary materials

It is tempting to shorten your stay in an archive or use those interlibrary loan books before they expire by taking photos or photocopies of everything, because you can always go back later and examine the photographs or the copies. Sometimes you have no

---

[7] Steven J. Ross, ed., *Movies and American Society* (Oxford: Blackwell, 2002).

choice, but working this way is sometimes a mistake. First, it is unlikely that you will get to it later. There will always be more pressing matters. Second, if you do look at these photos or copies later, they will be stale. You will not remember exactly how that telegram or letter or book fit into your argument, and you may be missing vital information. Instead, take notes as you go with three types of information:

1. *Bibliographical.* Record all the information you can: archive, collection, box, file, type of document (telegram, etc.), date, author, recipient, and today's date; if it is an Internet source or a primary printed source, look for as much information as you can including title, author, publication information, last update. *You need all the information required by The Chicago Manual of Style, the preferred citation method of historians precisely because it facilitates the citing of that particular source. So please look up what is needed for that particular source before you leave the source behind.* There is nothing worse for the thesis writer than realizing that you cannot use the perfect quote or image because you do not remember where you originally found it.

2. *Notes in your own voice.* Do not just type quotes. Putting what you read into your own voice begins your analysis. Students are often confused by the term "paraphrase," so it is good practice to both quote AND take notes in your own voice, because you do not always know how you are going to use the information in your final thesis. When primary sources inspire you to rethink your overall research questions and conclusions—and they do—you are actively analyzing. Students often freeze when told that they are expected to come up with their own original analysis. Those "a-ha" moments will happen as you encounter the primary materials. This is why you are encouraged to keep a research journal. When you have those insights, write them down as soon as possible, as well as the source that inspired them.

3. *Direct quotes.* Be careful to distinguish direct quotes from notes in your own voice by using quotation marks, plus perhaps some other system, such as changing the font for quotes or dividing your page into two columns: one for quotes, one for notes. Make sure that your transcription is accurate down to the punctuation and misspellings. When you quote a misspelled word, type [*sic*] directly afterward to indicate that the word is typed as it appeared in the original. If you are quoting from a document that is not written in standard English, such as a sermon from the 1600s, you will not need to use [*sic*] because the context of your source will explain the spellings. Be sure to make a note of every page number, because if you are going to use only part of a quote, you want to be sure to indicate exactly where you found it down to the page number. Sometimes each document within a file is numbered. Remember, you are creating a breadcrumb trail for the next researcher. When you use a quote in your assignment, you will need to identify the speaker of the quote, as well as the time and place and audience, so be sure that you have that information as well.

Interpreting primary documents. Hints regarding the interpretation of specific kinds of documents are sprinkled throughout this chapter. Several of the online guides included in this chapter offer more directed guidance, and George Mason University's

"History Matters" website offers useful advice to assist in the interpretation of many kinds of evidence (http://historymatters.gmu.edu/browse/makesense/).

In general, consider the following:

1. *Is it descriptive or prescriptive?* Is the source describing how things are, that is, *descriptive*, or suggesting how things should be, or *prescriptive*? It is not always clear which it is. For example, one scholar studying the history of diets found that weight tables published in the United States in the first half of the twentieth century were *descriptive*; that is, the weights reported were the average weight of adults of a particular height. A few decades later, the weights were *prescriptive*, that is, the charts listed *ideal* weights according to height, and the numbers were lower.[8] You do not want to mistake a prescriptive source for a description of reality. Fashion guides, etiquette books, health publications, budgets—many are quite useful to the historian, but beware of assuming that they describe the real rather than the ideal.

2. *How many examples do I need?* This depends on your particular thesis, so asking your professor is the best course of action. Generally you will need more than one example to make a point, but how many more is contextual. If you wish to pursue a cultural inquiry, for example, and want to see what women's magazines were saying in the 1950s, you could not possibly read them all. Work with your professor to come up with a reasonable sample, such as reading four issues a year of particular titles over a specified number of years.

3. *How do I know how influential this source was?* This question applies to public speeches and published or exhibited materials. Public opinion is unlikely to be influenced by what it cannot see: internal documents, personal letters, minutes of meetings, etc., unless they are published, which might happen in a court case. Who would have heard/read/seen your primary source, when, and how? How many eyes and ears were exposed to it? If it was in print, who might have read it? Who *could* have read it (literacy rates)? Think hard about audiences and sources in combination. Also think about technological change. Franklin D. Roosevelt's famous "fireside chats" over the radio in the 1930s were popular and influential, but the weekly radio addresses of sitting presidents in the twenty-first century rarely merit notice, largely because radio no longer plays the same role. Common sense goes a long way here. Research the author's name and the title of the piece in both scholarly sources and on the Internet. If your source was truly influential, in all likelihood you will find it mentioned. But an obscure source is still useful. A personal letter can shed great light on a topic although it was originally meant to be shared by only two people.

4. *Do not write beyond your sources.* Do not make broad claims that your sources do not support. The ability to declare "X represents what the public believed" with any certainty is extremely rare. Just because a movie or a book or an idea is popular does not make it the will of the people. Students often assume that for their thesis to be important the topic must be of great significance, and thus they tend to

---

[8.] Jesse Berrett, "Feeding the Organization Man: Diet and Masculinity in Postwar America," *Journal of Social History* 30, no. 4 (Summer 1997): 810.

exaggerate the significance of their evidence. But any glance at a scholarly historical journal will reveal that this is not so. Most scholarly articles are tightly focused as to time, place, and significance. From these bricks are built the large, significant histories that use the findings of dozens if not hundreds of scholars to make larger claims.

You are being asked to write a historical research paper based on primary sources: a small brick. Your assignment is as manageable as you make it. The purpose of this chapter is to help you realize that quality primary research is within the grasp of any history student. Begin by sitting down with your professor and your librarian, who can help you get started.

CHAPTER FIVE

Ensuring a Successful Research Outcome

A successful research paper cannot be conjured up overnight, over a weekend, or even over a couple of weeks. It requires thought, work, and planning. The process involves three major activities: research, critical analysis, and writing. Research includes selecting a topic, posing a research question, and identifying and assessing secondary and primary sources that will enable you to answer that question. Critical analysis includes reading your sources, questioning them, and challenging them with evidence that you find in other sources. Writing means presenting the results of your research in an organized, coherent manner, using the appropriate conventions for the discipline of history. This chapter takes you through the first part of the process, from the first entry in your research journal to the completion of your research prospectus. Chapter Six takes you through the third part, writing your paper. Exercises in the workbook chapters will hone your critical analysis skills.

The advice in this chapter is valid for any research paper. You may be working on a project in an upper-division history course, an honors thesis, a capstone paper in your senior year, or your first research paper in a master's program. You will devote an entire semester, perhaps two, to this project. You may find this prospect daunting, so you will be glad to know that there is a process that helps guide your every step. The process contains certain nonnegotiable items, but it offers considerable flexibility. Because it is not rigidly linear, you are able to revisit your decisions and change your direction as you work. The process is there to help steer you, not control you. Above all, you will want to be guided by the evidence you find through your research. You will learn to manage the process and become your own project coordinator.

The process begins as you work to decide on a topic and ends when you submit the final version of your research paper. In between these two end-points are several way stations; chief among them are the following:

1. Preliminary research to craft a research question;

2. Initial annotated bibliography of secondary sources;

3. Identification of key primary sources;

4. Research proposal;

5. Detailed outline of your paper;

6. The first draft of a section of the paper;

7. Introduction;

8. First full draft; and

9. Final draft.

Your professor will likely give you a schedule of the interim assignments with dates by which you need to accomplish them. If not, your first task is to draw up a list of deadlines to make sure that you stay on track during this long, complex, but ultimately rewarding assignment.

Completing your research paper is not your only task but it may well be the most important task in your year or semester. Time management is essential. If your college offers a course in time management, take it. Create a schedule that allows you to complete your research stage by stage and then stick to it as closely as possible. In addition, arrange time blocks, say two-hour stretches, that you use to devote to a particular task. For example, in one two-hour time block your task might be to read and annotate four primary sources. This way, you have a plan, and, as you work on your plan, you will see that you are making progress. You will even begin to look forward to your next block of time. Save a few minutes in each writing session to record your progress.

TIMELINE TO COMPLETE RESEARCH

We assume that you will have a full academic semester of approximately fourteen weeks to complete your research and writing, and we recommend that you devote the first five or six weeks to completing the steps leading to your research prospectus. If your college operates on a trimester or quarter basis, if you have an entire academic year for your project, or if you are engaged in an internship, work-study, or public scholar program, you will want to adjust your time scale accordingly. If you have less than a fourteen-week semester, you would be well advised to use part of your summer vacation or winter break to work on your prospectus. Take college breaks into account to make sure you complete your assignment on time.

TIMELINE: ADD REAL DATES TO ESTABLISH YOUR DEADLINES*	RESEARCH ACTIVITY	ASSIGNMENT
Weeks 1–3	Select subject area, focus topic, locate initial secondary sources, identify potential primary sources, craft preliminary research question	Research question with one-page explanation of its significance and preliminary list of sources
Week 4	Expand list of relevant scholarly monographs and articles	Annotated bibliography of secondary sources
Week 5	Confirm primary source collections	List of primary source collections with completed analyses (see worksheets) for five key sources
Week 6	Organize findings	Research prospectus

May be modified to suit course and trimester or semester sequences.

FIGURE 5.1. Establishing a timeline for your research.

Professional associations such as the American Historical Association and the Organization of American Historians have for some time called on their members to make their research relevant and more available to the general public. You may have an opportunity to do this yourself; indeed, if you are interested, whether or not you plan to make a career as a historian, you might want to consider seeking out such an opportunity. Talk to your professor about connecting your research to a work-study program, an internship, or a funded scholarship with a local historical association, archive, or museum that will allow you to present your work publicly through personal presentation, development of a videofilm, or creation of posters or databases that can be made available to schools, museums, or other such venues. The experience you gain working with other professionals will serve you well in the early stages of your professional life, and you can be proud that you have contributed to expanding historical knowledge.

Journaling: The record of your progress

Perhaps you keep a private handwritten diary to record your thoughts and activities. Perhaps you tweet your activities to the world. Either way, you understand these two different genres of journaling and the different purposes of recording elements of your daily life. Research journaling is another genre with its own purpose—to help you keep track of your experiences as you engage in the process of research, record the positive and negative results of your search strategies, jot down your questions and insights before you forget them, and avoid repeating unsuccessful strategies. We recommend that you keep a journal of this nature during the journey you are about to begin.

The journal is a separate exercise from note-taking and formal writing, although it can be combined with them, as we explain later in this chapter. It can be a handwritten entry in a special notebook, or an electronic file on a tablet or laptop, or whatever you feel most comfortable with. Record your thoughts at the end of every session of research and writing. It may seem strange at first, but you will soon become accustomed to noting down your questions, frustrations, and insights. No query or idea is too small. Treat the exercise as a one-person brainstorming session that you use to get your thoughts on paper. As you work through the process, you will find that you have new questions or a different interpretation, and we hope you will even experience some "a-ha!" moments. These epiphanies, fully developed and with the historical examples that support them, will comprise the heart of your thesis.

Choosing a topic

The next item on your agenda is to find a topic. Some students find this task easy: they have been waiting for the opportunity to spend a semester or two on a subject that has long intrigued them. Others find it a challenge because they manage to come up with several areas of interest and have a hard time choosing one and sticking to it. In some cases, your professor will help by assigning a theme, a period, or even a specific subject area. It should go without saying that you should choose a subject that interests you because you will spend a large amount of your time on it, and you want to be content to devote your energy to it. After deciding on a general area, you face the challenge of focusing on a feasible topic. Bear in mind two points: you must narrow it down to a project that you can accomplish within the time available, and you must have easy access to relevant primary sources because without them you will be unable to complete your assignment. In certain situations, you might be guided initially by a perusal of the primary sources available to you through your college library or local historical association. See Chapter Four for a discussion of primary sources.

Let's say you are interested in the history of human rights. You are a twenty-first-century student, so you go straight to the Internet. You type "human rights" into your favorite search engine and, in the top five hits, you see a Wikipedia entry. You click on the entry and find a long essay on human rights that expands your topic in fascinating ways. You see hyperlinks to the Universal Declaration of Human Rights, subjects as seemingly diverse as the Protestant Reformation, the American Declaration of Independence, and the French Revolution, issues as varied as slavery, women's rights, and child labor. You click on women's rights. In the contents box you begin to see the possibility of narrowing down your topic: suffrage, property rights, rape, and sexual enslavement are all pertinent areas for a research project. You also see the possibility of studying women's rights in different countries. You click on China. In September 2014, when we were completing this chapter, the entry on China was brief. The scant eight lines appeared to suggest that the only women's rights issue in China was foot-binding, a practice, now banned, that prompted American women missionaries in the nineteenth century to work to improve the health and status of women in that country. The entry is misleading. You might already know that if you have taken a course in Chinese history or women and global issues. In the meantime, you might well think that you have a topic to pursue.

You already know that Wikipedia is not necessarily a tool you can rely on for accurate information, but it can prove useful in helping you locate a topic for your research assignment. You have successfully narrowed down your interest in the history of human rights to two or three options. You might consider pursuing foot-binding as a facet of women's rights in China, or the work of American women missionaries in China, or the connections between Chinese and American women in the early twentieth century. Now go to your college's print or online encyclopedias and bibliographic guides to discover more about your potential topics. Your librarian will be able to direct you to specialized encyclopedias and annotated bibliographies that offer pertinent background information, suggest appropriate secondary sources, and likely open up more avenues for you to explore. Bear in mind if you consult printed bibliographic guides that they rapidly become out of date and do not contain the latest scholarly research. Check the date of publication to see how much you might be missing.

Remember that encyclopedias and bibliographic guides are **tertiary sources**; that is, they are of third-level significance after primary and secondary sources. As a rule, you do not cite tertiary sources in your research. You should use them to inform yourself about your general topic. Good specialized encyclopedias give you the background you need before you start looking for monographs, journal articles, and other sources. They offer an overview and put your topic in perspective. They help you develop lists of keywords to use in catalogs and databases. The best of them include recommended bibliographies. You should avoid broad, general encyclopedias aimed at the general public, such as *Encylopaedia Britannica*. Instead, ask your librarian to point you in the direction of specialized encyclopedias that contain entries written by recognized scholars. Some examples are *The Encyclopedia of Women and Islamic Cultures*, *The Encyclopedia of the Holocaust*, *The Encyclopedia of Religion*, second edition, and *Notable American Women*.[1] Most encyclopedias are available online, and many libraries have subscriptions.

Using and evaluating information in websites

Now that you have used the Internet to identify possible topics, you may feel inclined to do some more searching there before you consult the encyclopedias or even instead of going to them. You may do that. Let us return to your original topic of human rights. In your Internet search, you come across the term "child labor." You click on that term and discover that the abuse of children in workplaces is a centuries-old problem that continues in many parts of the world today. Among other issues of interest, you learn that child labor was associated with the growth of factories in Europe during the Industrial Revolution. The topic intrigues you, so you type "industrial revolution" into your search engine. You have moved your search from twentieth-century China to nineteenth-century Europe.

In the top five hits for your search term you find a BBC site entitled "Why the Industrial Revolution happened in Britain." By the time you have scrolled to the bottom of the page, you have forgotten all about the industrial revolution in favor of the intriguing headline "Why we became addicted to sugar." BBC stands for the British Broadcasting Corporation, and you learn that the corporation has in the past broadcast programs about the significance of sugar in contributing to an obesity epidemic in the United Kingdom. You also learn that addiction to sugar is not only a contemporary issue: the topic takes you farther back in history to early modern Europe and its connections with the sugar plantations of the Canary Islands and the Caribbean. A historical treatment of addiction to sugar is an excellent topic, although you still need to narrow your focus. At this early stage of exploration, a change of topic is perfectly reasonable. The research process is flexible.

Remember to use caution with information you find on websites. As with all your research, you must evaluate the reliability of the evidence you find there. Exercises in the corresponding Chapter Five of the companion workbook will enable you to make your own assessments, where you will determine the authority of the publishing organization, the credentials of its authors and compilers, and the value to your project of the information you locate.

Note the name of the site and its address or location, otherwise known as the uniform resource locator, abbreviated to URL. In the case of the BBC webpage, the URL is

---

[1.] Suad Joseph, ed., *The Encyclopedia of Women and Islamic Cultures* (Leiden: Brill, 2003–2007); Israel Gutman, *The Encyclopedia of the Holocaust* (New York: Macmillan USA, 1990); Lindsay Jones, *The Encyclopedia of Religion*, 2nd ed. (New York: Macmillan USA, 2005); Edward T. James, *Notable American Women, 1607–1950: A Biographical Dictionary* (Cambridge, MA: Belknap Press of Harvard University Press, 1971).

http://www.bbc.co.uk/history/0/20979973/. The name, "Why the Industrial Revolution happened in Britain," should give you a clear indication of the site's contents. The URL will let you know what kind of organization is responsible for it. For example, .gov means government, .edu means an educational institution, .org means a nongovernmental, noncommercial organization, and .com or .co usually indicates a business. Non-U.S. sites also indicate the country of origin of the material; in this case "uk" stands for United Kingdom. Many of these sites have a particular perspective or point of view that their authors wish to promote; none is entirely bias free. As with your critiques of all materials you discover, you will need to proceed with caution based on the type of bias you might expect to meet.

Check with your professor about the acceptability of the websites you may wish to use in your research. The BBC operates within the demands of journalism, and its target audience is the general public although the corporation does engage professional historians to consult on and present its programs. You might be able to cite the contents of the webpages if you wished to highlight the relevance of sugar addiction in our own time, but you would be advised to locate any scholarly sources listed on the website as evidence for a historical discussion of addiction or of sugar and slavery. When trying to decide whether you want to include a website, at the very least you will want to be able to find the names and contact information of its publisher or sponsoring institution, its authors, and the individuals chiefly responsible for the site or for specific sections of the site. You will also want to see some indication of the original source (citation) of the documents posted on the site and a discussion of attempts to ensure accuracy. If you can find none of this information, the website is likely inappropriate for your purposes. You will also want to assess the audience targeted by the website. Frequently, snappy sentences and short paragraphs suggest a journalistic style designed to appeal to the general public. Although such sites might trigger ideas and indicate sources, you should not rely on them to conduct your research. Another word of caution: some sites are written by schoolchildren for schoolchildren. The string of characters "k-12" in the URL should alert you to websites of this nature. You might find the stories they tell interesting, but you should not use the site for your college-level research. Finally, with the popularity of tweeting, blogging, **native advertising**, infomercials and other types of web writing, you will need to be increasingly alert to online publishing that masquerades as serious work. A critical eye will serve you well.

Focusing your topic

Locating scholarly monographs

Once you have perused tertiary sources to narrow down your subject of interest, you are ready to focus on a topic. Begin with some preliminary research in your library's online catalog to locate scholarly monographs. Although catalogs have their own peculiarities, they all have a similar search function, giving you the option to search by author, title, subject, and keyword. In the initial phase of your search, your best option is to search by keyword and subject. At this stage, particularly if you are new to online catalog searches, the work of selecting terms proceeds very much by trial and error. You can help yourself if you develop a search strategy, keep notes in your journal about your selected terms and their success rate, and modify the strategy as you discover which terms produce the most useful hits. It does not help you to find three hundred hits. You need a search that will produce, say, fifty. The numbers are arbitrary, but you are looking for quality, not quantity.

The keyword option offers you a broader starting point with any word you choose to begin with. It will provide an extensive hit list. To use the subject option, you need to know specific Library of Congress (LoC) search terms for the subject and you will receive a correspondingly specific hit list. The good news is that an initial keyword search will reveal the LoC subject terms to you. You can begin with a geographic location, your general topic theme, or the personal name of an individual you have read about in your encyclopedia grazing.

TESTING OUT YOUR SEARCH STRATEGIES IN YOUR COLLEGE ONLINE CATALOG

Take the example of women's rights in China and use the keyword option. If you type the word "China" into the search box, you will likely find thousands of hits. So, whereas using a geographical term might well be a useful start for some projects, you might not be surprised, given the vastness of the country and the richness of its history, that "China" alone as a term is not a useful keyword. If, then, you add your general topic to the geographic location using "China and women's rights" (or "China—women's rights") as a keyword phrase, you will find you have a usable list of titles. Try it and see how many hits you have. The number will depend on your library's holdings. We did this exercise using CYRIL, the Siena College catalog, and found 14 hits, all monographs. We then went to our library consortium, ConnectNY, and found 165 hits offering a combination of monographs, primary sources, and electronic sources. As it happens, "women's rights" is a specific LoC term, so the phrase aptly refined your term "China."

You may also be lucky to have selected a topic that enables you to conduct a rapid initial search. For example, you want to study slavery in the Ottoman Empire. If you type the words "Ottoman slavery" into the keyword option, you will likely find a short and useful list of titles. Among the titles we found was a monograph by Ehud R. Toledano entitled *Slavery and Abolition in the Ottoman Middle East*. We clicked on the link to this title and found additional information about the book in the library entry, including a list of useful subject terms, as shown in Figure 5.2. All these phrases represent specific LoC terms. You can use them to continue your search, expand it, or refine it. Follow the same steps using the hits in your original search to locate more specific subject search words.

Author	Toledano, Ehud R.
Title	**Slavery and abolition in the Ottoman Middle East / Ehud R. Toledano.**
Imprint	Seattle : University of Washington Press, c1998.

continued on next page

continued

LOCATION	CALL #	NOTE	STATUS
SECOND FLOOR	HT1316 .T65 1998		AVAILABLE

Full Record
More Details
Similar Subjects
Copy Status
Print Version

Call #	HT1316 .T65 1998
Phys. Description	xii, 185 p. ; 23 cn.
Bibliog.	Includes bibliographical references (p. 169–177) and index.
ISBN	029597642X (pbk. : alk. paper)

Author	Toledano, Ehud R.
Series	Publications on the Near East
	Publications on the Near East, University of Washington.
Subject	Slavery -- Middle East -- History.
	Slave-trade -- Middle East -- History.
	Slavery and Islam -- History.
	Turkey -- History -- Ottoman Empire, 1288–1918.
Alt Title	Slavery and abolition

LOCATION	CALL #	NOTE	STATUS
SECOND FLOOR	HT1316 .T65 1998		AVAILABLE

FIGURE 5.2. CYRIL catalog entry for *Slavery and abolition in the Ottoman Middle East* by Ehud R. Toledano.

Consider another example. You may have a vague interest in studying the history of colonial Mexico. You already know from our example with China that "Mexico" is likely to be a weak search term because it will yield a high list of hits, probably in the thousands. If you try "colonial Mexico" you will locate a more usable list of hits. Click on some of the titles that interest you. In their full entries you will find several subject search terms, the most general of which is Mexico—History—Spanish colony, 1540–1810. By clicking on this term, you will be introduced to a wide array of topics about colonial Mexico. Each time you click on a link you will be introduced to more books, more search terms, and more refined topics.

In short, once you have a useful list of titles from a keyword search, click on an entry that looks pertinent to your topic to locate the full record for that entry. You will then find specific associated subject search terms. Click on them to see how you might expand (or narrow) your search to find relevant books. Keep a journal record of your search terms and their results. You want to remember which terms work for you and which do not. Remember, too, to make a note of the books that you want to take a look at. Record their call numbers so that you can find them easily on your library shelves. Then, when you go to the stacks to collect your books, remember to browse the shelves to locate other relevant titles that your catalog search may not have found for you.

If you have selected a highly specialized area of study, you may find few monographs, or even none, in your college library. Your college may well belong to a consortium of institutions in your region, a midpoint between your home library and WorldCat through which you have access to a larger database of titles. If this is not the case, then take your search to WorldCat and use your library's interlibrary loan options. Always use the advanced search option in WorldCat; otherwise, you will receive hundreds (even thousands) of hits, most of them irrelevant. If your search reveals nothing of use to you, seek the assistance of your librarian.

Locating scholarly articles

College libraries usually subscribe to several databases that combine a large number of academic journals. JSTOR and Project Muse are among the most commonly used. They include only scholarly articles, that is, peer-reviewed research, which means that they were critiqued by other scholars in the field before they were accepted for publication. If unsure, check with your professor or librarian to see which databases you have access to. As with the search for scholarly monographs, keyword searches generate the most effective results. And, as with your experiences locating suitable monographs, the search proceeds largely by trial and error.

Always select the advanced search option in your chosen database because this will allow you to filter your searches so that you avoid as much irrelevant material as possible. Your first task is usually to enter your search term. JSTOR allows you to combine two terms and offers you drop-down boxes to define your terms as an author's name or to search for them in full text, title, abstract, or caption. As JSTOR now includes books and primary sources as well as journals, it asks you to narrow your search by checking a box for articles, books, pamphlets, reviews, or miscellaneous items. Then it asks you to enter a date range, which establishes a long or short publication period for your search. You

---

TESTING OUT YOUR SEARCH STRATEGY IN JSTOR

Take the topic of Chinese women we used earlier. Perhaps your search led you to consider the impact of the U.S. Chinese Exclusion Acts on Chinese women. Use the terms "women" and "Chinese exclusion" (include the quotes with your search term so that JSTOR understands that it needs to find those two words together) for your two search boxes and select "item title" from the drop-down boxes. To narrow down the search, click on the "articles" box, enter the dates 2005 to 2015, select "English" as the language, and check the boxes for "Asian Studies" and "History" to filter the disciplines. Then click on the search button. When we did this, we received only one search result. This result was very specific but you need more than one article. Use the option to modify your search and instead of selecting "item title" choose "full text" from the drop-down boxes next to your search terms. This change yielded us one hundred and thirty-nine search results. Bear in mind that the first page of articles presented is not always the most relevant. A quick glance through the results will enable you to select a smaller number of articles to read. JSTOR allows you to read online or download articles that are more than five years old. For more recent articles, check whether your library holds the respective journal titles. Whatever you do, please read carefully to ascertain that the articles are relevant to your topic before you decide to print.

---

also have an option to select a language. After this initial narrowing, you can filter your search by discipline or journal. When JSTOR returns with your search results, it also gives you an option to modify your search.

Once you have obtained the books and articles you wish to consult, use the "scanning a monograph" and "anatomy of a scholarly article" activities in Chapter Three of the companion workbook to help you grapple quickly with the information available to you. Then review the strong and weak annotations in that chapter before you proceed to annotate your own sources. At this point, you can still remain open to changing direction. Once you have a clearer direction, however, do not let diversions sidetrack you. Stay focused. You are now ready to formulate your initial research question.

Formulating a research question

Historians and journalists ask the same questions. They need to know the answers to the questions who, what, when, and where. But whereas the task of journalists is to report, the task of historians is to explain. You will go beyond a basic reporting narrative to offer an interpretive analysis. Your research will account for the why or the how. Your question must begin with one of those words and end with a question mark. This may seem a trivial point but it is important. If your professor asks you what your research question is, do not answer "sugar and slavery." Sugar and slavery is your broad topic, not your question. Note also that the BBC headline "Why we became addicted to sugar" is also not a question, although it begins with the word "why." More specific questions would be "How did sugar become a stable transatlantic commodity in the seventeenth century?" or "How did early modern Europeans become addicted to sugar?"

Formulating a research question that offers explanatory potential is a challenge. At this point, if you have not already done so, organize a peer group, that is a group of your fellow students who are also working on research papers. Share information about your tasks, your progress, your findings, and your frustrations. Ask them what they think about your questions. Do some brainstorming together. Although the stereotype of the historian buried alone in the archive is a common one, historians do not work alone all the time. They share their findings, ask for feedback on their interpretations, and cooperate on research projects. You can do the same and get help formulating your research question.

You may come up with several preliminary questions before you hit on the one that will guide your further research, and you will more than likely refine your question as you gather evidence. It helps to begin with a statement of your purpose that explains why you want to study a topic. For example, "I want to study Qiu Jin's life because I want to understand how women fought for their rights in early-twentieth-century China"; or "I want to study Qiu Jin's life because I want to find out about women revolutionaries in China." Now, turn your purpose into a question. One option is "What contributions did Qiu Jin make to the struggle for women's rights in early-twentieth-century China?" Note, however, that this question will lead you to write a narrative, describing Qiu Jin's contributions. Instead, you need an interpretive analysis that offers the readers different consequences to consider. A stronger question is "How did Qiu Jin's actions shape the struggle for women's rights in early-twentieth-century China?" This question forces you to make an argument about Qiu Jin.

Even at this early stage, you should try to gain an initial grasp of the **historical context** in which your topic is set and within which your historical actors are operating. Context means the larger historical background, or setting, for the individuals, events, and ideas you analyze so that the reader can understand the significance of your argument in its time and place. You will gain insight to this background by asking more questions. What else is happening that might shed some light on people's thinking or behavior? What can you learn about their situation that helps explain their actions? Jot these questions down in your journal. As you discover the answers, you will begin to understand the significance of your larger research question—and its answer—to larger historical processes.

You will also want to establish a **chronological trajectory** (an established timeline of events) to help you determine **cause and effect**, that is, which events or activities led to which consequences. For example, you may have heard that the sinking of the *Lusitania* led to the entry of the United States into World War I. This is a commonly held misperception. Just because an action precedes an event does not necessarily mean that it caused it. Apart from the fact that historical explanations are rarely monocausal, establishing even the simplest of timelines would lead you to question the statement. A German submarine sank the British liner *Lusitania* on May 7, 1915. The U.S. Congress approved President Wilson's war resolution on April 6, 1917. Clearly, other events in the almost two-year gap between these events would complicate an answer to the question "Why did the United States enter World War I?" A more detailed timeline will help you do this. Historiographical research will convince you that historians continue to differ on their interpretations of the origins of the war and the reasons for U.S. entry into the conflict.

When you begin to focus your research question, there are some traps that you should take care not to fall into. In particular, you will want to avoid the following situations.

Questions that facilitate descriptive narrative but may distract you from analytical rigor. You have probably written many descriptive essays that convey your understanding of an event. Such essays are particularly common in writing about battles or the passage of legislation, but they can be written on any topic. Questions guiding such descriptive essays usually begin with "What happened?" With questions like this, you will become mired in a tedious repetition of facts, what some professors call "one damned thing after another." You need a question that will enable you to make an argument. Begin with "why" or "how," instead of "what happened."

Broad questions with expansive projections. Remember that you have a limited amount of time and perhaps limited resources to complete your assignment. Your project must be doable. So, for example, the question "How did colonial slavery affect race relations in twentieth-century Britain?" is far too broad. You cannot deal with a centuries-long issue in one or two semesters.

Counterfactual questions. You have probably heard the question: What if Germany had won World War II? This might lead to a fun discussion on an evening out with friends, but the question is speculative, or counterfactual, that is, against the facts. You cannot find the evidence to craft the answer to such a question. Military strategists, among others, engage in "what if" games when they seek to cover all eventualities as they draw up plans for battle. They must know how to respond to any given action the enemy may engage in. For them, counterfactual questions are useful. Some prominent historians also wade into the muddy waters of counterfactual questions to offer fascinating interpretations of what might have been. Unless your professor agrees, however, we advise you to avoid such questions. They may be helpful to you as you work to develop a strong research question, but it is best to remember that the historian's work is based on evidence and pose a question to which you can find an answer, based on evidence from the past.

Questions that offer a yes-or-no answer. Some questions can box you into a corner, for example, Did women fight in the Soviet military during World War II? Your answer is yes or no, and you will find it difficult to construct an argument from there. A stronger initial question would be, How did the inclusion of women in the Soviet military affect the outcome of World War II?

Questions that express moral judgment. For example, do not pose the question: "Were missionaries right to take indigenous children in Australia away from their parents? Apart from the fact that this question elicits a yes-or-no answer (see above), it leads you to take a moral stance. Although you may be disturbed to learn about some of the consequences of the work of missionaries in Australia and elsewhere, you should make every effort not to judge them from the perspective of your own time. Seek, instead, to locate in the past the voices of contemporaries who supported missionaries and those who opposed them. Present your research as objectively and dispassionately as possible, explaining issues and actions within the context of the times in which they occurred. Our task as historians is to understand why people acted as they did in the past and what beliefs shaped their actions. A stronger question would be, "Why did missionaries remove aboriginal children from their parents and how did contemporaries respond?" This question continues to offer you options for a contentious discussion. It allows you to express a carefully worded opinion after you have presented your evidence.

Questions that contain assumptions. Do not pose a question that potentially contains its own answer, for example, "How did hostile American actions initiate a war between the United States and Mexico? If you make the assumption as you begin your research that the United States provoked a war with Mexico, you are likely to fall into the trap of gathering evidence that supports your position while disregarding information that could lead you to argue against it. A more neutral question would be, "Why did war break out between the United States and Mexico in 1846?" This question allows you to be more receptive to evidence of all kinds. In crafting your response, you will want to avoid a straight narrative of events and instead offer an interpretative explanation of the causes of the war.

Gathering more information

With your focused research question to guide you, you are now ready to continue with your research to find targeted scholarly monographs and articles that will help you construct the initial historiographical framework for your research. From your reading of Chapter Three (and the exercises in the companion workbook), you already know how to do this. By this stage, you should be able to scan your secondary sources rapidly to determine whether they will help shape your paper. If they are unhelpful, make a note to that effect in your journal and put them aside immediately. Remember to consult the bibliography and endnotes in the books you have already read to locate additional scholarly monographs and articles. Your professor will set the parameters for this stage of your research, for example, the minimum number of sources you require, their date of publication, and so forth. When in doubt, always consult your professor.

Next, look for additional primary sources that will help shape the answer to your question. The type, quality, and quantity of primary sources you locate will determine the successful outcome of your assignment. (See Chapter Four for assistance with the location of primary sources. See Chapter Five of the workbook for exercises that will help you develop close reading skills to assess their relevance and capture appropriate evidence.) If you are unable to locate sources relating to your question, you will be obliged to reconsider it. Let the sources guide you in this. Remember, you are engaged in a process. You can continue to focus your topic and refine your question as long as you are making progress. You will not be making progress if you cannot locate primary sources. It is much better to switch topics early on than to find yourself struggling halfway through the semester.

Processing information

You may have written previous papers directly from open books or open websites in front of you, but this assignment is too lengthy and complicated for that. Instead, you will be writing the final research paper from your notes, which will include precise quotes, paraphrases, and the original ideas (yours) that they inspired.

You have several options for the mechanical process of taking notes. We recommend that you become acquainted with a software program that organizes your notes for you and makes citations much easier to deal with. Several commercial programs are available. You can also download a free and reliable program called Zotero at http://www.zotero.org/. Zotero was developed for historians by historians at the Roy Rosenzweig Center for History and New Media at George Mason University. The website describes it as "a free, easy-to-use tool to help you collect, organize, cite, and share your research sources." If you think that Zotero looks daunting, ask your research librarian whether he or she would be willing to offer a skills development course on using the software program.

You do, of course, have other options. You can keep a notebook just for this assignment, although a regular notebook offers no help to organize your notes. You can use the tried-and-trusted card index system that at least allows you to organize alphabetically by author and cross-reference by subject matter. It keeps your note-taking to a minimum, a reality that you might view positively or negatively. We recognize that you are more likely to use your tablet, laptop, or computer to take notes. This option certainly has the advantage of speed, lets you take copious notes (not necessarily an advantage), allows you to cut and paste, and facilitates organization of ideas.

You must keep your notes safe. You most certainly do not want to lose them. Electronic note-taking offers a secure location as long as you back up your files or deposit them in a location such as Dropbox or other virtual spaces such as the "cloud" environment. Whatever you do, always keep your note-taking files separate from the files in which you begin to write your paper. If you do not, you risk deleting your notes in the writing process. Your hard work will be lost.

How does one combine taking notes while keeping a research journal? *Dialectical journaling* is one common form in which you divide the page into two columns, or set up columns in an electronic file, writing notes from the source in the left-hand column and your own reactions or thoughts in the right-hand column. Another way is to take notes from the sources in whatever fashion you choose, but, as you go, type or write your own thoughts in a different font or color so that they stand out. However you choose to combine note-taking with journaling, you must (1) take specific notes from the source in front of you and (2) capture your own thoughts, without confusing one with the other. It is a good idea to write all the necessary bibliographical information about the source in front of you, and be sure to keep careful track of page numbers. You might find yourself copying long quotes and virtually retyping the page of an interesting source. This can be useful in the beginning of the process, when you are not sure what part of the quote you will need in your final paper. If you type a long quote that runs more than two pages, note which word ends the first page and which word begins the new page. The part you may use might come from only one page, and your citation must be precise.

Remember that photocopying, photographing, or printing sources is simply gathering information, not analyzing it. If you are pressed for time and must return sources, copying without careful reading is a necessary expedient, but if you find yourself with lots of "research" and few "a-ha!" moments, you have not intellectually processed the sources you have gathered. Even if you copy a long quote, you should also rephrase it in your own words. Paraphrasing is a form of critical thinking.

Try to write primarily in your own words. As you take notes, carefully distinguish your own language from the language used in your source. Quote exactly, including punctuation. When you paraphrase, be certain to thoroughly change the original language and syntax. Remember that paraphrases, like quotations, must be cited in a footnote or an endnote. If you go back to your journal and are unable to remember whether something that you wrote was a quote, you will have to check it against the original source to avoid plagiarizing. Precise note-taking from the beginning pays off handsomely in time saved when you write the paper.

Avoiding plagiarism

Plagiarism, or academic dishonesty, means taking someone else's work and pretending that it is your own. It is cheating. It is intellectual theft, stealing other people's ideas. You do not want to be accused of plagiarism or of falsifying information. Your institution has an academic integrity policy and a committee to review accusations of intellectual theft and falsification. Be aware of it. Seek clarification if you do not understand it. Ignorance is no defense once you face an accusation. The credibility of professional award-winning historians Doris Kearns Goodwin and Joseph Ellis suffered when she admitted to inadvertently plagiarizing because of a lack of attention to detail when taking notes and he acknowledged having lied about his serving in the military during the Vietnam War.[2]

The roots of plagiarism lie in the note-taking stage. You can easily commit it unintentionally if you are negligent with your notes. Whichever system you choose for taking notes, you must make sure to take them carefully. Appropriate care here will avoid any potential for falling into traps. Be sure to use quotation marks to differentiate straight quotes from paraphrases, and always use your own words when paraphrasing. Your instructor will penalize you for misquoting and poor paraphrasing.

Intentional plagiarism is more egregious and usually occurs during the writing phase. (See Chapter Six of the companion workbook for exercises to help you detect plagiarism.) Examples include lifting entire paragraphs from books, copying and pasting from websites, submitting a paper you wrote in one course for another course, copying a fellow student's paper, and purchasing a paper from an Internet paper mill. Remember, too, if you are inclined to help out a friend in a tight spot, that if you give a fellow student your work to copy, you are an accomplice to plagiarism and you will face the consequences. Professors at many colleges and universities use plagiarism detection software to uncover egregious lapses in academic integrity. Please be assured that such programs will uncover your dishonesty. If in doubt, consult your professor.

We offer one final word of advice if you are tempted to resort to plagiarism. If you have procrastinated, are facing a deadline for an assignment, and cannot possibly do the work on time, you might think it is worthwhile to go ahead and take the risk. If you take the risk and are discovered, however, you will likely fail the assignment. You may also flunk the course and risk being reported to your college academic integrity committee with the upshot that you may be expelled from your college. The consequences are not

---

[2.] David D. Kirkpatrick, "Historian Says Borrowing Was Wider Than Known," *The New York Times*, February 23, 2002, http://www.nytimes.com/2002/02/23/us/historian-says-borrowing-was-wider-than-known.html (accessed May 12, 2015); "The Lies of Joseph Ellis," *The New York Times*, August 21, 2001, http://www.nytimes.com/2001/08/21/opinion/the-lies-of-joseph-ellis.html (accessed May 12, 2015).

worth the risk. Instead, talk to your professor, explain your situation, and ask for an extension. You may not get one. You may still fail the assignment. You will learn a hard lesson. But you will not face expulsion and disgrace.

Assembling your research prospectus

Your *research prospectus* provides the confirmation that you have a doable topic. It brings together the results of your research thus far and becomes the foundation on which you build. Yet it is not written in stone, nor is your research finished. Your prospectus serves as a flexible guide as you continue to refine your research question and locate and evaluate additional primary sources during the writing stage. Most important, it is the document in which you make your first attempt to answer your research question. This is the place where you take a bold step and commit your initial thesis statement, or argument, to paper.

If you have followed your time schedule and met your deadlines, assembling your prospectus is relatively straightforward and gives you a great sense of satisfaction. Your professor will likely provide instructions, but a research prospectus usually provides the following elements:

1. Brief introduction to set the context for your topic, pose your research question, and explain the significance of your work;

2. Historiographical sketch, based on key secondary sources (as explained in Chapter Three);

3. Preliminary thesis statement, or working argument;

4. Discussion of evidence from your primary sources to support your argument;

5. Attached annotated bibliography of key secondary sources;

6. Brief reflection of your experience of the research process based on your journal entries.

Crafting your initial thesis statement

An initial, or preliminary, *thesis statement* is your first working argument. It offers an interim answer to your research question based on an analysis of your primary sources. It does not describe your topic. It does not explain your purpose. It does not offer your opinion, and it does not rephrase your question. It is a one-sentence conclusion based on your evidence, and, as obvious as it sounds, it argues a point. After weeks or months of research, you will already have an idea what your argument is; yet you may still feel the need to be tentative. Instead, make a first stab at it. Be as bold as your evidence will allow you to be, but do not overstate your case. You are not restrained by your initial argument. You may change it later. You will certainly refine it as you write your final paper. In the first instance, however, craft a one-sentence thesis statement that begins like this: "In this paper, I argue that . . ." (See the companion workbook for examples and exercises.) The task is a challenging one but one you must complete before you start to write, indeed before you develop your outline, because your argument determines the way in which you begin to organize your evidence.

Preparing a prospectus is a challenge. By the time you reach the end of this chapter, you have met that challenge. You began the semester perhaps with only a vague idea of the topic you planned to research. Following the process outlined here, you grappled with different terms for keyword and subject searches and developed successful search strategies. You researched tertiary sources to narrow down the topic, secondary sources to craft an initial research question, and primary sources to confirm that you could answer the question. You came to appreciate the different types of research questions you can pose and mastered the skill of crafting a strong question that allows you to keep an open mind as you analyze your sources. You discovered the flexibility of the research process and learned that it does not constrain you. We hope the experience was a rewarding one. You are entitled to celebrate. You are now ready to begin the next stage of the project: writing the paper.

CHAPTER SIX

How Do Historians Write?

Like all writing, the writing of history is an art, a skill, and a science. It is an art because the writer develops his or her own style and color. It is a skill because the writer can acquire proficiency through regular practice. It is a science because the writer is obliged to follow the rules of grammar, structure, and evidence. Beyond these basic elements, each academic discipline has its own genres and tenets. This chapter introduces you to the principles of good practice in the writing of history and focuses on the research paper. You will learn about the conventions peculiar to the discipline, in particular, structure, argumentation, language, and documentation. You will appreciate the difference between narrative and analysis and understand key concepts in the writing of history, such as context, chronology, and causality. Finally, because all good writing is clear, concise, and free of jargon and colloquialisms, this chapter also includes tips to improve your personal writing style and a list of basic errors that all writers should strive to avoid. These skills will serve you well in other courses.

Becoming a strong writer is like becoming a powerful athlete or an exceptional musician. Practice is everything. Many historians, including the writers of this book, set themselves the task to write every day, even if it is only one page. We recommend that you develop a writing habit by setting an hour or two a day in which to write. Read regularly too, both fiction and nonfiction. Read the historians who have gone before you. You will get a sense of different styles, and you may well find one that you would like to emulate.

🖊 Structure: Organizing your time and your paper

A research paper has a formal structure. It begins with a title, which should reflect the contents of your paper. The title is followed by an introduction, in which you inform your reader about your topic and specific focus, discuss what other historians have written about the subject, introduce your work in the context of previous research (historiography), and offer your thesis statement, that is, your overarching argument. In the main body of your paper, you develop your analysis through a series of claims, supported by your interpretation of the evidence you have gathered. Your conclusion summarizes your findings, without restating in the exact same words the argument in your introduction, and explains the significance of your research. Your endnotes and bibliography provide the sources of your evidence. Before you begin to write, however, you must do three things: first, establish a schedule that will enable you to complete your work week by week in a timely fashion; second; develop a robust outline that will act as a framework for the presentation of your evidence; and third, exchange your outline with your peer reviewer and provide each other with feedback.

Schedule: **Planning your time**

Your professor will likely give you a schedule of the interim assignments required with dates on which you need to accomplish them. If not, draw up your own list of deadlines with appropriate stages according to the number of weeks available to you. We recommend the following steps:

1. Outline;
2. Introduction;
3. First five to ten pages;
4. First full draft;
5. Formal peer review; and
6. Final draft.

You may also be asked to present your findings orally. We offer suggestions for this option in the companion workbook.

   If you are unable to write a strong introduction at the outset, by all means begin writing your first five pages, drafting a section of your paper based on your strongest evidence. It may seem counterintuitive not to begin at the beginning, but the idea is to start writing. Because you are already familiar with your key sources, you may find it easier to draft an analytical section first. Organize a peer review group from the outset. The more you discuss your work with other students, the more firmly you will be able to grasp your argument.

EXAMPLE: TIMELINE TO COMPLETE RESEARCH PAPER

TIMELINE: (Add dates)*	WRITING ACTIVITY, WITH PEER REVIEW AT EACH STAGE	INTERIM ASSIGNMENT
Week 7	Map your ideas, then organize them	Formal outline
Week 8	Set the context for your thesis statement	Introduction
Week 9	Select your strongest evidence and build a section of your paper making claims that support your thesis statement	Five to ten pages
Week 10–12	Bring all your evidence together. Draft, revise, and rewrite.	First full draft
Week 13	Exchange papers with a fellow student and provide each other critical feedback	Final peer review
Week 14	Revise and rewrite, finalize title.	Final draft

As in Ch. 5, you may need to modify dates by course and trimester/semester.

FIGURE 6.1. Establishing a timeline for your writing.

Outline: **Planning your paper**

A formal outline is not merely a list of words. It is a carefully constructed framework on which you build your analysis. Your working thesis statement determines the elements of your outline and tells you what your paper needs to accomplish. No hard rules exist about the order of presentation of evidence. You begin with what you consider the most significant claim that supports your overall thesis, but the significance may change as you work. Start with a basic outline that sketches the bare bones of your paper. Once you have these initial ideas down on paper, you can develop them into an *expanded outline.* Each section of the outline focuses on a particular idea or issue, is driven by a claim, and includes the key supporting evidence you plan to use. Your outline is a tool to guide you. It can be revised as you work. Before they begin to write, some historians, including the authors of this book, produce expanded outlines of several pages that also include key quotes. We recommend this practice. It makes the process of writing easier.

Your research question, working thesis, and working title are integral parts of your outline. Remember to type them at the top of your page as you begin to structure it, and indeed, at the top of all your pieces of writing. They will serve as sign posts for you (and your peer reviewer and professor). Initially, you can craft a descriptive title. By the time you hand in your first full draft, you will have a more nuanced version. Before you submit your final paper, check the title to make sure that it reflects the key concepts and contents of your paper. Your *title* is the first thing your readers read. Try to catch their attention and introduce them to the main thrust of your paper, letting them know where you plan to take them.

STRONG TITLES FROM THE *AMERICAN HISTORICAL REVIEW*

- Indian Indentured Labor and the History of International Rights Regimes
- Between Eden and Empire: Huguenot Refugees and the Promise of New Worlds
- The Soviets at Nuremberg: International Law, Propaganda, and the Making of the New World Order
- The Profane and Imperfect World of Historiography
- Before Race Mattered: Geographies of the Color Line in Early Colonial Madras and New York

The following examples of a *basic* and *expanded* outline come from the work of Barbara Reeves-Ellington. As a historian of U.S. foreign relations broadly conceived, she explores the extension of American cultural ideals abroad in the nineteenth century. Her research examines the work of American Protestant missionaries, arguably the leading exporters of American culture at that time. Her geographic focus is the Ottoman Empire, the site of the largest mid-nineteenth-century American mission and yet a neglected region in the study of U.S. foreign relations. The article for which these outlines were developed was based on the discovery in the National Library of Bulgaria of a Bulgarian-language version of a mother's manual written by missionary Martha Jane

Riggs, which introduced the concepts of American domesticity to Orthodox Christian women in the Ottoman Balkans. Reeves-Ellington takes a gendered lens to examine this American–Bulgarian encounter, analyzing the content of Riggs's manual, tracing its impact through the Bulgarian press, illuminating the unintended consequences of American interventions in the Ottoman world, and raising methodological questions about earlier approaches to the study of missions.

BASIC OUTLINE

Topic: Gender and the Transfer of American Cultural Ideals in the Ottoman Balkans.

Initial question: How did American missionaries advance American cultural ideals among Bulgarian Orthodox Christians, and how did Bulgarians respond?

Initial working thesis: By rearticulating the domestic ideals promoted by American missionaries in the Ottoman Empire, Bulgarian women advocated a new Bulgarian understanding of female moral authority in the service of the nation, which male journalists adopted to counter Ottoman imperial reforms.

Working title: American missions, Bulgarian women, and the Protestant press in Ottoman Europe, 1864–1875.

   I. Introduction: missions, gender, domesticity, Ottoman context

  II. Martha Jane Riggs and her connections to the Protestant and Bulgarian presses
     A. Her background and influences
     B. Her writing about domestic ideals
     C. Her publications in mission magazines

 III. Evgeniya Kissimova and her connections to the women's movement
     A. Her background and influences
     B. Her writings about domestic ideals
     C. Her leadership in the Bulgarian women's movement

 IV. Journalism and the Bulgarian national movement
     A. Key Bulgarian newspapermen
     B. Connections to missionaries and women's movement
     C. Changes over time in their writings about women

  V. Conclusion: Gender, religion, incipient nationalism, and the significance of American–Bulgarian encounters

---

EXPANDED OUTLINE

Topic: Gender and the Transfer of American Cultural Ideals in the Ottoman Balkans

Revised question: How did missionaries advance American ideas about women among Bulgarian Orthodox Christians in the Balkans, how did Bulgarians respond, and what were the consequences?

Revised working thesis: By rearticulating American domestic ideals promoted by Protestant missionaries in the Ottoman Bulgarian press, Orthodox Bulgarian women advocated a new Bulgarian understanding of female moral authority in the service of the nation. Through their writings, Bulgarian women goaded male journalists into adopting gendered slogans as an anticolonial tool against both Ottoman reforms and American proselytizing.

Revised working title: Embracing Domesticity: American Missionaries, Bulgarian Women, and Nation Building in Ottoman Europe, 1864–1875*

I. Introduction
   A. Hook: Critiques of Evgeniya Kissimova's "Protestantism" in Bulgarian press
   B. American language of domesticity had its origins in U.S. expansionism and was redeployed in the Ottoman context by missionary Martha Jane Riggs (historiography on domestic discourse)
   C. Bulgarian women introduced new ideas about women that they encountered in mission publications (historiography on missions in Ottoman Empire)
   D. Unexploited sources demonstrate connections between the two groups and clarify the transfer of ideas at a time of extensive Ottoman social and political reform
   E. Thesis statement
   F. Significance: consider:
      1. Impact of American ideals on Christian subjects in a Muslim empire
      2. Cultural imperialism, cultural transfer, or cultural adaptation?
      3. Importance of local perspective and gendered lens to challenge previous historiographical interpretations

II. Translating domesticity: Martha Jane Riggs published *Letters to Mothers* as a way to attract Bulgarian women to Protestantism
   A. MJR experienced an upbringing typical for educated Presbyterian families in the early nineteenth century. Describe education and missionary career, and explain significance of personal library
   B. *Letters to Mothers* was widely published. Describe publication history and analyze key messages about women's contributions to national progress and prosperity
   C. Her messages found a wide audience through the mission magazine, which was widely distributed, inexpensive, and a unique medium for articles about women

III. Encountering domesticity: American Protestant ideas about women appealed to Evgeniya Kissimova and other Bulgarian women who sought to improve their status in Ottoman Bulgarian society, demand education for their daughters, and shape the principles of an incipient Bulgarian national movement
   A. EK belonged to a family of first-generation urban merchants, educated to primary level, unusual for the time; discuss Ottoman Bulgarian society
   B. She personally subscribed to mission magazine; explain her attraction to American domesticity in 1864
   C. Her actions and writings placed her in the vanguard of Bulgarian women's movement; analyze articles, explain how she reformulated ideas, 1869–1870

continued on next page

continued

IV. Nationalizing domesticity: American domestic ideals contributed to Bulgarian nationalism writ large only after Bulgarian women's articles had begun to appear in the Bulgarian Press and male journalists began to take note
   A. Petko Slaveykov, key, influential in Istanbul and across Balkans, 1863–1872
   B. He worked closely with missionaries: describe connections
   C. His writings about women during this period of Ottoman reform provoked change, as he began to understand how women could contribute to national progress

V. Conclusion: significance of gender and local perspective to studies of American missionaries in the Ottoman Empire
   A. Because women missionaries did much of the cultural work of nation and empire, historians must look at their contributions to American expansionism in the mid-nineteenth century, when the missionary impulse was a leading commitment to the extension of American ideals abroad
   B. Because the language of American domesticity was sufficiently malleable to serve nationalist, and even anticolonial, ends among Bulgarians, a framework of cultural encounter rather than cultural imperialism is a more robust tool through which to explore the interactions of American missionaries and the people among whom they worked around the world
   C. Because, despite the language of domesticity, neither American nor Bulgarian women exercised any real authority in their respective societies; future studies should explore power dynamics in missionary encounters

NOTE

* Subsequently published as Barbara Reeves-Ellington, "Embracing Domesticity: Women, Mission, and Nation Building in Ottoman Europe, 1832–1872," in *Competing Kingdoms: Women, Mission, Nation, and the American Protestant Empire, 1812–1960*, eds. Barbara Reeves-Ellington, Kathryn Kish Sklar, and Connie Shemo (Durham, NC: Duke University Press, 2010), 269–92.

🔊 Peer Review: **Getting critical feedback**

Peer review is an essential element of the historian's craft. Even senior historians seek out the comments of their colleagues on their work. Seeking another perspective on your work (in addition to your professor's comments) is something you should do. Your professor may well have assigned peer reviewers; if not, invite one of your fellow students and agree to critique each other's work. You cannot start too soon. It is a good idea to begin at the beginning with your expanded outline. At this stage, the feedback required is straightforward and takes little time. In the companion workbook, we offer more advanced suggestions for peer review of your final paper.

CHECKLIST FOR PEER REVIEW OF OUTLINE

❏ Is the research question clear?

❏ Does the thesis statement read like a reasonable answer to the question?

❏ Is the title clear and engaging?

❏ Is the outline driven by claims that support the thesis statement?

❏ Does the outline move the argument along in a logical order?

❏ Does the outline offer a clear chronological trajectory and establish cause and effect?

❏ Has the writer made an effort to craft the beginnings of a conclusion?

With feedback from your peer reviewer and a revised outline, you are ready to start building your paper.

Argumentation

As a student you may feel hesitant about critiquing the work of previous historians, developing strong arguments, and coming to forceful conclusions about your evidence. If so, you are in good company. Even seasoned historians are occasionally tentative about their findings. Remember three things. First, always be guided by your sources; your arguments are only as strong as your evidence. Second, you are offering an interpretation, not eternal proof; other historians may challenge your reading of the evidence. Third, your own classmates who pose different questions about your topic and find different sources may come to different conclusions. Historians disagree among themselves. As we discussed in Chapter Three, debate about the past is healthy.

Most historians writing today choose to blend analysis with narrative. Narrative is a form of writing that means to narrate, or tell, a story. Narratives provide descriptive accounts of what happened in the past in one long, uninterrupted text. Everyone likes stories, so narratives tend to be popular accounts. Historians are also versed in the art of narrative, but their writing is driven by arguments based on evidence that they have gathered from primary sources. They interpret the past to explain how or why things happened. Both narrative and analysis must establish a chronological trajectory, that is, a timeline of events in the order in which they occurred over time. Without a coherent chronology, historians are unable to understand continuity and change over time. The remainder of this chapter advises you how to write an analytical research paper and incorporates recommendations to develop your narrative skills.

Your task is to tell a story, but it is much more than that. You will use your skills of critical analysis and imagination in a disciplined way to combine the force of analysis with the power of narration. When we ask you to use critical thinking skills, we are not suggesting that you be critical of other historians or actors in history. An analytical research paper is not a **polemic**. It is not an opinion piece. It is a soundly argued analysis of evidence found in primary sources, written with skill, style, and restraint. You will explain why events happened the way they did, how individuals acted to influence events, what occurred as a consequence, and why your findings are significant.

📓 Introduction: **Engaging your reader**

The purpose of an introduction is to engage your readers in your topic, your main actors, and the time and place in which they lived. You will discuss what other historians have written (historiography), clarify your research question on the basis of that discussion, and offer your thesis statement (overarching argument). In the process, you will explain how your work contributes to furthering knowledge on the topic by offering a new perspective or adding nuance to earlier arguments. In a twenty-five-page paper, the introduction is likely to take up three to five pages.

The first paragraph of your introduction must communicate to your reader the scope of your topic. That sounds obvious, but too many students are tempted to begin their paper not with their topic but with some all-encompassing statement about all of history. Do not yield to this temptation. Do not begin your paper with bland assertions that include phrases such as "throughout history . . . ," or "everywhere in the world . . . ," or "women have always . . . ." You are not writing about all of history, you cannot possibly provide evidence about the entire world, and women do not all think and act alike. Moreover, the generalizations that follow such universalizing phrases are usually so vague as to be meaningless; your readers will be unable to grasp the topic of your paper.

If you are writing about slavery in the Mamluk sultanate, do not write as your first sentence a general assertion, such as "The Mamluks were slaves"" or "Slavery has always existed." Opt instead for a sharper introductory sentence that communicates to your reader your specific topic and its time and place in history or that is sufficiently intriguing by itself that they will want to continue. Consider the following more effective alternatives:

- Mamluk slaves created a powerful empire based in the eastern Mediterranean from 1250 to 1517.
- Slavery was a major component of the political system of the Mamluk sultanate in the early-modern eastern Mediterranean.

Both sentences answer the questions *who* (the Mamluks), *what* (slavery and politics), *when* (early modern era), and *where* (eastern Mediterranean). Providing this information clearly and succinctly, you have raised in your readers' minds the questions how and why. With one sentence, you have their attention. Because your readers may not have heard about the Mamluks, your next task is to expand on this initial identification and provide a context for their actions, that is, some background information that will help your readers follow the information you present. You will want to explain, briefly, who the Mamluks were, what events were transpiring at the time they rose to power, and why they were significant.

In a short research paper (five to ten pages), you usually include your thesis statement in your introductory paragraph. In a longer paper, including a capstone, you may delay delivery of your thesis statement. No hard and fast rule exists; you may find it appropriate to insert it before or after your historiographical discussion. In the final section of your introduction, you will explain how your findings contribute to the historical literature on your topic. Depending on your topic and approach, you may need to discuss your methodology and sources.

To illustrate the points we have made, we reproduce three examples of introductory paragraphs from articles in the journal *Diplomatic History*. Different in style and tone, each fulfills the requirements: an intriguing first sentence that draws in the reader, clarification of the key actors, topic, time and place, and a brief statement of context and significance. In the third example, about the fund-raising activities of young Canadians to end global hunger in the 1960s, we have reprinted the entire introduction. Note the author's thesis statement toward the end of the second paragraph and her brief discussion of other historians' work and the significance of her contribution in the third.

[Please note that the journal's style guide for footnotes does not follow exactly the conventions of *The Chicago Manual of Style*, which we recommend in the documentation section of this chapter.]

EXAMPLE 1

Bauer, Jean. "With Friends Like These: John Adams and the Comte de Vergennes on Franco-American Relations." ***Diplomatic History*** **37, no 4 (2013): 664–92.**

On July 29, 1780, Charles Gravier, the Comte de Vergennes and Foreign Minister to Louis XVI of France, decided he was quite finished with John Adams. Adams had reached a similar conclusion about Vergennes two days earlier and was already on his way from Paris to Amsterdam. For five weeks, the two men had crossed epistolary swords over America's status in the Franco-American Alliance, specifically the level of sovereignty to be enjoyed by the United States following the American Revolution. When they both became so angry with the situation in general, and each other in particular, they committed far more damning truths to paper than good sense or diplomatic convention would have otherwise allowed. Vergennes and Adams were among the primary architects and implementers of their nations' foreign policies. Their letters encapsulate the fundamental conflicts over American trade policy which kept the allies at (or near) each others' throats until 1815.[1]

NOTE

[1] Strangely, these letters have never been subjected to any serious political analysis. Instead of appreciating this rich record of disagreement, historians have allowed Adams's famous temper to divert attention from the dispute. All discussions of this debate have centered on Adams's psychological state and ignored the geopolitical implications of both Adams's and Vergennes's positions. Orville Murphy and Jonathan Dull each give the episode one dismissive paragraph in their books. Orville Murphy, *Charles Gravier, Comte de Vergennes: French Diplomacy in the Age of Revolution, 1719–1787* (Albany, NY, 1982), 328; and Jonathan Dull, *A Diplomatic History of the American Revolution* (New Haven, CT, 1985), 118. Often the exchange is not even mentioned—for example, Lawrence Kaplan, ed. *The American Revolution and "a Candid World"* (Kent, OH, 1977); nor Ronald Hoffman and Peter J. Albert, eds., *Diplomacy and Revolution: the Franco-American Alliance of 1778* (Charlottesville, VA, 1981). For examples of the pro-Adams view, see Page Smith, *John Adams*

continued on next page

continued

(Garden City, NY, 1962), 474–80; John Ferling, "John Adams, Diplomat," *The William and Mary Quarterly* 51, no. 2 (1994): 227–52; and James Grant, *John Adams: Party of One*, 1st ed. (New York, 2005). For the anti-Adams view, see James Hutson, *John Adams and the Diplomacy of the American Revolution* (Lexington, 1980). There is one exception. Samuel Bemis gives a brief but balanced account of the issues in two pages of *The Diplomacy of the American Revolution*. Samuel Bemis, *The Diplomacy of the American Revolution* (Westport, CT, 1983 [1957]), 176–77.

EXAMPLE 2

Guillory, Sean. "Culture Clash in the Socialist Paradise: Soviet Patronage and African Students' Urbanity in the Soviet Union, 1960–1965." *Diplomatic History* 38, no. 2 (2014): 271–81.

The (mis)recognition of the Other plays a vital role in cultural diplomacy and international relations. Although many of us assume cultural exchange promotes understanding, encounters with the Other often reinforce preexisting assumptions. These presuppositions frequently structure relations between nations.[1] The dialog between self and Other greatly influenced African–Soviet relations during the Cold War. Maxim Matusevich has noted the "exercise in mutual misunderstanding and frustrations" in Soviet–Nigerian relations that contributed to Nigerians' reticence to form strong ties with the Soviet Union.[2] But as Matusevich's work implies, these misunderstandings went beyond the level of diplomacy and informed the everyday interactions between Africans and Russians.

NOTES

[1] Iver B. Neumann, *Uses of the Other: "The East" in European Identity Formation* (Minneapolis, 1999), 20–37.

[2] Maxim Matusevich, "Visions of Grandeur . . . Interrupted: The Soviet Union through Nigerian Eyes," in *Africa in Russia, Russia in Africa: Three Centuries of Encounters*, ed. Maxim Matusevich (Trenton, 2007), 366; Maxim Matusevich, *No Easy Row for a Russian Hoe: Ideology and Pragmatism in Nigerian–Soviet Relations, 1960–1991* (Trenton, 2003), 6.

EXAMPLE 3

Myers, Tamara. "Local Action and Global Imagining: Youth, International Development, and the Walkathon Phenomenon in Sixties' and Seventies' Canada." *Diplomatic History* 38, no. 2 (2014): 282–93.

On a cool November morning in 1968, 34,000 residents of Calgary, Alberta, most of them students, set out to walk a grueling thirty miles in one day. Across the country similar events had taken place that year involving hundreds of thousands of participants. The occasion was a new fund-raising event designed to raise awareness of, and money to resolve, hunger and poverty in the developing world. Aptly named the Miles for Millions walkathon, or simply the Walk, it stood out amid other charity events of the fifties and sixties: a considerable test of endurance, it annually amassed a good size army of young Canadians and generated millions of dollars. At the astonishing length of more than a marathon distance, it was designed to be physically challenging, even impossible for some, to evoke bodily empathy with the people it was intended to aid. With so many young people committed to the Walk, it would become a yearly display of Canada's place in an imagined global community.

Beyond the great physical effort inherent in the walkathon, its striking feature was young Canadians' confidence that social and political change would result from such exertion. Walk Day, youthful organizers claimed, was "a chance for every one of us to act . . . to do something about the world we live in—and the better world we all want."[1] While fundamentally misapprehending the complexities of global hunger and ignoring the politics of foreign aid programs, the core idealism driving the Miles for Millions walkathons is remarkable for its sense of purpose and, more critically, is emblematic of its time, illuminating the optimism among young Canadians that compassionate foreign policy could address global inequities in the developing world; the secularization and expansion of humanitarianism in the name of international development; the exuberance of Canada's 1967 centennial celebrations; and the emergent role of children and youth in Canadian civic culture and movement politics. As a cultural expression of its time, this national effort permitted Canadians to cultivate a new transnational identity, with youth representing the new face of global citizenship. The Walk reveals the centrality of young people's embodied and affective political labor in this process and how the symbolic potential of youth was harnessed for reimagining the nation in a transnational context.[2]

This article contributes to the growing scholarship on children as powerful symbols in Cold War transnational imaginings by focusing on how the putative traits of Canada's young—able-bodiedness, pluck, determination, and global mindedness—were mobilized for the Walk and, in turn, how this new symbolism of the nation's young was used to reinforce a benevolent Canadian identity in the global community. Youth as conceptual category, in a Cold War context, had multiple meanings and was put to use in varied ways. Emerging from the devastation of World War II, states operationalized "youth" as a way forward. Citing one example, Richard Ivan Jobs writes of Fourth Republic France: "youth and youthfulness now became the image, the goal, and the means of cultural reconstruction."[3] Beyond the youthful characteristics nations adopted, young people were also national subjects and icons imbued with changing meaning during the Cold War years. In the early days of refugee camps and orphans, nuclear proliferation, and North American domestic containment, the iconic postwar child was the vulnerable object around which international policy was forged, fallout shelters were built, and for whom a more peaceful future was imagined.[4] In the late forties and fifties, Cold War youth represented vulnerability and required protection. When the duck-and-cover generation grew up, a more activist subjectivity superseded this passive youthful category: in the sixties, "youth" meant college-aged students whose historical agency has been well documented as they challenged old governing structures and authority around the globe.[5] Dissembling the binary between the passive Cold War child and the sixties' activist college student, this article draws attention to school-aged children in the Canadian context, their curiosity about global issues, and involvement in intercultural exchange.

NOTES

[1] "Those Walks," *The Blister* 1 (1970).

[2] Internal political and cultural crises in Canada—involving Quebec distinctiveness, and eventually sovereignty, and multiculturalism's triumph over Britishness and the two-founding nations idea

continued on next page

continued

of Canada—made reimaging Canada as a global nation all the more attractive. See Bryan Palmer, *Canada's 60s: The Ironies of Identity in a Rebellious Age* (Toronto, 2009).

[3.] Richard Ivan Jobs, *Riding the New Wave: Youth and the Rejuvenation of France after the Second World War* (Stanford, CA, 2007), 22.

[4.] Dominique Marshall, "Children's Rights and Children's Actions in International Relief and Domestic Welfare," *JHCY* 1, no. 3 (2008), 351–88; Tara Zahra, *The Lost Children: Reconstructing Europe's Families after World War II* (Cambridge, MA, 2011); Tarah Brookfield, *Cold War Comforts: Canadian Women, Child Safety, and Global Insecurity* (Waterloo, ON, 2012).

[5.] Gael Graham, *Young Activists: American High School Students in the Age of Protest* (DeKalb, Ill, 2006).

Main body of evidence: Convincing your reader of the validity of your analysis

Will your readers find your argument compelling? Your task is to convince them. You will do this when you bring together the advice in this handbook. Craft robust topic sentences in well-developed paragraphs where you identify actors, clarify agency, and establish distinct causal relationships; support your claims by judicious use of quotes; reinforce the significance of your evidence with appropriate explanation; and make good transitions between paragraphs. Successful completion of this task requires proficiency, which you build with practice as you hone your writing skills, apply your organizational talents, and harness your creativity.

From your expanded outline, you will see that you can craft *subheadings* for your paper that will act as guideposts for your reader. Check with your professor whether you should use them. In institutions where the discipline of history is housed in the humanities, scholars tend to eschew subheadings, but where the discipline is housed in the Social Sciences, they use them. Narratives generally do not contain subheadings; analytical pieces usually do. In short essays, say six to ten pages, they are unnecessary. In a longer paper, they serve a useful purpose. Subheadings allow you to divide your paper into sections, each with its own introduction, main body of evidence, and conclusion. This makes your first draft easier to write because you can select your evidence to focus on one section at a time instead of worrying about the development of the paper as a whole. When crafting the wording of your subheadings, always make sure that they indicate to your reader that you are moving their attention to the next stage in your argument.

Paragraph structure influences the force of your argument

A successful paragraph focuses on one idea that is connected to and supports your thesis statement and the overarching argument of a section of your paper. It begins with a topic sentence that alerts the reader to that idea and makes or is followed by a claim about the idea, offers evidence (including quotes and paraphrases) to support the claim, and closes with a sentence that interprets the significance of the evidence, that is, brings meaning out of the quote for your reader. As you construct your paragraph, try to be sure that your sentences are connected logically and transition smoothly.

ROBUST PARAGRAPH STRUCTURE: AN EXAMPLE

In his book on U.S.–Nicaraguan relations, Michel Gobat devotes a chapter to Nicaraguan economic nationalism, which he argues arose in response to U.S. dollar diplomacy between the years from 1912 to 1927. The following paragraph analyzes just one element of the Nicaraguan critique of dollar diplomacy. All sentences flow smoothly and logically, with strong transitions. Note the paragraph's strengths, as numbered.

1. Strong topic sentence, includes claim.

2. Key players (actors, agents) are identified.

3. Evidence supports claim in topic sentence; quote is appropriately framed.

4. Significance of evidence is explained.

Gobat, Michel. *Confronting the American Dream: Nicaragua under U.S. Imperial Rule*. Durham, NC: Duke University Press, 2005, 135. CC: Permission

Many prominent Nicaraguans shared the view that dollar diplomacy had triggered a crisis of elite masculinity. [1] A leading Liberal politician denounced the Banco Nacional and the Compañía Mercantil de Ultramar as "octopuses that have impoverished and dishonored many of our capitalists."[42] [2 and 3] And one of Nicaragua's most famous Liberal ideologues, Salvador Mendieta, claimed that dollar diplomats were "emasculating" (*desvirilizando*) his countrymen.[43] [2 and 3] So acute was this concern that "Crisis of Men" was the title a Granadan newspaper chose for an article that denounced dollar diplomats for having ruined many agroexport producers.[44] [2 and 3] The 1920s campaign against dollar diplomacy was thus not just about recovering Nicaragua's sovereignty. It sought to rescue elite entrepreneurs and the economy from Wall Street's "diabolical machine." [4]

NOTES

[42] Berrios, *Réplica*, 14. [a shortened citation after an initial full citation]

[43] Mendieta, *Enfermedad de Centro-América*, 1:319.

[44] "Crisis de hombres," *El Correo*, 11 April 1933.

Use quotations judiciously as evidence to support your own statements. Do not succumb to the temptation to sprinkle quotes liberally through your text to try to demonstrate that you have located numerous primary sources. Overreliance on quotes suggests that you have not done the hard work of analysis. Quotes from secondary sources are acceptable in your historiographical section but you should try to limit them otherwise. You might make an exception for particularly unusual expressions that make a strong point and would be difficult to paraphrase. As a general rule, however, rely on quotes from your primary sources to support your own arguments.

When you want to use a quote that offers strong support for your argument, do not simply drop it into the middle of your paragraph as an unformed sentence or even an entire sentence. Do not use quotes as substitutes for your own words. Instead, frame them appropriately so your readers understand why you are using them. No matter how fascinating you find the quotes, your reader will not appreciate them as you do unless you incorporate them carefully into your analysis. You must also integrate them grammatically into your text.

Finally, do not begin or end a paragraph with a quote, and do not rely on long quotes. Although you are aware of the significance of a selected quote, your readers will not understand its relevance at the beginning of a paragraph; they need a topic sentence first to introduce your key idea or claim. It is acceptable to include a short quote in the concluding sentence of your paragraph, but it is unwise to leave a long quote hanging at the end of a paragraph without alerting your reader to its importance. Although long quotes are appropriate in some disciplines, for example, literature, excessive use in a history paper is out of place. If you do need to use one long quote to make a point, remember to indent it within your text.

Crafting sentences and paragraphs with effective transitions takes discipline and imagination. It is a skill that you will acquire with practice. Connecting words and phrases such as *likewise, yet, in contrast, subsequently, consequently*, and *therefore* help guide the reader through your text; but take care not to overuse them. No one will tell you how many sentences you need to write to construct a robust paragraph, but one sentence is unlikely to do the job. Equally unsuitable are excessively long paragraphs that include too many different issues and ramble on through a series of unconnected ideas. If you have a paragraph that extends to more than one page, try to separate out your ideas and construct two or three shorter paragraphs. (You will find exercises and examples of effective paragraphs and weak and strong transitioning in the companion workbook.)

To illustrate the points we have just made, we reproduce the text that precedes Gobat's paragraph illuminating Nicaraguan perceptions of the impact of dollar diplomacy on masculinity among elite entrepreneurs in his chapter "Economic Nationalism." The perceptions formed part of an overall critique of the actions of Wall Street financiers in this excerpt from a section of the chapter signaled by the subheading "Confronting Wall Street's Antimodern Impact." In this section, Gobat argues that Nicaraguan views of U.S. financiers turned critical when, unlike other Latin American countries, Nicaragua failed to secure loans from U.S. banks to finance public improvements after the global economic depression of 1920–1921. Consequently, Nicaraguan elites were unable to recover from the economic downturn and began to blame U.S. financiers for their plight and for the country's inability to modernize. Their critiques eventually contributed to the development of a particular feature of Nicaraguan nationalism. The author's evidence includes a government economic survey, newspaper and journal articles, and novels from the 1920s. Each of Gobat's topic sentences clearly indicates the central idea of the paragraph, which he develops in subsequent sentences. Using transitioning words and phrases such as *yet, however, as a result, above all, indeed*, and *more than anything*, he smoothly moves between sentences and paragraphs, marshalling his evidence to establish relationships between people, their actions, and events. Note that several citations use the shortened form because they have appeared previously in the chapter.

DEVELOPING AN ARGUMENT WITH SMOOTH PARAGRAPH TRANSITIONS

Gobat, Michel. *Confronting the American Dream: Nicaragua under U.S. Imperial Rule.* **Durham, NC: Duke University Press, 2005, 132–34. Extract from the chapter "Economic Nationalism."**

Nicaraguans' negative views of dollar diplomacy were critically reshaped by the world depression of 1920–21. To overcome this crisis, most Latin American governments undertook public improvements to promote the agroexport economy. These efforts included the modernization of the transport system, the creation of new state-controlled credit institutions catering to agroexporters, and the establishment of state-owned mercantile institutions. This heightened state activism was largely financed by the post-1921 boom in U.S. loans to Latin America.[33] Nicaragua, however, failed to benefit from this capital inflow, as U.S. bankers refused to extend large loans. Moreover, dollar diplomats ideologically opposed Nicaraguan efforts to enhance the state's economic role. As a result, Nicaragua failed to develop the kind of state interventions implanted elsewhere in Latin America. If "Wall Street" succeeded in restoring fiscal stability to Nicaragua, it came at the cost of being newly vilified as a promoter of economic backwardness.

The rise of anti–Wall Street sentiments is reflected in the 1923 economic survey commissioned by President Bartolomé Martínez (1923–24).[34] The survey asked prominent Nicaraguans from all political, regional, and economic sectors to identify the causes of the country's "distressing economic problem." Of forty-two responses published in newspapers, thirty-seven blamed dollar diplomacy. Many pointed out that dollar diplomats had promoted a highly politicized and thus inefficient administration of public finances or, as one complained, "too much politics and too little administering."[35] They also criticized dollar diplomats for blocking important public investment projects, as well as for their racist views.

Most, however, reserved their harshest criticism for Wall Street's control of Nicaragua's main financial institution: the Banco Nacional de Nicaragua. Above all, they lashed out at the bank's extreme reluctance to provide credit to agroexporters. Indeed, the 1920–21 depression had led the bank to reduce its output of loans drastically.[36] Although international markets recuperated shortly thereafter, the bank continued its restrictive lending practices. Moreover, its Wall Street owners prevented Nicaragua from participating in the post-1921 financial bonanza that swept much of Latin America. To most respondents, then, Wall Street was the main force blocking Nicaragua's development. Or, as one put it, dollar diplomacy was nothing but "a source of misery for Nicaraguans [and] an insurmountable wall for any honorable effort to promote the nation's progress."[37] More than anything, the 1923 survey underscores how dollar diplomacy generated much elite anxiety at a time when many Latin American upper classes were enjoying renewed prosperity. This discrepancy only reinforced Wall Street's peculiarly antimodern image in Nicaragua.

Nowhere did Nicaraguans more vividly depict Wall Street's antimodernism than in literature. The most acclaimed of such novels was Hernán Robleto's *Los estrangulados*.[38] Linked via kinship to parvenu elites, Robleto (1892–1969) was a prominent Liberal journalist who had fought with General Zeledón in the 1912 revolution. Set in the 1920s, *Los estrangulados* [The Strangled Ones] traces how "Wall Street" drove the twenty-four-year-old Gabriel Aguilar to bankruptcy. Like the author's family, Aguilar owns a large coffee plantation in the Sierra of Managua. In charting Aguilar's economic downturn, the novel denounces the U.S.-owned Banco Nacional for forcing the country's most entrepreneurial producers to turn to "antiquated methods of exchange or barter: cacao, beans, corn,

continued on next page

continued

and other grains for salt, butter, and basic medicine."[39] But the novel also vividly illustrates that Wall Street's stranglehold over Aguilar and his like is not limited to financial matters, as the Banco Nacional monopolizes the coffee trade through its subsidiary, the Compañía Mercantil de Ultramar (Overseas Mercantile Corporation); owns the country's sole railroad; and controls the all-important customhouses. Working in unison, Wall Street's chosen instruments are depicted as forming a diabolical machine bent on paralyzing Nicaragua's coffee economy. So great is Wall Street's regressive impact that local producers are forced to turn to premodern forms of credit and transportation. If Wall Street thus fueled the engines of "progress" in most Latin American countries during the 1920s, *Los estrangulados* stresses that in Nicaragua it forced the economic vanguard to turn to "antiquated" business methods.

Yet *Los estrangulados* is more than just an attack against Wall Street. It chronicles how Wall Street nefariously undermines the virility of Nicaraguan agroexporters. For this purpose, *Los estrangulados* begins by presenting the successful, modernizing coffee hacendado Gabriel Aguilar as the paradigm of (elite) manliness. It goes to great length to describe not only Aguilar's mental and business capacities but the physical prowess of this man "formed by fieldwork, strong, a bundle of muscles and nerves."[40] The tragedy that then unfolds centers on Aguilar's heroic yet futile efforts to maintain his economic independence, the basis of modern manhood. His economic problems begin with the sudden fall in international coffee prices—surely a reference to the depression of 1920–21. This unexpected drop prevents Aguilar, who never before faced financial problems, from repaying the loan he had recently received from the Banco Nacional at extremely onerous conditions. For Aguilar, there is no doubt that "Wall Street" orchestrated the devastating decline in coffee prices. And however much he tries to find a way out of the quagmire, Wall Street throws one obstacle after another in his way. In the end, Aguilar succumbs to Wall Street's "diabolical machine" and joins the long line of prominent Nicaraguans whose coffee fincas had been swallowed up by the "Ultra-tomb," that is, the Compañía Mercantil de Ultramar. As the narrator emphasizes, "the most characteristic trait of [Nicaragua's] current men is that they have been unable to defend themselves or defend a legacy of dignity."[41]

Many prominent Nicaraguans shared the view that dollar diplomacy had triggered a crisis of elite masculinity. A leading Liberal politician denounced the Banco Nacional and the Compañía Mercantil de Ultramar as "octopuses that have impoverished and dishonored many of our capitalists."[42] And one of Nicaragua's most famous Liberal ideologues, Salvador Mendieta, claimed that dollar diplomats were "emasculating" (*desvirilizando*) his countrymen.[43] So acute was this concern that "Crisis of Men" was the title a Granadan newspaper chose for an article that denounced dollar diplomats for having ruined many agroexport producers.[44] The 1920s campaign against dollar diplomacy was thus not just about recovering Nicaragua's sovereignty. It sought to rescue elite entrepreneurs and the economy from Wall Street's "diabolical machine."

NOTES

33. Thorp, "Economy, 1914–1929," 57–81.
34. *Encuesta económica propuesta a la consideración nacional por el Señor Presidente de la República Don Bartolomé Martínez.* Thanks to Jeffrey Gould for providing me with a copy of this survey.
35. *Encuesta economica,* 115.
36. Greer, "Hughes and Nicaragua," 102.
37. *Encuesta economica,* 57.
38. See also Silva, *Jacinta*; Chamorro Zelaya, *Entre dos filos*; Toruño, *Mariposa negra*; and Aguilar Cortés, *Ramón Diaz.*
39. Robleto, *Estrangulados,* 29.

40. Ibid., 30–31.

41. Ibid., 75.

42. Berrios, *Réplica*, 14.

43. Mendieta, *Enfermedad de Centro-América*, 1:319.

44. "Crisis de hombres," *El Correo*, 11 April 1933.

SOURCE

🖋 Conclusion: Answering your reader's "so what?" question

A successful conclusion explains why your findings are important. It reformulates (not repeats) your thesis statement, recapitulates the key evidence supporting your thesis, and reinforces the significance of your analysis. In other words, your conclusion should answer the "so what?" question: why should your readers care about your findings, what new connections or perspectives do they learn about, in what way have you contributed to the historiographical debate? Your conclusion should be a tight summary of what you have presented. It does not repeat your introduction. It should not introduce new or extraneous information. If you have not discussed an issue within the main body of your paper, do not introduce it in your conclusion. You may briefly point out any gaps in your research that might affect your analysis; but do not ruin all your hard work by offering a well-researched interpretation and then countering it with a speculative assertion about what might have been in different circumstances with different actors. Note in the following example how successfully Tamara Myers connects her final paragraph with her thesis statement and explains how, by championing young children in developing countries, Canadian youth helped position Canada as a benevolent actor in a global world, but they also contributed to increasing the divide between developed and developing nations by emphasizing differences based on racial distinctions and implying that people of color could not solve their own problems, a perception that became reinforced in subsequent international programs.

CONCLUDING PARAGRAPH: AN EXAMPLE

Myers, Tamara. "Local Action and Global Imagining: Youth, International Development, and the Walkathon Phenomenon in Sixties' and Seventies' Canada." *Diplomatic History* **38, no. 2 (2014): 282–93.**

Empathic, idealistic, and at times naïve, Canadian young people met the challenge of the Miles for Millions walkathon and were responsible for the millions of foundational dollars raised for the era's international development projects. With hindsight we can see that

continued on next page

continued

while clearly embracing a spirit of change, and perhaps even a need for the radical re-alignment of global capital, youth demands and activism around international development ultimately may have helped reinforce, rather than eradicate, global systems of power and colonial North–South relations. This resulted in part from the racialization of the needy child, a powerful symbol of reform in the Miles for Millions project, but one that tended to divide, rather than connect, North and South, rich and poor, sated and hungry. The process of imagining the developing world's children through the annual walkathon campaigns contributed, to an extent, to Canadian children's consciousness of global suffering, but by representing brown children as "other," the Miles for Millions experience delimited young people's compassion, creating, one might argue, a youthful Canadian identity based on a help-mate image in which whiteness and privilege were inherent to the solution of developing world problems. The millions of dollars Canadian children and youth raised in these walkathons were funneled into established Western aid organizations and development projects that would be criticized in subsequent years for serious limitations and too often having paradoxical effect on the targets of those charities.[54] Interestingly, it was these youngsters who embraced empathy and activism at a young age who would be, as adults, responsible for the critique of Canada's international development projects.[55] For better or worse, Canadian children and youth participated in and were integral to the history of international development in the late sixties and into the seventies.

NOTES

[54.] See Heron, *Desire for Development* and Hoffman, *All You Need Is Love.*

[55.] Heron, *Desire for Development*, 13.

 # History and language

As you write and revise your paper, remind yourself of the conventions of history writing regarding the use of English itself. Here are some guidelines.

Evidence, not proof. As you learned in Chapter One, history is an interpretive discipline. Historians provide interpretations of events and phenomena in the past. They offer a careful analysis to argue their case. They make claims about the past and support their claims with evidence. But most historians do not claim to be able to prove what happened in the past. Try to avoid the words "prove" in favor of "argue" and "proof" in favor of "evidence."

Past tense, not present or conditional. Historians write about the past. They use the past tense. We recommend that you write in the simple past tense, taking care to observe the rules governing sequence of tenses, and avoid switching from past to present and back again. Some writers use the historical present in narrative writing and also in historical fiction as a way to make their story alive in the present to their readers. It is rarely appropriate for analytical writing when you are trying to establish a convincing chronological trajectory. Even in expert hands it can lead to confusion. That said, historians sometimes use the present tense when they analyze literary texts, as in the example from Michel Gobat's *Confronting the American Dream*, cited earlier in this chapter. Use of the conditional is also inappropriate to discuss the past although it has its own use to describe a future event from a past perspective, as you have seen in the final sentence of the introductory paragraph from Tamara Myers's article "Local Action and Global Imagining."

> Write: *American whalers sailed from Salem for the Sandwich Islands, expecting to spend several months at sea before they reached their destination.* (past tense)
> Avoid: *American traders sail from Salem for the Sandwich Islands, expecting to spend several months at sea before they reach their destination.* (present tense)
> Avoid: *American traders would sail from Salem for the Sandwich Islands, expecting to spend several months at sea before they reached their destination.* (conditional, but inappropriate because they *did* sail; however, "would" in the sense of "used to" is correct to describe repeated or habitual action in the past.)

> Note: *American traders sailed from Salem for the Sandwich Islands. They knew that they would spend several months at sea before they reached their destination.* (appropriate use of conditional)

Active voice, not passive. The passive voice has its purpose and can be used effectively on occasion. For example, in Michel Gobat's introduction to a section of his chapter on economic nationalism, we find this opening sentence: "Nicaraguans' negative views of dollar diplomacy were critically reshaped by the world depression of 1920–21." Gobat could have written this sentence in the active voice as follows: "The world depression of 1920–21 critically reshaped Nicaraguans' negative views of dollar diplomacy." But his purpose was to emphasize the views of Nicaraguans, not the world depression; hence his use of passive voice. You may use passive voice for emphasis as long as you can clarify agency; but you should use it sparingly. When you write in the active voice, you will find it easier to state who did what to whom. You might be tempted to use the passive if you are unclear about the connections among individuals, actions, and consequences. In such a case, your better option is to try to clarify those connections.

> Passive: *China was forced to trade in opium in the mid-nineteenth century.*
> Active: *British merchants smuggled opium into China against the wishes of the Chinese government until the British and French governments forced the Chinese to accept legalization of the trade in the Treaty of Tientsin at the conclusion of the Second Opium War (1856–60).*

Neutral language, not bias, disrespect, or familiarity. People in the past had different ideas from us. They did not think as we do, they did not behave as we do. As L. P. Hartley put it in his book *The Go-Between* (1953), "the past is a foreign country, they do things differently there." We may be shocked at some of the beliefs and actions of people in the past, but we should be careful to explain rather than judge them. We may like to convince ourselves that we would not have joined the Nazi Party in the 1930s, for example, but we cannot know how we might have thought and acted had we been born into a different time and space. We may think that we know better than individuals in the past, but it is inappropriate to call them misguided, barbaric, neurotic, inferior, and backward or label them by other such derogatory terms. You will find in your sources terms that we consider inappropriate today. Although it was commonly used in the nineteenth century, we no longer use the term "Negro." The word "heathen," a term frequently used by European and American missionaries, is likewise unacceptable. You may use them in quotes, with quotation marks, to explain earlier perceptions, but you should avoid them in your own writing.

At the same time, try to avoid referring to actors in the past as "we." We are actors in our own time, but we could not act before we were born. You may like to feel a sense of oneness with the women and men in your own national history, but they are far removed from you in time, culture, beliefs, and understanding. When you have properly identified actors in the past, the appropriate pronoun to use is "they." Compare the following sentences:

> Weak: *We beat the British at the Battle of Saratoga and won the war.*
> Strong: *American forces conquered the British army at the Battle of Saratoga. Although they experienced many hardships in intervening battles, the Americans went on to win the Revolutionary War.*

Similarly, develop the habit of using gender-neutral terms. Some older textbooks refer to an essentialized student who is always referred to as *he*; however, many (although not all) historians agree that it is no longer appropriate to use the masculine pronoun *he* to encompass all of humankind or small groups of mixed-gender individuals. Perhaps you have used the masculine pronoun to avoid the somewhat awkward repetition of the phrase *he or she*. Occasional use of the joint pronoun is not a problem, although excessive use becomes irritating to most readers. You can often avoid it, however, by choosing plural nouns rather than singular nouns. For example, throughout this chapter, we have frequently used the plural noun *readers*, for which the pronoun *they* avoids gendered language. That said, you will want to avoid neutral terms if they displace agency or responsibility. Always try to aim for clarity.

Specific claims, not generalizations. Do not make broad claims about entire groups of people. Although certain features and identity traits allow us to group individuals by nationality, religion, gender, sexuality, race, or ethnic group, for example, they do not allow us to argue that all people in the group believed, thought, or acted in the same way. Statements such as "American women did not go out to work before World War I" or "African Americans in the South supported Booker T. Washington" are inappropriate and incorrect. Instead, clearly identify your agents. Which American women? What particular group of African Americans?

Basic errors of grammar and syntax. Such errors disrupt meaning, confuse your readers, and can contribute to misunderstandings. If your readers are baffled and have to work hard to follow your argument, they will eventually give up. Your professor might also stop reading and invite you for consultation. Professors need to spend their time helping you develop your skills of historical analysis. They cannot do this if they have to spend time correcting grammar and improving clarity. Failure to use good English will impair the impact of your research paper and result in penalties. Although it is beyond the scope of this handbook to provide writing instruction, the following tips, culled from years of grading assignments, alert you to the most prominent errors that recur in student papers. If you can avoid them, you will save yourself substantial time and effort. For more detailed assistance, please consult the sections on grammar and punctuation in *The Chicago Manual of Style*. (Many libraries have online subscriptions.)

1. **Write complete sentences.** A full sentence requires, minimally, a subject and a verb. Sentence fragments that begin with the relative pronouns *who, which,* or *that* need repair.

   Compare the following:

   > Sentences: *Reformers were well aware of shifting patterns of consumption among the new urban middle classes. The changes were reflected spatially in the new neighborhoods of the expanding capital.*
   > Sentence and sentence fragment: *Reformers were well aware of shifting patterns of consumption among the new urban middle classes. Which were also reflected spatially in the new neighborhoods of the expanding capital.*

2. **Make your subjects and verbs agree.** A singular subject requires a singular verb. A plural subject requires a plural verb.

   > Singular: *Hwang Keum-ja, who endured forced labor as a "comfort woman" during World War II, has recently died.*
   > Plural: *The few surviving Korean women whom the Japanese military compelled to work as "comfort women" during World War II have since the 1990s staged weekly protests in front of the Japanese embassy in Seoul. They have continued to demand an apology from the Japanese government for forcing them into sexual slavery.*

3. **When possible, use strong active verbs in preference to weak auxiliary verbs (to be, to have) and specific vocabulary rather than vague terms.**

   Compare the following:

   > Weak: *French-Canadians were south of the Great Lakes long before the British got there in 1763.*
   > Strong: *French-Canadians had inhabited the lands south of the Great Lakes for a century before the British gained control of the area by the Treaty of Paris in 1763.*

4. Be concise. Avoid empty or verbose phrases. A "lean and mean" style will serve you better.

   Compare the following:

   > Weak: *It is evident from this document that the Indians believed that they were vulnerable.*
   > Strong: *The Indians believed that their location rendered them vulnerable.*

   Examples of other redundant phrases you want to avoid:

   > As mentioned before, . . .
   > *It should come as no surprise*
   > *Needless to say*
   > *It should be noted that*
   > *Thus one can conclude that*

5. Revise impersonal constructions that contribute words but not meaning.
   Weak: *There were threats to Bolshevik rule.*
   Strong: *Several threats to Bolshevik rule loomed ahead.*

6. Watch for dangling modifiers, that is, phrasal constructions that do not agree with the subject of your sentence.

   Compare the following:
   Incorrect: *Like many Jewish children of his age in the Ottoman Empire, Gabriel Arié's parents enrolled him in the nearby Alliance school. While in school, the experiences were harrowing.*
   Correct: *Like many Jewish children of his age in the Ottoman Empire, Gabriel Arié attended the nearby Alliance school. While in school, he experienced several harrowing events.*

7. Select language that reflects a more formal writing style than speech. Avoid slang and colloquialisms.
   Weak: *Germany got ripped off in the Treaty of Versailles.*
   Strong: *Many Germans viewed the Treaty of Versailles as excessively punitive.*

8. Learn the difference between the words *their* and *there*. The possessive pronoun *their* refers to people. The word *there* is an adverb of place.

   Compare the following:
   Their: *Many Germans reacted with disbelief to the Treaty of Versailles. Their earlier optimism gave way to anger against the Allies.*
   There: *Many Germans reacted with disbelief to the terms of the treaty proposed in Versailles. They had hoped for a more lenient outcome to emerge from negotiations there.*

9. Try to be aware of the appropriate use of the singular and plural forms of common nouns, particularly man and woman, men and women. Some confusion can result from their use in earlier sources; for example, in the nineteenth century the phrases *woman suffrage* and *woman's rights* were normal usage. When referring to these topics in their historical context, it is fine to use them in quotation marks; otherwise, we should write about women's suffrage and women's rights.

10. Distinguish the possessive case, indicated by the use of apostrophes, from plural forms of words.

    Note the differences in the following sentences:
    The butler housed the visiting servant in the attic of the abbey. (Singular form of servant)
    The butler obliged the visiting servants to assist with daily chores at the abbey. (Plural form of the singular servant)
    The servant's room in the attic resembled a monastic cell. (Apostrophe required before the "s" for possession in singular)
    The servants' quarters in the attic resembled monastic cells. (Apostrophe required after the "s" for possession in plural)

11. Match pronouns with preceding nouns.

    For example:
    > *The suffragettes marched in the parade carrying their banners.*
    > *The suffragette chained herself to the railings in protest still holding her banner.*

12. Distinguish between *it's* (contraction for *it is*) and *its* (denoting possessive case). Note the following:
    > *The government relied on its military intelligence when making the decision to intervene in the border skirmishes.* (possessive)

13. Do not use informal contractions:
    > *It is* (not it's) *a courageous act.*
    > *The soldiers would have enjoyed the march had it not been snowing.* (not would've or would of)

14. Appreciate the difference between count and noncount nouns.
    > *A large number of soldiers contracted pneumonia.* (You can count soldiers, so it is ungrammatical to write "large amounts of soldiers.")
    > *Fewer soldiers died after being treated with antibiotics.* (Fewer, not less)
    > *Large amounts of penicillin were required to treat the soldiers.* (You cannot count penicillin.)
    > *Less penicillin was required to treat the younger soldiers.*
    > *Fewer doses of penicillin were required to treat the younger soldiers.* (You can count doses)

15. Try not to use the adjectives *most* or *many* standing alone as nouns, such as "most believed" or "many came" because the sentence may be unclear to your reader. Most who? Most what? Clarify by adding a noun. You may use the words standing alone if you have clarified the noun to which they refer in a preceding sentence.
    > Clear: *Most Germans resented the impositions of the Treaty of Versailles.*
    > Clear: *Of forty-two responses published in newspapers, thirty-seven blamed dollar diplomacy. Many pointed out that dollar diplomats had promoted a highly politicized and thus inefficient administration of public finances . . .* (from Michel Gobat's extract on Nicaraguan economic nationalism)

16. Avoid sentences that begin with the demonstrative pronoun *this*, standing alone in place of a noun. They are weak. It is rarely clear what *this* refers to. You must clarify. Write, for example, *this event* or *this battle*.

17. Avoid repetition. Read your writing carefully, revise it, and edit it. When editing, eradicate redundant phrases and repetitious sentences.

18. Simplify awkward constructions. Read your writing aloud, slowly, and listen for meaning. If it does not make sense to you, it will not make sense to your readers.

Documentation

The discipline of history requires you to document all your sources, whether your final assignment is a written research paper, a visual presentation, or an oral report. Appropriate bibliographic documentation and incorporation of footnotes or endnotes establishes your credibility as an author and helps convince your readers of the power of your argument. The information you provide enables other historians to read the evidence themselves, evaluate your analysis, and perhaps challenge your interpretation. Documentation is a time-consuming task, so be sure to plan enough time to complete it successfully. The more attention you pay to documenting your sources in the early stages of your research and writing, the easier the task is. You want to make sure that your documentation is complete for each piece of writing you submit to your professor.

Each academic discipline has its system of documentation. The existence of multiple systems makes students' lives difficult because they must follow different methods for different classes. If you are taking classes in literature, psychology, and history in one semester, you have three systems to contend with—the Modern Language Association, the American Psychological Association, and *The Chicago Manual*. Until such time as scholars get together to simplify the situation (an eventuality that we do not anticipate), you are unfortunately burdened with this reality. Historians generally follow the models codified in *The Chicago Manual* because it allows for stronger documentation of primary sources. Unless your professor instructs you otherwise, you will not go wrong if you follow the guidelines of *The Chicago Manual*.

As you learned in Chapter Three, a *bibliography* is a list of sources, organized alphabetically, that you add at the end of your paper, following the endnotes. Cite all the sources you use, including visual images and interviews. Include in the list only those sources you actually cite. Do not include sources you consulted early on in your work and decided to discard for your final paper. Organize primary and secondary sources separately. Within your primary source section, organize unpublished and published sources separately, listing the unpublished sources first.

Your professor will advise you whether to use *footnotes* or *endnotes*. Footnotes have the advantage of being readily accessible at the bottom of the page but become cumbersome when long. Placed at the end of a research paper, endnotes are less accessible to the reader, but their position allows the writer more flexibility with regard to the length of comments alongside the citation. More and more, publishers dictate the choice of adopting endnotes or footnotes. The decision is partly a matter of cost; endnotes entail less expense. Doctoral dissertations remain the key publication in which footnotes are preferred to endnotes.

Historians document sources within their text by adding a superscript number at the end of the sentence in which a quote or paraphrase occurs. (See examples in the excerpts from Michel Gobat's *Confronting the American Dream*.) Although in the past historians might have included two or three superscripted numbers within one sentence for a string of quotes, publishers have reduced the frequency of this practice, again for cost reasons, although the practice is also unwieldy. Indeed, some publishers insist on only one superscript endnote per paragraph. Unless otherwise instructed by your professor, you are advised to insert no more than one superscript in a sentence and place it at the end of the sentence. Superscript numbers follow sequentially, but you no longer have to worry about getting this right. Most word-processing software packages include an easy endnote insertion tab. They keep track of the numbering for you even when you cut and paste your text. If you have not yet learned how to do this with the software available to you, now is a good time to investigate. It will save you a lot of headaches. And remember to click on the option for Arabic numerals (1, 2, 3) rather than Roman (i, ii, iii).

Commercially available note-taking software can also be integrated into your word-processing software to create your bibliography and endnotes. Zotero, which we mentioned in Chapter Five, is one such option. The existence of this software makes the lives of historians much easier; however, your professor may want you to learn and demonstrate the basics of creating your own endnotes and bibliography. As always, check with your professor.

A fully comprehensive catalog of all the documentation models historians might possibly need is beyond the scope of this handbook. In the remainder of this section, we provide examples for citing the single-author book and article as the basic documentation model. An appendix offers a quick guide in tabular presentation of the most common bibliographic and endnote models for your ease of comparison. For models not included here, please consult the *The Chicago Manual* or the style guide your professor recommends.

Single-Author Book

We begin with the single-author book as the general model. Please pay careful attention to font use (*italics* for book title), punctuation, and capitalization. In general, in titles in English, prepositions and articles (a, the) are not capitalized unless they appear as the first letter of the first word of the title.

Bibliography: A single-author book entry is listed with the following elements. Second and subsequent lines are indented.

- Author's last name [comma]
- Author's first name(s) and initial(s) [period]
- Title of work [in italics followed by period, note capitalization]
- Place of publication [colon]
- Publisher [comma]
- Year of publication [period]

Example:

Hall, Catherine. *Civilising Subjects: Metropole and Colony in the English Imagination, 1830–1867*. Chicago: University of Chicago Press, 2002. (Note the British spelling in the word "*Civilising*." Always retain spellings in the original publication.)

If the place of publication needs clarification, then an abbreviation of the state or country is added. If the title page of a book lists two places of publication, for example, London and New York, include only the first.

Example:

Hasegawa, Tsuyoshi. *Racing the Enemy: Stalin, Truman, and the Surrender of Japan*. Cambridge, MA: Belknap Press, 2005.

Footnotes and endnotes. Models differ from those for bibliographic citation. Please take care to note the distinctions. A single-author book entry is listed with the following elements. No indentation is required.

- Author's first name
- Author's last name [comma]
- Title of work [in italics, no punctuation]
- Publishing information all in parentheses [comma outside last parenthesis]
- Place of publication [colon]
- Publishing company [comma]
- Year of publication
- Page number(s) of quote or paraphrase [period] (if required)

Example (no indentation):

Catherine Hall, *Civilising Subjects: Metropole and Colony in the English Imagination, 1830–1867* (Chicago: University of Chicago Press, 2002), 191.

After the first full citation, you may use a shorter option for subsequent citations, using page numbers where appropriate.

Example:

Hall, *Civilising Subjects*, 191.

If you cite the same work immediately in the next endnote, you may use the Latin abbreviation *ibid*. Page numbers may differ because they can be added after *ibid*.

Example:

Hall, Civilising Subjects, 191.
Ibid., 191.
Ibid., 200.

This usage is becoming increasingly uncommon, however, because it can lead to confusion. The better option is to use the model of author and short title.

Several items in the same endnote are separated by semicolons.

Example:

Robert J. C. Butow, *Japan's Decision to Surrender* (Stanford, CA: Stanford University Press, 1954); Leon V. Sigal, *Fighting to a Finish* (Ithaca, NY: Cornell University Press, 1988); Richard Frank, *Downfall: The End of the Imperial Japanese Empire* (New York: Random House, 1999); and Forrest E. Morgan, *Compellence and the Strategic Culture of Imperial Japan: Implication for Coercive Diplomacy in the Twenty-First Century* (Westport, CT: Praeger, 2003).

Journal Articles

Bibliography: A single-author article is listed with the following elements. Second and subsequent lines are indented.

- Author's last name [comma]
- Author's first name(s) [period]

- Title of article in quotation marks [period inside quotation marks]
- Title of journal in italics [no punctuation]
- Volume number (without the contraction vol.) [comma]
- Issue number (preceded by the contraction "no.") [no punctuation]
- Year of publication (in parentheses) [colon]
- Inclusive page numbers, separated by hyphen [period]

Example:

Bossler, Beverley. "Gender and Empire: A View from Yuan China." *Journal of Medieval and Early Modern Studies* 34, no. 1 (2004): 197–223.

Endnote or footnote for single-author journal article.

- Author's first name(s)
- Author's last name [comma]
- Title of article in quotation marks [comma inside quotation marks]
- Title of journal in italics [no punctuation]
- Volume number (without the contraction vol.) [comma]
- Issue number (preceded by the contraction "no.") [no punctuation]
- Year of publication (in parentheses) [colon]
- Inclusive page numbers, separated by hyphen [period]

Example:

Beverley Bossler, "Gender and Empire: A View from Yuan China," *Journal of Medieval and Early Modern Studies* 34, no. 1 (2004): 197–223.

Subsequent citations

Bossler, "Gender and Empire," 197–223.

Primary Sources

Published primary sources can be treated the same way as secondary sources. If a published source lacks the name of the author, organize it within the bibliography alphabetically by the first letter of the first word. If the first word is a definite or indefinite article (the, a), then organize alphabetically by the first letter of the second word.

Unpublished primary sources receive special treatment. For bibliographies, list only the name and location of the archival collection in which you worked, not individual pieces of correspondence. List only the names of the newspapers you consulted, not every article in every newspaper. For endnotes, it is impossible to cover all the possibilities. You will find examples of the most common options in the appendix.

Final peer review

Peer review is arguably one of the most useful services that a historian can offer to a colleague. We discuss, read, and comment on each other's work. We are expected to offer and be prepared to accept critical feedback, and we revise our work on the basis of the comments received. You will want to take the task seriously before you complete the final version of your paper. The following questions will help you craft a peer review of your fellow student's outline that offers feedback on the strength of his or her argument and the logic and flow of the structure. The questions also serve as a checklist for your paper.

QUESTIONS FOR FINAL PEER REVIEW

Structure

1. Is the paper well organized? Does it have a strong introduction and conclusion? Do the subheads clarify the sections of the text? Does each paragraph deal with one key point? Has the author crafted strong topic sentences with pertinent paragraph development of content? Do the paragraphs transition well? Is the order of presentation of information logical?

Analysis

2. What is the thesis statement? Does the author make a strong argument?

3. Is the argument clear and convincing? Does the author provide adequate analysis (not just description and summary) to convince you? Does s/he provide answers to the "how" and "why" questions, or does s/he simply provide a chronological narrative that lacks analysis? Are the author's sources adequate and appropriate? How does the author use sources to support his/her arguments? Are quotes and examples appropriately framed?

Context

4. Is the paper well contextualized? Does the author engage in historiographical debate? Is there enough background information to help you understand the argument and its significance?

Readability/Use of English

5. How "readable" (clear and coherent) is the draft? Does the narrative flow smoothly and logically? What, if anything, is missing? Is terminology appropriate? Comment on grammatical errors only if they seem excessive to you.

Documentation

6. Is the bibliographic information correctly cited? Are all the citations mentioned in the endnotes listed in the bibliography? Note discrepancies. Are the endnotes properly cited?

Suggestions for Revision

7. Provide three focused suggestions for revision.

When you submit your final paper, you will experience a great sense of achievement, as well as relief. Congratulate yourself. You have mastered a complex process of research and writing. You have learned to structure your thoughts and express them cogently. You appreciate the importance of organizing evidence to support your arguments. You have acquired the delicate art of providing and accepting critical feedback. These skills will serve you well in the world of work.

PART TWO
DOING HISTORY

CHAPTER ONE

What Is the Discipline of History?

Workbook Exercises

❶ Scholarly versus popular history books

As discussed in Chapter One of the textbook, certain topics generate a great deal of interest from both scholarly and general audiences. Professional historians are not the only authors of history books. Journalists, writers, and amateurs with a passion for a particular area of inquiry produce texts that rest on the shelves of libraries and bookstores alongside the works of academics. The quality and significance of history books varies; historians and other writers have published numerous outstanding studies, but a number of mediocre and questionable titles appear in print as well. As a student, you want to be able to tell the difference between scholarly books and popular books and look for clues to help you identify the better titles in both areas. Generally speaking, for a major research paper or capstone project you will want to consult primarily scholarly books. However, popular titles can be quite useful in helping you to get an overview of a particular field of study and leading you to questions that are currently on the minds of the general reading public.

ACTIVITY: Is it a scholarly or popular book?

EXAMPLE ONE—THE HOLOCAUST

The Holocaust is one of the most horrible tragedies in human history and thus one of the most studied. Historians and other writers have long tried to understand how it was possible for the Nazis to exterminate more than 6 million Jews and 6 million others as World War II raged on. What was deemed the "final solution" to Adolf Hitler's and the Nazis' "Jewish problem" resulted in mass executions in death camps across Germany and Eastern Europe. Although we now know a great deal about the process of ghettoization, internment, and murder organized by the SS and faced by millions of men, women, and children labeled as undesirables, we are still left with many questions: Who knew what was going on? Why didn't anyone stop it? Had anything like this ever happened before? Was there something peculiar about the German state? Was it all because of Hitler?

Turning to recent publications on the Holocaust will allow us to grapple with some of these questions while becoming more familiar with the distinctions between books intended for slightly different audiences. Let's say you have the following two titles in front of you but you are not sure which one is a better choice to include in a bibliography of scholarly sources. What steps can you take to quickly evaluate them before reading on?

continued on next page

continued

Bloxham, Donald. *The Final Solution: A Genocide.* New York: Oxford University Press, 2009.

McMillan, Dan. *How Could This Happen? Explaining the Holocaust.* New York: Basic Books, 2014.

_____Who is the author?

You have their names, but who are they? Look for the author information. It is usually located on the back cover, inside flap of the dust jacket, or toward the beginning or end of the text. Does the author hold a Ph.D. in history or a related field? Is the author currently employed by an academic institution, such as a college or university? Has the author published anything else on this subject?

Donald Bloxham is Professor of Modern History at Edinburgh University. An expert in the history of genocide and the punishment of genocide, he is the author of *Genocide on Trial* (2001), *The Holocaust: Critical Historical Approaches* (with Tony Kushner, 2005), and *The Great Game of Genocide: Imperialism, Nationalism, and the Destruction of the Ottoman Armenians* (2005), which won the 2007 Raphael Lemkin Award for Genocide Scholarship. He is also co-editor of the forthcoming *Oxford Handbook of Genocide Studies* (2009) and the monograph series *Zones of Violence*.

DAN McMILLAN holds a Ph.D. in German history from Columbia University and a law degree from Fordham University and has worked as a history professor and a prosecuting attorney. He lives in New York City.

If comparing these two authors, you might note that there is no mention of Bloxham's degrees but at the time of publication he was a professor at Edinburgh University and he has published several other books on genocide and won an award for his scholarship. McMillan holds a Ph.D. in history and a law degree and has taught history and worked as a lawyer. There is no mention of his current position. Both authors have impressive credentials. We might assume McMillan is an independent scholar, that is, someone who conducts research and writes without the support of an academic institution.

_____Who is the publisher?

This information is located on the title page and/or copyright page and likely on the back cover or spine as well. Publishers housed within a university, such as Oxford University Press, generally publish mostly academic or scholarly nonfiction titles and may also publish textbooks, fiction, or popular nonfiction. Some scholarly presses are not affiliated with an academic institution. You will need to look for additional clues if you are not sure or ask a librarian or your professor.

We are sure Bloxham's book is with a scholarly press, Oxford University Press. Basic Books, McMillan's publisher, does not appear to be housed in a university so we will have to investigate further. Your professor would tell you that Basic is a trade press, that is, a publisher of books for general audiences.

_____Are there footnotes or endnotes and a bibliography? What sorts of sources did the author consult?

The Final Solution
A GENOCIDE

DONALD BLOXHAM

OXFORD
UNIVERSITY PRESS

HOW COULD THIS HAPPEN

EXPLAINING THE HOLOCAUST

DAN McMILLAN

BASIC BOOKS
A Member of the Perseus Books Group
New York

A few presses still print footnotes, which are found at the bottom of the page. Most publishers, however, now use endnotes. You will find them either at the end of each chapter or collected all together at the end of the book. The bibliography, if included, generally follows the notes. You should expect to see more extensive notes and bibliographies in scholarly books as well as titles in the languages of the countries or peoples featured in the study. Top-notch scholars rely heavily on primary sources (see Chapter Four), whereas other authors may mainly refer to secondary sources, that is, to books and articles published by other writers who were not witness to the events at hand.

Bloxham

NOTES

INTRODUCTION

[1.] See Chapter 6.

[2.] Berel Lang, "The Evil in Genocide," in John K. Roth (ed.), *Genocide and Human Rights: A Philosophical Guide* (New York: Palgrave Macmillan, 2005), 5–17, here 12. On Cambodia, see Ben Kiernan, *The Pol Pot Regime: Race, Power, and Genocide in Cambodia under the Khmer Rouge, 1975–79* (New Haven, CT: Yale University Press, 1996): on Latin America, see Daniel Feierstein, *El genocidio como práctica social* (Buenos Aires: Fondo de Cultura Económica, 2007).

[3.] Mark Levene, *Genocide in the Age of the Nation State*, vols. i and ii (London: Tauris, 2005), is the best attempt at a comprehensive history of the subject for the modern period.

continued on next page

continued

[4] Daniel J. Goldhagen, *Hitler's Willing Executioners: Ordinary Germans and the Holocaust* (New York: Knopf, 1996).

[5] See Chapter 8.

[6] Michael Marrus, *The Holocaust in History* (Harmondsworth, UK: Penguin, 1989), and Dan Stone (ed.), *The Historiography of the Holocaust* (Basingstoke, UK: Palgrave, 2004) cover many of the historiographical issues splendidly.

[7] e.g., Saul Friedländer's superb two-volume *Nazi Germany and the Jews* (New York: Harper Collins, 1997, 2007).

DOCUMENTARY TRACES

[1] Federation of the Romanian Jewish Communities, neg. 11561. Courtesy of United States Holocaust Memorial Museum (USHMM) photograph archives, W/S 58558.

[2] Ibid. W/S 58559.

[3] Aimé Césaire, *Discourse on Colonialism* (New York: Monthly Review Press, 1972), 14.

SELECT BIBLIOGRAPHY

PRIMARY SOURCES

Arad, Yitzhak, et al. (eds.) *Documents on the Holocaust* (Lincoln: University of Nebraska Press, 1999).

Benz, Wolfgang, Konrad Kwiet, and Jürgen Matthäus (eds.), *Eintatz im "Reichskommissariat Ostland": Dokumente zum Völkermord im Baltikum und in Weissrussland* (Berlin: Metropol, 1998).

Berenstein, Tatiana, et al. (eds.), *Faschismus—Ghetto—Massenmord: Dokumentation über Austrottung und Widerstand der Juden in Polen während des zweiten Weltkrieges* (Berlin: Rütten and Loening, 1960).

Deutsche Geschichte im 20. Jahrhundert Online. Nationalsozialismus, Holocaust, Widerstand und Exil 1933–1945. Online-Datenbank, ed. K. G. Saur Verlag.

Domarus, Max (ed.), *Hitler. Reden und Proklamationen 1932–1945*, 2 vols. (Neustadt: Schmidt, 1962).

Friedman, Tuviah (ed.), *Die drei verantwortlichen SS-Führer für die Durchführung der Endlösung der Judenfrage in Europa waren: Heydrich—Eichmann—Müller: eine dokumentarische Sammlung von SS- und Gestapo-Dokumenten über die Vernichtung der Juden Europas 1939–1945* (Haifa: Institute of Documentation in Israel, 1993).

Goebbels, Joseph, *Die Tagebücher von Joseph Goebbels*, ed. Elke Fröhlich, (Munich: Saur, 1996).

Gruner, Wolf (ed.), *Die Verfolgung und Ermördung der europäischen Juden durch das nationalsozialistische Deutschland 1933–1945* (Munich: Oldenbourg, 2008).

Himmler, Heinrich, *Geheimreden 1933 bis 1945*, ed. Bradley F. Smith and Agnes F. Peterson (Frankfurt Am Main: Propyläen, 1974).

Hoess, Rudolf, *Commandant of Auschwitz: The Autobiography of Rudolf Höss* (London: Phoenix Press, 1961).

International Military Tribunal, *Trial of the Major War Criminals before the International Military Tribunal*, 42 vols. (Nuremberg: IMT, 1947–9).

Jäckel, Eberhard, and Axel Kuhn (eds), *Hitler, Sämtliche Aufzeichnungen 1905–1924* (Stuttgart: Deutsche Verlags-Anstalt, 1980).

McMillan

NOTES

INTRODUCTION

[1.] Elie Wiesel, "Plea for the Dead," in *Legends of Our Time* (New York: Holt, Rinehart and Winston, 1968), 181–82. The second and third sentences of the quoted passage are separated by roughly a page of text. Emphasis in original.

[2.] Primo Levi, quoted in Inga Clendinnen, *Reading the Holocaust* (New York: Cambridge University Press, 1999), 88; Elie Wiesel, "Plea for the Dead," 180–81. At 181 Wiesel also asked: "We dare interpret the agony and anguish, the self-sacrifice before faith and faith itself of six million human beings, all named Job? Who are we to judge them?"

[3.] With Himmler I have departed slightly from a literal translation to make this passage more readable. I have also left out a significant (but in my view misleading) comment on the nature of the Nazi belief system. The complete passage was as follows: "Mit dem Antisemitismus ist es genauso wie mit der Entlausung. Es ist keine Weltanschauungsfrage, daß man die Läuse entfernt. Das ist eine Reinlichkeitsangelegenheit. Genauso ist der Antisemitismus für uns keine Weltanschauungsfrage gewesen, sondern eine Reinlichkeitsangelegenheit, die jetzt bald ausgestanden ist. Wir sind bald entlaust. Wir haben nur noch 20,000 Läuse, dann ist es vorbei damit in ganz Deutschland." Excerpt from Himmler's speech to SS-Korpsführer, April 24, 1943, in Heinrich Himmler, *Geheimreden 1933 bis 1945*, Bradley F. Smith and Agnes Peterson, eds., with an introduction by Joschim C. Fest (Frankfurt: Propyläen, 1974), 200. On the complete extermination and other unique features of the Holocaust, see Chapter 2.

[4.] Historians and psychologists generally agree that most perpetrators of the Holocaust were psychologically normal, at least before they began committing mass murder. See, for example, Victoria Barnett, *Bystanders: Conscience and Complicity during the Holocaust* (Westport, CT: Greenwood Press, 1999), 23; Zygmunt Bauman, *Modernity and the Holocaust* (Cambridge, UK: Polity Press, 1989), 19.

Bloxham's book has both notes and a bibliography. Both are extensive and include German-language titles. The bibliography is divided by primary and secondary sources, making it easy to see that he relied on firsthand accounts as well as what other authors have written on the subject. McMillan's notes are also numerous. He has referenced fewer German language titles and did not include a separate bibliography. On first glance, it appears he has used *Mein Kampf* as a major primary source and relied more on important secondary works than on primary sources.

Pause: Have you made a determination yet? Both authors measure up as scholars in their field. Both clearly conducted extensive research and carefully cited their sources. Bloxham made it easy for us to understand that he used primary sources in German and we are sure we can rely on OUP for quality scholarship so we might give an edge to *The Final Solution* at this point and list it in our bibliography. I certainly would not return *How Could This Happen* to the library before looking it over some more, however.

Other points to consider:

_____Is it illustrated?

Photographs, maps, and reprinted images can enrich our understanding of a subject. Look to see whether these items are discussed in the text, however, or if they are simply there to embellish. A scholar is more likely to explain why a particular image has been added and

continued on next page

continued

will offer some interpretation of it, whereas a popular author may simply include related images to allow for visualization but without offering a specific analytical framework.

_____How does it read?

Most authors strive for clarity in their prose but academic writing sometimes follows conventions less commonly found in books intended for a broad audience. The vocabulary in popular texts may be simpler and the sentence structure less complex. Scholarly authors are likely to refer to the historiography (see Chapter Three) in their field and their approach may be more analytical than narrative. Or, putting it another way, popular authors may tell you principally what happened rather than explain in depth how or why it happened and they may not tell you what other authors had to say about the subject matter before they wrote their book.

EXAMPLE TWO—D-DAY

Another facet of World War II that excites most readers is that of the Allied invasion of Normandy in May 1944 known as Operation Overlord. The largest amphibious assault in history involved 2 million soldiers launched from southern England assisted by thousands of planes, landing craft, and amphibious vehicles and nearly three hundred naval ships. The Normandy landing was a military undertaking of unprecedented scale and turned the European theater of the war decisively in the Allies' favor. Historians and popular authors have been interested to understand exactly what went into the planning of the attack and what risks were involved. They have collected the oral histories of participants at all levels—from new recruits to the top generals and admirals. They have also examined how the operation shifted the course of the war and speculated about other possible outcomes. In fact, the "what ifs" of D-Day generate a great deal of debate. Students, however, should be cautious about becoming mired in these discussions and must take care to separate serious scholarship from texts that mainly provide an interesting read and general coverage. This is true not only for books about D-Day but also for an array of historical topics.

As above, you will want to examine the texts before determining their value for your project. The following two titles are a good starting point:

Symonds, Craig L. *Neptune: The Allied Invasion of Europe and the D-Day Landings.* New York: Oxford University Press, 2014.

Van der Vat, Dan. *D-Day: The Greatest Invasion, A People's History.* Introduction by John S. D. Eisenhower. New York: Bloomsbury, 2003.

Again, we have included an Oxford book and we can be reasonably sure it will work well for our research bibliography. The author is a distinguished military historian with an impressive list of published books and awards. The press is credible and the research is impeccable.

The second book also looks appealing, however. We know from the title page that a relative of Dwight D. Eisenhower wrote the introduction. The text is richly illustrated with photographs, maps, and examples of primary sources. The style is accessible and lively. Our library copy has had the dust jacket removed so we went to the Internet to look up the author and saw that he is a journalist who has published several books on naval history and has worked for the leading British daily, *The Guardian*. We also searched for the publisher, Bloomsbury, and noted that they publish academic and popular titles. All of this is useful information because we can determine that the book is credible. Yet, there is no notes section and no bibliography and the text seems to provide an overview with several compelling stories, but we do not see evidence of interpretation or debate. The book is a nice tribute to the D-Day landings and we will read it with interest to refresh our memories on the events at hand, but we will not list it as a scholarly source and may just cite it in our notes as a narrative account of this event. Chances are your professor will be more impressed with the first book.

ACTIVITY: Your own search

Locate three or four books in the catalog of your college library on the general topic of your research. Go through each to determine whether it is scholarly or popular and decide if you will want to read it for your project or return it to the library right away. Keep in mind the items on our checklist:

_____Is the author a historian or a journalist or something else?

_____Is the publisher an academic press or a popular (trade) press or unknown?

_____Are there notes and/or a bibliography of sources? Are they mostly secondary or primary?

_____Are there integrated images?

_____Is the tone more appropriate for a general or a highly educated reader?

Answering these few basic questions will help you to quickly determine the best sources to begin with for your research. You do not necessarily have to exclude all popular books but do make sure they are credible and consider showing them to your professor or a librarian if you have any doubts.

❷ Historical analogies

In Chapter One of the textbook, we explained some of the pitfalls of working from the notion that history repeats itself, but at the same time suggested that historical analogies can be useful in understanding certain events in the present day. We cannot discount the importance of historical study in seeing how we have arrived in our current time. Presumably, we would also like to believe that errors committed in the past can be evaded in the future if we recognize specific patterns or signs. But what sorts of analogies are effective? How can we make accurate comparisons of events in the present and past? What do we need to know to avoid making misleading claims that may do more harm than good? The following exercises will help you to critically evaluate claims of history's repetitiveness.

ACTIVITY: Comparing Russia's annexation of the Crimea in 2014 to Germany's taking of the Sudetenland in 1938

READ   **03/31/2014 01:01 PM Fighting Words: Schäuble Says Putin's Crimea Plans Reminiscent of Hitler. By Christian Reiermann.**

He's not the first to do it, but he's a big enough player that it could worsen tensions. On Monday, German Finance Minister Wolfgang Schäuble said he saw parallels between Vladimir Putin's annexation of Crimea and Adolf Hitler's land grab of Sudetenland.

As Germany's Mr. Euro, Wolfgang Schäuble is one of the country's best-known politicians abroad. When the finance minister speaks, people generally tend to listen. But on Monday morning, public statements at his ministry raised eyebrows. Schäuble made statements drawing parallels between the politics of Adolf Hitler and Russian President Vladimir Putin.

Schäuble said Russia's actions in Ukraine remind him of the expansionism of Nazi Germany. "Hitler already adopted such methods in Sudetenland," Schäuble said at a public event at the Finance Ministry in Berlin on Monday morning. "That's something that we all know from history." Schäuble's comments were directed at the justification provided by the Russians for annexing Crimea. Russian officials claim ethnic Russian residents of the peninsula are threatened by Ukraine. The Nazis argued similarly in the 1938 that "ethnic Germans" in peripheral regions of what was then Czechoslovakia required protection.

Given stewing tensions between Russia and the West and the finance minister's political prominence in Europe, Schäuble's comments could further intensify discord.

The finance minister made the comments while speaking to 50 school children from Berlin participating in a government-organized EU Project Day. Schäuble answered children's' questions about European unity and the euro crisis. He made his remarks after a student asked if the Ukraine crisis could potentially intensify the euro zone's problems. Schäuble said the most important thing was to prevent Ukraine from becoming insolvent. He said if the government in Kiev were no longer able to pay its security forces, "then of course some armed bands would seek to take power." That, he warned, could serve as a pretext for a Russian intervention. "The Russians would then say they can't accept that, that they are threatening our Russian population. Now we have to protect them, and that is our reason for invading."

Eastern Europeans 'Quite Scared'

The finance minister also explained to the students how Russia's occupation of Crimea came about. "At some point the situation escalated and then Putin said, 'I actually always wanted Crimea anyway.'" Schäuble said Putin had justified the action because the Russian Black Sea fleet is located on the peninsula. He said Putin must have told himself, "And the current opportunity is the right one." Schäuble also claimed the Russian president deployed troops near the Ukrainian border, "to show that I can take care of ensuring order if need be."

Schäuble also told the students that concerns about Russian actions are widespread among his colleagues in the EU member states that used to be part of the Eastern Bloc—particularly Hungary, Poland and the Baltic states. "They're quite scared," he said. He said the finance ministers of these countries have told him personally that they planned to expand their military expenditures. But Schäuble said there were no plans to increase Germany's defense budget. "That would be of no use," he said.

URL:http://www.spiegel.de/international/germany/schaeuble-compares-putin-moves-in-crimea-to-policies-of-hitler-a-961696.html

Reflect on the following:

1. What is the basis of Wolfgang Schäuble's claims that Putin's actions in the Ukraine in 2014 are comparable to Hitler's actions in the Sudetenland in 1938? Is it surprising that a German would compare Putin to Hitler? What might motivate other European leaders to make a historical analogy between these two men, their aims, and the surrounding circumstances? Why does Schäuble say leaders of former communist states are especially concerned about Putin's words and actions? What is at stake in using a phrase such as Schäuble's statement "that's something we all know from history"?

2. What other information would help you determine whether the Crimea - Sudetenland analogy is valid? What primary source evidence would help you further evaluate the correctness of the comparisons made in the article [see below]? What is the current situation in the Ukraine and Russia? Have new developments made such an analogy more accurate or less so? [Look up a recent article from a reputable news source such as BBC News http://www.bbc.com/, CNN http://www.cnn.com/, NPR http://www.npr.org/]

Additional Reading:

See also the website of the British National Archives on the background for Munich: http://www.nationalarchives.gov.uk/education/resources/chamberlain-and-hitler/.

On the Sudetenland and the "policy of appeasement" agreed to at the Munich Conference see the following related primary sources.

FROM THE HISTORY GUIDE—HTTP://WWW.HISTORYGUIDE.ORG/EUROPE/MUNICH.HTML

On September 27, 1938, when negotiations between Hitler and Chamberlain were strained, the British Prime Minister addressed the British people. Excerpts of this speech and another before the House of Commons are included here.

First of all I must say something to those who have written to my wife or myself in these last weeks to tell us of their gratitude for my efforts and to assure us of their prayers for my success. Most of these letters have come from women—mothers or sisters of our own countrymen. But there are countless others besides—from France, from Belgium, from Italy, even from Germany, and it has been heartbreaking to read of the growing anxiety they reveal and their intense relief when they thought, too soon, that the danger of war was past.

If I felt my responsibility heavy before, to read such letters has made it seem almost overwhelming. How horrible, fantastic, incredible it is that we should be digging trenches and trying on gas masks here because of a quarrel in a far-away country between people of whom we know nothing. It seems still more impossible that a quarrel which has already been settled in principle should be the subject of war.

continued on next page

continued

I can well understand the reasons why the Czech Government have felt unable to accept the terms which have been put before them in the German memorandum. Yet I believe after my talks with Herr Hitler that, if only time were allowed, it ought to be possible for the arrangements for transferring the territory that the Czech Government has agreed to give to Germany to be settled by agreement under conditions which would assure fair treatment to the population concerned . . .

However much we may sympathize with a small nation confronted by a big and powerful neighbor, we cannot in all circumstances undertake to involve the whole British Empire in war simply on her account. If we have to fight it must be on larger issues than that. I am myself a man of peace to the depths of my soul. Armed conflict between nations is a nightmare to me; but if I were convinced that any nation had made up its mind to dominate the world by fear of its force, I should feel that it must be resisted. Under such a domination life for people who believe in liberty would not be worth living; but war is a fearful thing, and we must be very clear, before we embark upon it, that it is really the great issues that are at stake, and that the call to risk everything in their defense, when all the consequences are weighed, is irresistible.

For the present I ask you to await as calmly as you can the events of the next few days. As long as war has not begun, there is always hope that it may be prevented, and you know that I am going to work for peace to the last moment. Good night. . . .

Since I first went to Berchtesgaden more than 20,000 letters and telegrams have come to No. 10, Downing Street. Of course, I have been able to look at a tiny fraction of them, but I have seen enough to know that the people who wrote did not feel that they had such a cause for which to fight, if they were asked to go to war in order that the Sudeten Germans might not join the Reich. That is how they are feeling. That is my answer to those who say that we should have told Germany weeks ago that, if her army crossed the border of Czechoslovakia, we should be at war with her. We had no treaty obligations and no legal obligations to Czechoslovakia and if we had said that, we feel that we should have received no support from the people of this country. . . .

When we were convinced, as we became convinced, that nothing any longer would keep the Sudetenland within the Czechoslovakian State, we urged the Czech Government as strongly as we could to agree to the cession of territory, and to agree promptly. The Czech Government, through the wisdom and courage of President Benes, accepted the advice of the French Government and ourselves. It was a hard decision for anyone who loved his country to take, but to accuse us of having by that advice betrayed the Czechoslovakian State is simply preposterous. What we did was to save her from annihilation and give her a chance of new life as a new State, which involves the loss of territory and fortifications, but may perhaps enable her to enjoy in the future and develop a national existence under a neutrality and security comparable to that which we see in Switzerland to-day. Therefore, I think the Government deserve the approval of this House for their conduct of affairs in this recent crisis which has saved Czechoslovakia from destruction and Europe from Armageddon.

Does the experience of the Great War and the years that followed it give us reasonable hope that, if some new war started, that would end war any more than the last one did?

One good thing, at any rate, has come out of this emergency through which we have passed. It has thrown a vivid light upon our preparations for defense, on their strength and on their weakness. I should not think we were doing our duty if we had not already ordered that a prompt and thorough inquiry should be made to cover the whole of our preparations, military and civil, in order to see, in the light of what has happened during these hectic days, what further steps may be necessary to make good our deficiencies in the shortest possible time.

SOURCE

Neville Chamberlain, *In Search of Peace* (1939), p. 393; and *Parliamentary Debates, House of Commons* (London: HMSO, 1938) vol. 339, 12th vol. of session 1937–1938, pp. 361–369, 373.

AGREEMENT CONCLUDED AT MUNICH, SEPTEMBER 29, 1938, BETWEEN GERMANY, GREAT BRITAIN, FRANCE AND ITALY [PUBLIC DOMAIN]

GERMANY, the United Kingdom, France and Italy, taking into consideration the agreement, which has been already reached in principle for the cession to Germany of the Sudeten German territory, have agreed on the following terms and conditions governing the said cession and the measures consequent thereon, and by this agreement they each hold themselves responsible for the steps necessary to secure its fulfillment:

1. The evacuation will begin on 1st October.

2. The United Kingdom, France and Italy agree that the evacuation of the territory shall be completed by the 10th October, without any existing installations having been destroyed, and that the Czechoslovak Government will be held responsible for carrying out the evacuation without damage to the said installations.

3. The conditions governing the evacuation will be laid down in detail by an international commission composed of representatives of Germany, the United Kingdom, France, Italy and Czechoslovakia.

4. The occupation by stages of the predominantly German territory by German troops will begin on 1st October. The four territories marked on the attached map will be occupied by German troops in the following order:

   The territory marked No. I on the 1st and 2nd of October; the territory marked No. II on the 2nd and 3rd of October; the territory marked No. III on the 3rd, 4th and 5th of October; the territory marked No. IV on the 6th and 7th of October. The remaining territory of preponderantly German character will be ascertained by the aforesaid international commission forthwith and be occupied by German troops by the 10th of October.

5. The international commission referred to in paragraph 3 will determine the territories in which a plebiscite is to be held. These territories will be occupied by international bodies

continued on next page

continued

until the plebiscite has been completed. The same commission will fix the conditions in which the plebiscite is to be held, taking as a basis the conditions of the Saar plebiscite. The commission will also fix a date, not later than the end of November, on which the plebiscite will be held.

6. The final determination of the frontiers will be carried out by the international commission. The commission will also be entitled to recommend to the four Powers, Germany, the United Kingdom, France and Italy, in certain exceptional cases, minor modifications in the strictly ethnographical determination of the zones which are to be transferred without plebiscite.

7. There will be a right of option into and out of the transferred territories, the option to be exercised within six months from the date of this agreement. A German–Czechoslovak commission shall determine the details of the option, consider ways of facilitating the transfer of population and settle questions of principle arising out of the said transfer.

8. The Czechoslovak Government will within a period of four weeks from the date of this agreement release from their military and police forces any Sudeten Germans who may wish to be released, and the Czechoslovak Government will within the same period release Sudeten German prisoners who are serving terms of imprisonment for political offences.

Munich, September 29, 1938.

ADOLF HITLER,

NEVILLE CHAMBERLAIN,

EDOUARD DALADIER,

BENITO MUSSOLINI.

NEVILLE CHAMBERLAIN'S SPEECH ON SEPTEMBER 30, 1938, AFTER THE MUNICH CONFERENCE

We, the German Führer and Chancellor, and the British Prime Minister, have had a further meeting today and are agreed in recognizing that the question of Anglo-German relations is of the first importance for our two countries and for Europe.

We regard the agreement signed last night and the Anglo-German Naval Agreement as symbolic of the desire of our two peoples never to go to war with one another again. We are resolved that the method of consultation shall be the method adopted to deal with any other questions that may concern our two countries, and we are determined to continue our efforts to remove possible sources of difference, and thus to contribute to assure the peace of Europe.

SUBSEQUENT STATEMENT MADE BY CHAMBERLAIN AT 10 DOWNING ST:

My good friends, for the second time in our history, a British Prime Minister has returned from Germany bringing peace with honour. I believe it is peace for our time . . . Go home and get a nice quiet sleep.

ON THE REFERENDUM IN THE CRIMEA SEE THE SPEECH OF FOREIGN SECRETARY WILLIAM HAGUE IN THE HOUSE OF COMMONS ON MARCH 18, 2014: HTTPS://WWW.GOV.UK/GOVERNMENT/SPEECHES/RUSSIAS-ACTIONS-IN-CRIMEA

The crisis in Ukraine is the most serious test of European security in the 21st century so far, and the United Kingdom's interests are twofold:

First, we want to see a stable, prosperous and unified Ukraine able to determine its own future free from external pressure or interference. Second, we have a vital interest in the upholding of international law and the UN charter, the honouring of treaties, and the maintenance of a rules-based international system. Russia's actions in Crimea run roughshod across all of these fundamental principles and threaten the future of Ukraine.

I pay tribute to the extraordinary restraint shown by the Ukrainian government, its military forces and its people in the face of immense provocation, with part of their country invaded and tens of thousands of forces massed on their border by a neighbour that refuses to rule out further military intervention against them.

There is a grave danger of a provocation elsewhere in Ukraine that becomes a pretext for further military escalation. We are working urgently to agree the mandate for an expanded OSCE monitoring mission to all parts of the country in the coming days.

On Friday I met US Secretary of State John Kerry and Russian Foreign Minister Sergei Lavrov before their bilateral talks here in London. Russia was presented with a series of proposals to de-escalate the crisis and to address the situation in Crimea. After six hours of talks Russia rebuffed these efforts, and on Sunday the referendum went ahead. The Crimean authorities claimed a turnout of 83% of the population, with 96.8% voting in favour of joining Russia. Yesterday the Parliament of Crimea formally applied to join the Russian Federation, and President Putin signed a decree recognising Crimea as a "sovereign state."

He has now announced, in the last two hours, new laws to incorporate Crimea into the Russian Federation.

It was regrettable to hear President Putin today choosing the route of isolation, denying the citizens of his own country and of Crimea partnership with the international community, and full membership of international organizations, and Russia's right to help shape the 21st century in a positive manner. No amount of sham and perverse democratic process or skewed historical references can make up for the fact that this is an incursion into a sovereign state and a land-grab of part of its territory, with no respect for the law of that country or for international law.

continued on next page

continued

The referendum was clearly illegal under the Ukrainian Constitution, which states that the Autonomous Republic of Crimea is an integral constituent part of Ukraine, can only resolve issues related to its authority within the provisions of the Constitution, and that only the Ukrainian Parliament has the right to call such referendums.

This was a vote in circumstances where Crimea is occupied by over 20,000 Russian troops, and indeed the meeting of the Crimean Parliament that announced the referendum was itself controlled by unidentified armed gunmen and took place behind locked doors.

This referendum in the Crimea took place at ten days' notice, without the leaders of Ukraine being able to visit Crimea, without meeting any of the OSCE standards for democratic elections. These include verification of the existence of an accurate and current voter registration list and confidence that only people holding Ukrainian passports were eligible to vote. The OSCE mission to Ukraine was refused entry to Crimea on 6th March, and there are reports of considerable irregularities including voting by Russian citizens, Crimean officials and militia taking mobile ballet boxes to the homes of residents, a blackout of Ukrainian television channels. The outcome of the referendum also does not reflect the views of minorities in Crimea, since the region's Muslim Tatar minority, who make up 14–15% of the population, boycotted the referendum.

Furthermore, the ballot paper asked the people of Crimea to decide either to become part of the Russian Federation, or to revert to the highly ambiguous 1992 Constitution. There was no option on the ballot paper for those who support the status quo. The House should be in no doubt that this was a mockery of all democratic practice.

The Organisation for Cooperation and Security in Europe unequivocally stated last week that the referendum was illegal and should not go ahead. On Saturday the UN Security Council voted on a resolution condemning the referendum as "unconstitutional" and "illegitimate," which was co-sponsored by 42 nations. Russia was completely isolated in vetoing the text, while 13 members of the Security Council voted in favour and China abstained.

Indeed the House should be clear about the illegality not only of the referendum but also of all of Russia's recent actions in Crimea. Russia has advanced several wholly spurious arguments to try to justify what it has done:

First, that it has acted in defence of Russian compatriots who were in danger from violence and a humanitarian crisis. However the OSCE High Commissioner for National Minorities has stated that there is "no evidence of any violence or threats to the rights of Russian speakers" in Crimea. There is no evidence of Russians being under threat anywhere in Ukraine, or of attacks on churches in Eastern Ukraine, as Russia has alleged. It is not true that thousands of refugees are fleeing Ukraine into Russia. Nor is there any threat to Russian military bases in Crimea, since the Ukrainian government has pledged to abide by all existing agreements covering those bases.

Numerous international mechanisms exist to protect the rights of minorities, and Russia's own actions are the greatest threat to stability in Ukraine. On top of evidence of gangs of thugs being bussed across the Russian border to provoke clashes within communities in Eastern Ukraine, over the weekend the Ukrainian government reported that Russian forces have seized an oil and gas facility five miles outside Crimea.

Second, Russia claims not to be bound by any of its previous agreements with Ukraine, including the 1994 Budapest Memorandum, on the grounds that the new government in Ukraine is illegitimate. However the interim government, formed when former President Yanukovych fled his post, was approved by an overwhelming majority in a free vote in the Ukrainian parliament including representatives from Yanukovych's Party of the Regions. The government has restored the 2004 Constitution and scheduled Presidential elections. Its legitimacy and its commitment to democracy are clear. Moreover Treaties and international agreements are between States, not between governments. A change in government does not in itself affect the binding force of those agreements. The commitments in the Budapest Memorandum still stand, and Russia has flagrantly breached its pledge to, in the words of the Memorandum, "refrain from the threat or use of force against the territorial integrity of political independence of Ukraine."

Third, although Russia still denies that its troops are in Crimea, they maintain that former President Yanukovych, whom they describe as the 'legitimate President of Ukraine,' is entitled to request military assistance from Russia. This too is false, since the Ukrainian Constitution is clear that only the Ukrainian Parliament has the authority to approve decisions on admitting foreign troops. The President has no such right, nor does the Crimean Parliament. In law and as a matter of logic it is clearly ludicrous to argue that a President who abandoned his post and fled the country has any right whatsoever to make decisions about the future of that country let alone inviting foreign troops into it.

Fourth, Russia argues that the people of Crimea have a right to self-determination and that it is their basic right to choose to join Russia, citing Kosovo as an alleged precedent. But there is no equivalence whatsoever between Crimea and Kosovo, and as Chancellor Merkel has said, it is "shameful" to make the comparison. NATO intervention in Kosovo followed ethnic cleansing and crimes against humanity on a large scale. An International Contact Group, including Russia, was brought together to discuss the future of Kosovo after the conflict. The independence of Kosovo followed nine years of work by the Kosovan authorities to satisfy the conditions of independent statehood, and mediation by a UN Special Envoy. None of these circumstances apply to Crimea.

In all these areas Russia is attempting to find justifications in precedent or law to excuse its actions in Ukraine and to muddy the waters of international opinion. What we are actually witnessing is the annexation of part of the sovereign territory of an independent European state through military force. The fall of President Yanukovyn and the change of government in Ukraine was a massive strategic setback for the Russian government, which had made no secret of its desire to prevent Ukraine from moving towards closer association with the EU. Seen in this light the annexation of Crimea is a bid to regain the advantage, to restore Russian prestige and permanently to impair Ukraine's functioning as a country. And given that Russia still maintains it has the right to intervene militarily anywhere on Ukrainian soil, there is a grave risk that we have not yet seen the worst of this crisis.

If we do not stand up to such a profound breach of international agreements and the use of force to change borders in Europe in the 21st century, the credibility of the international order will be at stake and we will face more crises in the future. Russia and others will conclude that it can intervene with impunity in other countries where there are either Russian compatriots or orthodox populations. Indeed it has been a Russian policy over a number of years to encourage such links and dependencies, through the issuing of millions of Russian passports in Ukraine and other countries bordering Russia. Events in Crimea form part of a pattern of Russian behaviour including in South Ossetia, Abkhazia and Transnistria.

continued on next page

continued

Our national interest depends on a rules-based international system where nations uphold bilateral and global agreements in a whole variety of areas from trade to security. We have worked with Russia in recent years to uphold such agreements, such as the Nuclear Non Proliferation Treaty. The credibility of the international system rests on there being costs attached to breaking binding commitments and refusing to address disputes through peaceful diplomacy.

The door to diplomacy of course always remains open, as it has been throughout this crisis. We have continued in recent days our efforts to persuade Russia to enter into direct talks with Ukraine and to take part in an international coordination group.

But faced with these actions it will be necessary to increase the pressure and our response.

Following the invasion of Crimea, the European Union took action at the Emergency European Council meeting on 6th March to suspend visa liberalisation talks with Russia and talks on a new EU–Russia Cooperation Agreement.

The European Council also agreed that unless Russia de-escalated the crisis, we would move to a second stage of sanctions including travel bans and asset freezes against named individuals.

Yesterday the European Foreign Affairs Council meeting that I attended decided to introduce additional measures, including travel restrictions and an assets freeze against 21 individuals, not just in Crimea but also in Russia, people responsible for actions that undermine or threaten Ukraine.

These measures have been taken in close coordination with the United States and allies such as Canada, Japan and Australia.

Preparatory work is underway for a third tier of sanctions, including economic and trade measures. The European Council will consider further measures later this week in the light of President Putin's speech today and Russian's actions in recent days. In the British Government we are clear that further measures need to be taken and in the light of President Putin's speech today we will argue at the Council for the strongest position and range of measures on which agreement can be obtained in the European Union.

We have already decided with our G7 partners to suspend preparations for the G8 Summit in Sochi this summer.

We are also determined to ensure that we are taking all appropriate national measures. The Prime Minister announced last week that we would review all UK bilateral military cooperation not subject to treaty obligations with Russia. I can announce now that we have suspended all such cooperation, including the finalizing of the Military Technical Cooperation Agreement, the cancellation of this year's French, Russian, UK, US naval exercise, and the suspension of a proposed Royal Navy ship visit to St Petersberg and of all senior military visits, unless in direct support of UK objectives.

We believe that under current circumstances there is a compelling case for EU member states to act on defence export licences.

The UK will now with immediate effect suspend all extant licences and application processing for licences for direct export to Russia for military and dual use items destined for units of the Russian armed forces or other state agencies which could be or are being deployed against Ukraine. We will also suspend licences for exports to third countries for incorporation into equipment for export to Russia where there is a clear risk that the end product will be used against Ukraine.

All such licences were reviewed following the Prime Minister's Statement to the House on 10th March, and so we are able to act immediately. We encourage other European nations to take similar action.

As well as responding to Russia's aggression in Crimea, it is also vital that the international community increases its financial and technical support to Ukraine through the IMF and European Union, to ensure that an economic crisis does not contribute to further political instability. We are absolutely clear with the Ukrainian authorities that this support must be matched by economic and political reforms. I gave them this clear message when I was in Kyiv two weeks ago, and yesterday I met the Acting Foreign Minister. Given that they have got many difficult decisions to take it is vital that they build up support in Ukraine and in the international community, and part of the way to do that is to tackle corruption at the very outset. We will insist on such reforms and use the technical assistance I announced to the House in my last Statement to help bring them about.

We are sending technical teams to Kyiv to support reforms to the energy and social security sectors, and to work with them on their business environment and strengthen public financial management. We are also working up UK support for a flexible and rapid funding mechanism to support economic reform, further work on asset recovery, a partnership with Germany on public financial management, support to Parliamentary and local elections and so on.

At the emergency European Council, in response to a request by the Ukrainian Prime Minister, Heads of State and Government agreed to sign the political parts of the EU–Ukraine Association Agreement. This is an important symbol of the EU's support for Ukraine.

In taking these steps Ukraine should not and is not being asked to choose between Russia and the EU. It should be possible for Ukraine to enjoy strong relations with both, and it is in Russia's own economic interest that it does. I found on my visit to Ukraine that even in the South and East of the country Ukrainians do not welcome Russian intervention. And even those with many links to Russia or from the Party of the Regions believe in the independence and territorial integrity of their country.

By treating the situation in Ukraine as a zero-sum context Russia itself will lose strategically. Russia miscalculated its ability to control and influence the political situation in Ukraine in the events leading up to President Yanukovych's departure. And I would argue that by seizing Crimea the Russian government has miscalculated again, since it has alienated a huge majority of public opinion in Ukraine, done immense damage to Russia's reputation over the world, and increased the likelihood of European countries taking long term-action to reduce the balance of leverage in the relation with Russia.

We should be ready to contemplate a new state of relations between Russia and the West in the coming years that is different from the last twenty years; one in which institutions such as the G8 are working without Russia, military cooperation and defence exports are curtailed, decisions are accelerated to reduce European dependence on Russia energy exports, foreign policy plays a bigger role in energy policy, Russia has less influence in Europe, and European nations do more to guard against the flagrant violation of international norms we have seen in Crimea in recent weeks from being repeated. This is not the relationship that we want to have with Russia, but it is the relationship which Russia's actions look like they will force us to adopt.

continued on next page

continued

Over the last four years we have worked to improve relations with Russia and we have worked closely with them on Iran and many areas of UN Security Council business. But there is no doubt however that if there is no progress on Ukraine relations between Russia and many nations in the world, including ours, will be permanently affected in this way.

Russia should be clear about the long term consequences and in the United Kingdom we will not shy away from those consequences, on that, in this House and with our allies we will be clear and clear about our own national interest, which is in Ukraine being able to make its own decisions and in the upholding of international law and the UN charter, and the prevention of future violations of independent European states.

ACTIVITY: Why historical analogies sometimes fail but are important anyway: genocide before and after the Holocaust

In this chapter we have already pointed out that historians continue to seek answers to explain how and why the Holocaust happened. The desire to never forget is motivated by the desire to prevent future such atrocities from occurring. The sad reality is, however, that millions of men, women, and children around the world have continued to be slaughtered because of ethnic and religious hatreds and territorial conflicts. Sometimes it appears we have learned few lessons from the past and fail to recognize historical patterns.

The United States Holocaust Memorial Museum in Washington, D.C., offers several resources on its website to help visitors understand how the international community defines and attempts to combat genocide. As noted on its site,

> More than six decades after the Holocaust, the horrors of Bosnia, Rwanda, and Darfur are sobering reminders that preventing future genocides and mass atrocities remains an enormous challenge. Yet genocide is not the inevitable result of ancient hatreds or irrational leaders, and, learning more from past genocides about the risk factors, warning signs and triggering events of these crimes, we are also learning that they can be averted and that genocide can be prevented.

—*http://www.ushmm.org/confront-genocide/how-to-prevent-genocide*

As historians, we look to uncover facts, evaluate evidence, and determine cause and effect. If we wish to compare genocides that occurred in different places and at different times, we must take care not to expect that events would have unfolded in the same fashion. History never repeats itself exactly because the historical actors are never the same. However, looking for precedents and situations that are analogous can take our analysis beyond a direct comparison of the specific details to a broader understanding of how potentially devastating consequences can result when the world community is ignorant of or confused by problematic situations.

Using the website of the Holocaust Museum, see whether you can identify the similarities in two or more cases of genocide since the Holocaust (http://www.ushmm.org/confront-genocide/cases/).

Some questions to ask:

Who were the groups targeted?

Who was primarily responsible for the violence committed?

What rationale did the perpetrators offer for their actions?

Did they try to deny or hide evidence of what they did?

What evidence did the survivors collect?

How did the international community come to find out about events in this case?

What was the response?

Was anyone prosecuted for the crimes committed?

What happened in the aftermath? Did anything change?

Activity: The Analogy Trap. Students and the general public are often fairly well educated about the details of the Holocaust, but they do not always recognize that other cases of genocide, although they share important characteristics, may also look quite different. Historians have been reflecting on what it means to make the Holocaust the main model against which all other genocides are defined. One such example is the following paper by international relations expert and Professor Emeritus Martin Shaw, "Understanding Today's Genocides: The Snare of Analogy," also available at http://martinshaw.org/2013/08/30/understanding-todays-genocides-the-snare-of-analogy-2/.

Read the essay below and respond to these questions about it:

Why does Shaw argue that comparing other genocides to the Holocaust is problematic?

Why is the Holocaust seen as the ultimate evil in the modern world?

Should we compare other genocides to it?

How has genocide been defined historically?

How does the idea of "distinctiveness" interfere with our ability to recognize the warning signs of genocide?

What does Shaw say is the difference between colonial genocides and modern genocides?

When did this shift occur?

How did the Cold War and decolonization contribute to genocidal conflicts?

How have such conflicts changed again since the end of the Cold War?

What do you think is meant by referring to "ethnic cleansing" as the "dark side of democracy"?

How would you define genocide to allow for historical accuracy?

Can you apply the analogy of genocide to anything in your own project?

UNDERSTANDING TODAY'S GENOCIDES—THE SNARE OF ANALOGY

The spectre of genocide is always that of a repeat of the last genocide. Many Israelis, faced with the prospect of an Iranian nuclear weapon, fear a "second Holocaust." The UN works to prevent "another Rwanda," and genocide campaigners believe that one happened in Darfur. Genocide politics is about recognition—claiming the label for the particular set of atrocities with which people are concerned—and it generally proceeds by analogy with previous events. The Holocaust remains the defining episode: as Jeffrey Alexander has argued, it has been constructed as a "sacred evil," the ultimate embodiment of evil in the modern world, so that all other evils must be related to it. Defining "other" genocides requires "bridging" from (or to) the Holocaust, so that some of its sacred-evil quality rubs off on them. Indeed, genocide as such has become something of a "sacred evil": without its recognition, atrocities become second class, "only ethnic cleansing," and the demand for intervention or justice is strangely diluted.

Bridging, or reasoning by analogy, may be understandable politics, but it is inadequate for academic understanding. History may repeat itself, as tragedy or farce, but genocides do not repeat themselves in the ways that elections or football tournaments do. It may be utterly unscientific to claim that the Holocaust is "unique" in a metaphysical sense, but there is a profound sense in which all large-scale historical episodes are distinctive from each other. Of course, the argument about the uniqueness of each historical episode does not take us very far, as it risks a loss of generalising perspective. But it is important if it reminds us that history involves change as well as repetition, and that each historical period needs to identify the danger of genocide in its own terms. One tires of the kind of transhistorical "analysis" that always looks for similarities with the Holocaust, whether it be in the earlier events in Armenia or the later ones in Rwanda, let alone its variant that dismisses events in places like Bosnia and Darfur because of their insufficient conformity to the Holocaust paradigm.

This paper argues, therefore, that genocide research requires a more radical historical understanding if we are to understand the specific dangers of genocide in our time. There is, of course, a great deal of historical research on genocide, but as the contents of Dan Stone's edited volume, *The Historiography of Genocide* (2008) suggest, most of this consists of isolated case-studies rather than attempts to analyse developmental tendencies in modern history. The one "world history" of the problem, Ben Kiernan's *Blood and Soil* (2007), does not develop a coherent narrative of historical change, but attempts to trace thematic similarities across widely varied historical periods. Yet what if, despite all the similarities and continuities across periods, there are in fact crucial differences and discontinuities? What if the danger of genocide in the twenty-first century is not a repetition of the Holocaust or Armenia, or even of Rwanda, but takes significantly different forms, reflecting the distinctive features of social, political and international relations in our own times? This paper argues that we are in danger of being deeply misled by our need to find repetition and analogy.

The Core Elements of Genocide

Of course to identify the "same" substantive social phenomenon in different historical forms requires a clear and coherent idea of what constitutes "genocide." The big problem of genocide research is that there is no consensus on this definitional question: the idea that genocide is always the same, i.e. that it is similar to the Holocaust, gains plausibility in this situation. However the idea of genocide as first proposed by Raphael Lemkin in his *Axis Rule in Occupied Europe* (1944) is a broad notion of the violent "destruction" of a social collectivity, which is potentially a rich tool of social understanding. Although at that point Lemkin restricted its scope to the destruction of national and ethnic groups (earlier he had defined the threatened groups more broadly), it is now widely accepted, as Frank Chalk and Kurt Jonahsson argued in their *History and Sociology of Genocide* (1990), that it refers to the destruction of any group, the definition of the group being according to the perpetrators' ideology (which often does not match the self-understanding of the attacked population or any "objective" criterion). Rather, as I have argued in my *What Is Genocide?* (2007), geno-cide can be coherently understood as destructive violence against any civilian population, to be distinguished on the one hand from war (destructive violence exchanged between two armed forces) and on the other from those forms of coercion and even violence which do not seriously threaten to destroy a population group and its social relations.

This means that genocide should be understood, as Lemkin argued, as a broad category of violent and coercive actions that reflected destructive goals towards social groups. Lemkin stressed economic, political and cultural alongside physical and biologi-cal destruction; we might also emphasise territorial destruction, since the most com-mon method of destroying a particular group, its social networks and culture is to uproot it from where it has lived, and sexual violence, since rape is almost invariably used to help shatter the integrity of communities. Genocide cannot be coherently limited to mass murder, in terms of which some writers have tried to define the phenomenon, because mass killing is only one of the methods of group destruction, the extent of whose use varies widely between cases, and which is always combined with other methods such as expulsion, rape and cultural attacks.

If genocide is understood as a type of social action carried out by perpetrators, it must also be recognised as a type of conflict, generating civilian as well as armed resis-tance and intervention, either from the attacked population or from third parties, or both. Moreover as a type of political and/or armed conflict, it generally occurs in the context of other, more "conventional," political and armed conflicts. Genocidal conflict is usually an outgrowth of either political conflict or war, and frequently causes new political conflict and war. A crucial analytical problem in the study of genocide is to simultaneously distin-guish and show the relationships of genocide and other forms of conflict.

Indeed a major fallacy of the field is the idea that episodes of genocide can be neatly constructed as "genocides," discrete from other political and armed conflict. This fallacy is encouraged by the idea of the Holocaust as a discrete attack of Nazi Germany on European Jews: but conceptualising this as a distinct "genocide" abstracts it from both the larger com-plex of destructive Nazi antipopulation policies of which it was apart (which Lemkin called "the Nazi genocide" rather than 'the Holocaust'), and from the larger field of political and armed conflict (the Second World War) in which it was enmeshed. The idea of "genocides," of large, distinct, sustained episodes of group destruction, needs to be understood as a way of recognising genocidal violence and conflict of a certain scale and duration, not as a substi-tute for "genocide" as a generic concept of socially destructive action and conflict.

This point is important because genocidal action and conflict may occur in relatively limited episodes in conflicts which, taken as wholes, are not genocidal. Leo Kuper (1981) proposed the concept of "genocidal massacre" to describe small-scale, localised geno-cidal killing. We can extrapolate from this the need for ideas of genocidal expulsions,

continued on next page

continued

genocidal mass rape, etc., and propose the concept of "genocidal violence" as a general term for such localised destructive action.

This concept is applicable across all historical periods, but may be particularly important in periods in which the scope for large-scale, sustained destructive violence *à la* Holocaust is more restricted. Genocidal massacres have been particularly identified in colonial history; I shall argue that our own period is another in which localised genocidal violence is an important theme.

Historicising Modern Genocide

In this perspective, we can see that genocide has been deeply embedded in modern history, but in hugely varying forms. The archetypal Holocaust-type genocides of twentieth-century Europe were preceded by centuries of "colonial genocide," as European empires spread across the world. While European genocide in its Second World War nadir was large-scale, state-centric and systematically murderous—albeit there were many smaller episodes, much societal involvement and many destructive policies that fell short of mass murder—the genocide of colonisation was very often smaller-scale, perpetrated by settler militias and local authorities rather than imperial governments and armies, with more sporadic killing. In this sense, European genocide involved not only a refocusing of violence used against colonial "natives" onto the inhabitants of the metropoles themselves, but its centralisation, statisation and further radicalisation.

Why did this change in genocide take place? We can only answer this question by looking at the development of crisis and tensions inside the inter-imperial international system, and how this combined with the generalisation of nationalism in the system, as I argue in my book, *Genocide and International Relations* (2013). Industrial capitalism powered the empires of Western Europe to wider colonial conquests, leading in turn to sharper conflicts in Europe itself, culminating in the Great War. Failing to match the power of the Western empires, in this war the old Ottoman, Romanov and Habsburg empires disintegrated amidst increasingly destructive nationalist rivalries, which at their worst became genocidal, most notoriously (but not only) against the Armenians in 1915. The subsequent polarisation of international politics saw radical totalitarian regimes arise in the Soviet Union and Nazi Germany, and their genocidal tendencies, already visible before 1939, were greatly deepened in the all-out struggles of the Second World War. This war generalised genocide in the international system, in large parts of Europe and Asia, so that many lesser states also pursued genocidal policies. Even the Western Allies condoned them, for example when the USSR, Czechoslovakia, Poland and other states murderously expelled their ethnic German populations at the end of the war.

It is the argument of this paper that this huge development in Europe, which transformed the world history of genocide, was only one of a number of key international junctures in which the phenomenon has been radically transformed. The outcome of the war, indeed, led to a radical change in the situation. The best-known face of this transformation was the international criminalisation resulting from the Genocide Convention of 1948. But alongside this benign change, even in the period of the Convention's drafting, were more troubling new phenomena: the settlement in Europe that legitimated the Soviet-led population upheavals of the war's conclusion; the massive violence directed against population groups on both sides in the Chinese Civil War; the huge forced migrations, mass murders and rapes of the Indian Partition; and the more limited but still destructive forced removal of Palestinian Arabs, precipitated partly by the United Nations' own plan for partition.

As the Cold War set in, defining a new international order dominated by superpower and bloc rivalries, quite different patterns of genocide developed from those of the previous period of interimperial crisis. Some were closely linked to Cold War conflicts, like the genocidal violence of the Korean War, the mass murder of Communists in Indonesia in 1965, and the later violence against populations linked to leftists in Guatemala, Argentina, Chile, Colombia and elsewhere in Latin America. Others were indirect reflections of Cold War polarisation, like the genocidal famine of Mao Zedong's Great Leap Forward, during the period when China was in conflict with both superpowers, and the Khmer Rouge genocide in Cambodia, where the regime was likewise pitted both against the USA and Vietnam, a Soviet ally. Other strands reflected the terminal crises of the European empires—many wars of decolonisation saw genocidal violence—and the power struggles of the new post-colonial states. These arose both in contests over who controlled the state—for example the ethnopolitics of Rwanda and Burundi from the early 1960s onwards—and secessionist wars over the shape of the state, perhaps the most widespread context of genocidal war during the Cold War period, in states like Pakistan, Nigeria, Sudan and Iraq.

Post–Cold War, Global-Era Genocide

Cold War genocide was, therefore, quite different in location, context and (often) form from the genocide of the high imperial period in Europe. But by the same token, the end of the Cold War also signalled important changes in genocide. As after 1945, there was huge optimism about a more peaceful and less genocidal world, and some important developments in policies to affect genocide: ideas of "humanitarian intervention" and the "responsibility to protect" partly shaped Western and UN policies; and international criminal tribunals were established to try perpetrators of the worst new genocidal violence in Yugoslavia and Rwanda, finally followed at the beginning of the twenty-first century by the International Criminal Court that had been envisaged when genocide was criminalised half a century earlier.

However once again these developments were offset by new threats, other effects of the Cold War's unwinding. The dissolutions of the Soviet Union and Yugoslavia, like the collapses of earlier multinational empires, produced series of genocidal wars, and a similar pattern could be seen in Indonesia, where the anti-Communist Suharto regime collapsed precipitating a series of genocidal conflicts. The new international balance of power enabled the USA to use its military power not just in limited "humanitarian" ways but in serious power-projections like the Iraq wars of 1991 and 2003, both of which led to genocidal crises: in the first case, the weakened Saddam Hussein regime attacked the emboldened Shia and Kurdish populations, while in the second its Sunni guerrilla successors initiated a low-level genocidal conflict, attacking the Shia population, to which Shia-based militia responded with violence against the Sunni population.

Beyond these effects that can be linked directly to the post–Cold War transition, what patterns of genocidal violence can be seen in the "global" era of the twenty-first century? First, we can note a near-disappearance of the problem in East and South-east Asia, and also a marked diminution in Latin America, effects comparable to the disappearance of genocide in Europe [after 1949]. Towards the end of the Cold War period, following Mao's

continued on next page

continued

death in 1976, the party dictatorship in China was normalised in a way similar to the nor-
malisation of Soviet power following Stalin's death in 1953. Under Deng Xiaoping, China
industrialised by expanding into world markets, achieved rapprochements with the USA
and USSR/Russia, and replaced terror with more normal bureaucratic repression as its
mode of rule. In these circumstances, neither international nor domestic tensions had
genocidal outcomes. By the 1990s, even Cambodia underwent some sort of normalisa-
tion, as the Khmer Rouge threat finally disappeared.

Second, a changed pattern of genocidal wars could be seen. Some of the conflicts of the
Cold War period—for example in Angola, where the protagonists were closely linked to
Cold War sponsors and allies—ended, albeit sometimes after continuing in new forms
for a period. Others, however, like the conflicts in Sudan, were exacerbated by new local
tensions and stoked by new international rivalries. In general, the focus of genocidal
wars shifted overwhelmingly to Africa, including the Rwandan civil war that led to the
1994 genocide. Rwanda was also a catalyst for a new regional pattern of war, focused
on Zaire (which became the Democratic Republic of the Congo), in which many different
states became involved and multiple genocidal episodes developed, committed by different state and militia actors. What was noticeable not only in the Great Lakes Region but
also in North-east and West Africa was a developed regionalisation, in which patterns of
genocidal war spilled across borders.

Third, it became evident that democratisation, a key process of the post–Cold War
world, was linked to new genocidal dangers. As local populations demanded more free-
doms, Western governments withdrew support from Cold-War authoritarians, and local
elites saw they must increasingly manage electoral processes, new contexts of violence
developed. Not for nothing did Michael Mann (2005) call "ethnic cleansing" the "dark side
of democracy"; as he and others have pointed out, while stable democracies may not
be contexts of genocide, unstable democratising countries are often more violence-
prone that stable authoritarianisms. And contemporary democratisation has a specific
genocide-producing mechanism: ethnopolitically polarised electoral politics. Implicated
in the genocidal wars in Yugoslavia and Rwanda in the 1990s, electoral politics was also a
crucial context of violence in places like Kenya, Cote d'Ivoire and Zimbabwe in the 2000s.

Conclusions

The argument of this paper has been that the contexts and forms of genocide are historically specific in ways that the genocide field, dominated by transhistorical forms of
comparative study, has barely recognised. In particular, the problem of genocide is inti-
mately linked to the nature of the international order, and we can trace radical changes in
genocide together with epochal changes in the international system. This means that we
should not be looking, in the twenty-first century, for repetitions of the classic twentieth-
century genocides. On the contrary, genocidal violence in our period is taking, and will
take, new forms, some of which I have tried to indicate. Some are even closely linked to
apparently benign international developments like democratisation.

Martin Shaw, Emeritus Professor of International Relations at the University of Sussex, is Research
Professor at the Institut Barcelona d'Estudis Internacionals (IBEI) and Professorial Fellow at the
University of Roehampton, London.

CHAPTER TWO

The Development of the Discipline of History
Workbook Exercises

ACTIVITY: What kind of history is it? Identifying historical fields and subfields

Students and professional historians may be passionate about history, but that does not necessarily mean we enjoy all kinds of history equally. It is important to identify your own preferences in the history articles and books you read so you can better try to emulate what others have done. You also want to maintain a high level of interest through what could be a lengthy period for your historical research and writing. If you know you love reading about how ordinary people in the past experienced their day-to-day lives—what they ate, how they dressed, what pursuits occupied their time—there may be little utility in collecting numerous publications on diplomatic history for your latest project.

Once you know that a particular historical subfield interests you, look for articles for your research in the most appropriate journals. Broader searches are, of course, also necessary, but beginning with recent scholarly work in high-quality, relevant journals will provide you with good models for your work while you learn more about your topics. Although it is easy to remain fixed on a general subject matter and therefore look only for materials about it, you should also become more familiar with historical subfields and their related methodologies. Historians build complexity and advance the discipline of history by applying theories or frameworks to the primary and secondary sources they gather. Understanding how professional historians conceptualize the motors of history and analyze facts and data will make you a better student historian.

There are many excellent history journals that publish articles written primarily from the vantage point of specialized historical subfields. Oxford University Press, for example, oversees the publication of the following journals: *Diplomatic History; Environmental History; Enterprise & Society: The International Journal of Business History; European Review of Economic History; Journal of Social History;* and *The Oral History Review.* The titles alone alert you to the main approaches taken by their authors. There are other ways to recognize historical frameworks, however. The following exercises will help you learn to do just that and therefore to use your time in the most productive way possible.

EXAMPLE 1: READ THE TITLE AND ABSTRACT OF THE FOLLOWING SCHOLARLY ARTICLE

"'A Peculiar Species of Felony': Suicide, Medicine, and the Law in Victorian Britain and Ireland" by Georgina Laragy

Abstract

This paper examines the relationship between suicide and insanity in the eyes of both legal and medical professionals in nineteenth century Britain and Ireland. Both jurisdictions had a similar historical legacy in relation to the treatment of suicide, punishing sane suicides, those found *felo de se*, by ignominious burial and forfeiture. Legal changes between 1823 and 1882 negated the need for a verdict of temporary insanity as suicide essentially became a crime without legal punishment. Nevertheless, the rise of forensic psychiatry within the legal system meant that definitions of the temporary insanity of suicides became a controversial question for medical professionals. Similarly, the retention of distinctions of sanity and insanity for religious and insurance purposes ensured that there were spiritual and practical ramifications to a verdict of *felo de se* even if there were no legal consequences. The debate among doctors and legal professionals suggests that the process of "medicalization" of suicide was not, as MacDonald has suggested, driven by these elite professional groups, but rather by public opinion. While legal punishments for attempted suicide remained in force and in use, by the end of the nineteenth century medicine was seen as the main actor in the fight against this "social disease."

Answer the following questions:

_____What appear to be the main areas of interest to this author?

We see that the article looks at the relationship between suicide and insanity. The author mentions the medical and legal professions as the major determinants of how suicide was conceived and labeled.

_____What phrases or terms can help us determine the author's methodological framework?

Laragy wants to suggest that "professional elites" had less to do with suicide being medicalized than did "public opinion." The key historical actor thus appears to be the general public whose opinions about suicide and mental illness shaped the responses of medical and legal professionals. The author also notes that suicide came to be labeled a "social disease," which leads us to conclude that it was seen as a problem produced by society.

_____What kind of history is it?

Since the driving force behind the author's argument is public opinion and she uses the idea of a social component to suicide, we can reasonably conclude that the article can be categorized as social history with subfields in legal and medical history.

In fact, the article appeared in the *Journal of Social History*. Among other applications, it could easily be used as a secondary source in a paper about changing attitudes about suicide over a long period of time or in a paper about Victorian British society.

FULL CITATION

Laragy, Georgina. "'A Peculiar Species of Felony': Suicide, Medicine, and the Law in Victorian Britain and Ireland." *Journal of Social History* 46, no 3 (Spring 2013): 732–43.

EXAMPLE 2: READ THE FOLLOWING ENDNOTES FROM A SCHOLARLY ARTICLE

8. Kathryn Marshall, *In the Combat Zone: An Oral History of American Women in Vietnam, 1966–1975* (Boston: Little, Brown, 1987); Sandra C. Taylor, *Vietnamese Women at War: Fighting for Ho Chi Minh and the Revolution* (Lawrence: University Press of Kansas, 1999); Karen Gottschang Turner, *Even the Women Must Fight: Memories of War from North Vietnam* (New York: Wiley, 1998); Keith Walker, *A Piece of My Heart: The Stories of 26 American Women Who Served in Vietnam* (New York: Ballantine Books, 1985).

9. Pamela A. DeVoe, "Refugee Work and Health in Mid-America," in *Selected Papers on Refugee Issues*, ed. Pamela A. De Voe (Washington, DC: American Anthropological Association, 1992), 112.

11. Hai, first contact with author, Boston area, July 10, 1994.

13. Hai, interview with the author, Boston area, July 10, 1994.

14. Mr., Mrs., and Grandmother Nguyen, interview with the author, Boston area, July 12, 1994.

15. Hai, interview with the author, Boston area, July 18, 1994.

16. American Community Survey available on the U.S. Census Bureau's website at http://factfinder.census.gov/home/saff/main.html?_lang=en (accessed June 29, 2011).

19. Cao, interview with the author, central New Jersey, June 10, 2007.

20. Ibid.

21. John Tenhula, *Voices from Southeast Asia: The Refugee Experience in the United States* (New York: Holmes & Meier, 1991), 13.

Answer the following questions:

_____What kinds of sources are listed in Note 8? What are the major themes they appear to address based on their titles?

There are several books listed, many of which mention American women and their stories from the Vietnam War.

_____What kind of sources are indicated in Notes 11, 13, 14, and 19?

These are all interviews conducted by the author with women with Vietnamese names in the United States.

_____What is the subject of sources 9 and 21?

Both mention refugees in the United States.

_____What kind of history is it?

From just this select group of endnotes, we can reach the reasonable conclusion that the article is a work of women's history based especially on data collected through oral history. Moreover, we might expect to learn something about women refugees from war-torn Vietnam, considered by many historians a postcolonial Cold War conflict, which would also suggest a possible framework from postcolonial studies.

Reading the full title and abstract below confirms our assessment of the notes. The article appeared in *The Oral History Review* and seeks to shed light on the firsthand experiences of a select group of women during the Vietnam War. It would therefore be more appropriately referenced in a student paper that examines experiences of warfare outside those narrowly defined by direct combat.

continued on next page

continued

FULL CITATION

Gustafsson, Mai Lan. "'Freedom. Money. Fun. Love': The Warlore of Vietnamese Bargirls." *The Oral History Review* 38, no. 2 (Summer/Fall 2011): 308–30.

Abstract:

Memories of the Vietnam War abound in the minds of those who survived it, be they veterans or civilians, Vietnamese or American. Vietnamese refugees, forced to flee their homeland after the war ended in 1975, tell particularly poignant stories of loss—of country, of family, of tradition, and of identity. Not so the women featured in this article. During the war, they served as bargirls in Saigon, entertaining American soldiers. The stories they tell of the war paint an entirely different picture: one of good times, and camaraderie, and the exhilaration of being young and free in the city. They were able to break free from tradition and the expectations imposed on their gender because of the war, and because of that, remember the war as the best time of their lives.

EXAMPLE 3: READ THE FOLLOWING SELECTION FROM AN ARTICLE TITLED "SELLING LIBERIA: MOSS H. KENDRIX, THE LIBERIAN CENTENNIAL COMMISSION, AND THE POST–WORLD WAR II TRADE IN BLACK PROGRESS" BY BRENNA W. GREER

In narratives of twentieth-century US history, stories of black capitalists and their entrepreneurialism tend to exist in isolation from US postwar civil rights and foreign relations, granting some important exceptions.[3] In recent years, a handful of historians have shone an increasingly brighter light on the contributions of a small cadre of African American (male) marketers—"the Brown Hucksters"—to developing black consumer markets, driving black consumption, and representing black consumers.[4] Collectively, these histories document how black marketers helped large white corporations—including Lever Brothers, Pepsi-Cola, The Coca-Cola Company, Esso Oil, and Philip Morris—target black consumers and in the process integrated corporate America and altered representations of blackness in the United States.[5] Kendrix's public relations work on behalf of Coca Cola in the 1950s places him squarely in this narrative of US business history. Tracing Kendrix's reliance on black consumers to sell Liberia in the immediate postwar period, however, expands this history of African Americans defining themselves as consumers by considering the global and transnational dimensions of this enterprise.

The history of Kendrix's public relations work for Liberia draws direct links between postwar black enterprise, black politics, and international commercial and diplomatic relations. Exploring the connections reveals how commercial interests—domestic and international—intersected with civil rights agendas, which exposes African Americans' role in larger political projects. For example, the notions of black progress that Kendrix generated to sell Liberia engaged discourses of race and racial progress that were, as detailed by historian Mary Dudziak, essential to propaganda produced by the state in the early Cold War years to counter international criticism of US antiblack racism. Kendrix's story, in other words, shows that African Americans not only figured within Cold War race propaganda, they also produced it.[6] Finally, Kendrix's Liberian Centennial Commission experience provides another angle from which to consider the postwar turning inward of African Americans to focus on domestic matters. Within the civil rights historiography, historians have convincingly explained this phenomenon as civil right institutions' strategic responses to a repressive Cold War political climate.[7] Kendrix's Liberian Centennial Commission efforts make plain that business concerns also affected African American conceptions of and commitment to other black populations. What happened when black commercial interests coincide with US commercial imperialism and how did black imperialist attitudes affect relations and politics of the African Diaspora in the postwar moment? As Tiffany Ruby Patterson and Robin Kelley argue, the diaspora is a process "always in the making," and Kendrix's combined venture of selling himself and Liberia dramatizes this process through which African Americans, Africans, and Africa are "continually reinvented."[8]

NOTES

3. In recent years, historians have increasingly studied the role of black entrepreneurialism in civil rights campaigns. Notable examples include: Weems, *Desegregating The Dollar*; Cohen, *A Consumers' Republic*; Ward, *Radio and the Civil Rights Struggle in the South*; Chambers, "Presenting the Black Middle Class: John H. Johnson and *Ebony Magazine*, 1945–1974"; Chambers, *Madison Avenue and the Color Line*; Weems and Lewis, *Business in Black and White*; and Smith, *To Serve the Living*. Others have exposed the relationship between civil rights politics and US foreign relations and policy in the mid-twentieth century. See Plummer, *Rising Wind*; Von Eschen, *Race against Empire*; and Dudziak, *Cold War Civil Rights*.

4. See Weems, *Desegregating the Dollar*; Chambers, "Presenting the Black Middle Class: John H. Johnson and *Ebony Magazine*, 1945–1974"; Chambers, *Madison Avenue and the Color Line*; Delton, *Racial Integration in Corporate America 1940–1990*; and Weems and Lewis, *Business in Black and White*. In addition, *Ebony* publisher John H. Johnson's biography provides a detailed and illuminating firsthand account of post–World War II black entrepreneurialism. See Johnson with Lerone Bennett Jr., *Succeeding against the Odds*, chapters 18–36. "Brown Huckster" is the term that John Johnson's *Ebony* magazine used to reference African American marketers and lobbyists. "The Brown Hucksters," *Ebony*, May 1948, 28.

5. Chambers, *Madison Avenue and the Color Line*, 61–83. See also David J. Sullivan, "The Negro Market," *Negro Digest*, February 1943; and "The Negro Market: An Appraisal," *Tide*, March 7, 1947.

6. Dudziak explains how US state officials produced propaganda following World War II that emphasized Africans Americans' progress within (and, as the propaganda would have it, because of) American democracy. See Dudziak, *Cold War Civil Rights*, introduction, chapter 1. My research reveals that, due in part to openings created during the New Deal, African Americans also produced propaganda concerning civil rights and blackness after World War II that engaged Cold War concerns and official discourses of race and democracy.

7. In her important study of black anticolonialism, Penny Von Eschen details how, within the context of the rampant anticommunism that emerged after World War II and the corresponding political suppression, American black political leaders and civil rights organizations retreated from critiques of empire. To avoid the accusations and challenges of being identified as a threat to US interests, they chose instead to concentrate on domestic civil rights agendas. Von Eschen, *Race against Empire*.

8. Patterson and Kelley, "Unfinished Migrations," 11, 13, 29–31.

continued on next page

continued

Answer the following:

_____What kind of history is it?

From just these two paragraphs, you are probably already aware that there are many layers of history at work here. There is a transnational component—the United States and Liberia. The author is also interested in exploring race relations and international economic and diplomatic questions during the Cold War and decolonization. All of these subfields can then be tied together under the large category of economic history, with an emphasis on business and capitalism. In fact, this article appeared in the journal *Enterprise & Society*.

FULL CITATION

Greer, Brenna W. "Selling Liberia: Moss H. Kendrix, the Liberian Centennial Commission, and the Post–World War II Trade in Black Progress." *Enterprise & Society* 14, no. 2 (June 2013): 303–26.

EXAMPLE 4: READ TO IDENTIFY SUBFIELDS

A number of historical journals are not easily recognizable for their subfields by their titles alone but are well known to professional historians. Several Oxford journals are among them. The *American Historical Review* is the official journal of the professional organization the American Historical Association and is generally regarded as the most prestigious scholarly journal in the discipline of history. The American Historical Association publishes articles that appeal to historians across subfields as well as across geographical and temporal boundaries. *History Workshop Journal* is known for cutting-edge scholarship and a tendency to feature work about more radical groups in history. *Past & Present* is particularly strong in ancient, medieval, and early modern history.

The following example comes from *Past & Present* and looks at ancient Rome. Read the selected passage from the introduction and reach your own conclusions about the author's major subfield(s).

Fales Cooper, Catherine. "Closely Watched Households: Visibility, Exposure and Private Power in the Roman Domus." *Past & Present, no. 197* (November 2007): 3–33.

> Think of your brothers, think of your mother and your aunt, think of your
>
> child, who will not be able to live once you are gone. Give up your pride!
>
> You will destroy all of us! None of us will ever be able to speak freely again
>
> if anything happens to you![1]

In the prison diary kept before her execution in the spring of 203, the 22-year-old Roman matrona Vibia Perpetua recorded a disturbing encounter with her father, who had come to visit her on the eve of her audience with the proconsul Hilarianus. The father is reduced to tears and pleading, behaviour rarely attested by a Roman father to his child. The episode is well known, yet it touches on dimensions of life in the Roman household, and of the role of the paterfamilias within it, that have yet to be fully understood.

What did Perpetua's father mean when he warned that "none of us will ever be able to speak freely again"? That a paterfamilias should be accountable for the conduct of his dependants does not surprise. Roman men were expected to show themselves impervious to "womanly influence"—the self-interested persuasion of wives, lovers (whether male or female) and other objects of their affection—as a way of broadcasting their willingness to place the common good ahead of private interest. The present study considers another aspect of the calculated performance of domestic virtue by Roman men, the terms on which they laid their households open to scrutiny by peers and rivals. Roman law and custom accorded far-reaching powers to the property-owner and head of household, so it is perfectly logical that mechanisms for evaluating his performance in that capacity should have evolved. Far from being contained or excluded, the dominium of the paterfamilias benefited from substantial protection. Many of the duties of a man in public office were accomplished by drawing on resources which he owned or controlled in his capacity as a private citizen. Indeed, I shall argue, it is precisely because the powers centred on the domus were so important to the Romans that the domus was placed under such intense scrutiny.

(1) Aspice fratres tuos, aspice matrem tuam et materteram, aspice filium tuum qui post te vivere non poterit. Depone animos; ne universos nos extermines. nemo enim nostrum libere loquetur, si tu aliquid fueris passa': Passio of Perpetua and Felicitas, x5, in Herbert Musurillo, *The Acts of the Christian Martyrs* (Oxford, 1972), 112–13 (trans Musurillo).

Explanation: If you noted that "men" and "women," "male" and "female," and "paterfamilias" are among the key terms mentioned in this selection and you recognized the author's juxtaposition of the idea of public versus private life, you would be rightly led to the subfield of gender history. In this article, we would expect a significant discussion of the rights and duties of male heads of Roman households as well as their impact on the women of the domus. Even if you were not studying ancient Rome, the article could offer a nice perspective on gender relations and the privileges assigned to men of a certain status that you could compare to later historical periods.

ACTIVITY: Debates on the current state of historical subfields

Historians regularly enter into direct discussions about changes in the teaching and writing of history outside the realm of scholarly publications. A recent study in Texas engaged college professors in a lively debate about the place of subfields in American history courses and put them in front of many important questions. Is there an ideal balance among the subfields of diplomatic, intellectual, social, and economic history faculty should try to achieve? Should race, class, and gender be woven into the curriculum or separated into special units? Are students missing out on learning about military history or religious traditions because professors are obligated to focus on such questions as slavery or civil rights? In other words, what subfields are being covered in the majority of college classrooms today and is anything being overlooked as a result?

To begin to think about these questions, read the following two short responses to a report by the National Association of Scholars about the teaching of historical subfields.

The articles appeared in the January 28, 2013, edition of the Chronicle of Higher Education and are available at http://chronicle.com/article/An-Undisciplined-Report-on-the/136845/ and http://chronicle.com/article/The-Obsession-With-Social/136865/. The original full report is available as a pdf file at http://www.nas.org/images/documents/Recasting_History.pdf/.

"AN UNDISCIPLINED REPORT ON THE TEACHING OF HISTORY" BY JAMES GROSSMAN AND ELAINE CAREY

Historians welcome informed debate. It is precisely what attracted many of us to the discipline in the first place. Thus our initial reaction to a recent report by the National Association of Scholars, "Recasting History: Are Race, Class, and Gender Dominating American History?", was to engage the ideas, explore the research model, and open a conversation about different ways of understanding history. This report, however, does not contribute to informed debate.

"Recasting History" presents itself as a detailed study of lower-level history courses at the University of Texas at Austin and Texas A&M University—and by extension at colleges and universities across the nation. Its critique is straightforward: "All too often the course readings gave strong emphasis to race, class, or gender (RCG) social history, an emphasis so strong that it diminished the attention given to other subjects in American history (such as military, diplomatic, religious, intellectual history). The result is that the institutions frequently offered students a less-than-comprehensive picture of U.S. history." The report condemns "narrow, specialized, and ideologically partisan approaches, largely driven by faculty research agendas."

Any historian who writes or teaches about the dynamics of power in a context that includes black people is understood by this report to be interested exclusively in "race," American slavery being merely a "racial" topic with little of consequence for political, intellectual, religious, diplomatic, or military history.

The biography of a prominent Virginia planter is categorized solely under "race" and "class"—not political or intellectual history, fields supposedly underrepresented in syllabi. To study Abigail Adams is an exercise in gender history—never mind her writings about the political ramifications of the American Revolution (much less recognizing that any study of her husband and other founding fathers will be equally gender-related). A classic study of 17th-century Massachusetts—one that has taught two generations of students about Puritan notions of community, religion, and governance—is dismissed as "class" analysis, ducking the "big questions" of American history.

The Great Depression, too, falls into the "class" category, as any study of that period will by definition focus exclusively on workers and employers rather than on banking, politics, and diplomacy, not to mention the history of ideas or politics.

This all seemed at first glance odd, tendentious, and uninformed. Upon careful reading, it turned out to be that and worse. Despite its denunciation of "ideologically partisan approaches," the report itself is based on an idiosyncratic and ideologically driven taxonomy of the books, articles, and syllabi of historians, compiled with little knowledge of the scholarly literature and even less inclination to engage historians in serious conversation about our work.

Although ostensibly analyzing how American history is taught at two universities, the authors neither attended classes nor spoke with instructors. They did not examine lectures, in-class activities, or audiovisual presentations; their report signals no knowledge of digital materials or discussions, assignments, or examinations. The document tells us little about teaching or learning; it merely surveys reading assignments, many of which the authors seem to have either not read or not understood. Moreover, they assume that to the extent that faculty members focus on so-called RCG subjects, they necessarily sacrifice coverage of broader themes in American history.

A "course" is never simply a set of readings. This report fails to consider how instructors design their classes, integrating lectures with readings and various other assignments, presentations, and discussions. Instead, the authors erroneously assume that the percentage of readings dealing with a particular topic mirrors the proportion of overall course time devoted to that theme.

The authors use the acronym "RCG" as shorthand for a kind of social history that they believe presents "a constrained version of the past." They list 11 more-traditional subfields in American history to argue that a growing majority of faculty ignore or neglect those subfields in favor of "broad content categories" delineated by race, class, and gender. But those subfields are not discrete subjects of study. They constitute overlapping categories that historians have, over the past two generations, built into conceptual frameworks capable of taking into account how individuals fit into meaningful social categories. In the authors' zeal to pigeonhole the faculty and the scholarship under review, they confuse "topics" with the useful concepts that enable historians to weave a more nuanced and comprehensive view of the past and the dynamics of historical change.

The enemy at the door in this report is the commitment shared by historians of nearly all stripes to expand traditional categories of historical analysis. In the past, the study of U.S. history focused almost exclusively on white Protestant men of standing—the political campaigns they waged, the wars they fought, the treaties they negotiated. Today historians offer an enriched tapestry, and one that helps us to better understand the dynamics of change.

Military and diplomatic historians now consider the implications of their work for the study of gender, and the implications of gender for understanding military leaders and their troops. Intellectual historians examine the writings of all sorts of people, regardless of class, gender, or race. Civil War historians study the home front and the process of emancipation rather than accepting outdated references to Lincoln's freeing the slaves all by himself—a notion plainly belied by the primary sources we read and assign.

By freezing in historiographical time what the authors consider 11 clearly delineated subfields of American history and then underestimating the extent to which those subfields overlap with one another and with new historical insights, the report betrays a limited understanding of the nature of historical scholarship and the collaborative ethos of historians who work in different fields and see the past in different ways.

Just how little the authors know about history as a discipline is casually betrayed by this sort of detail: a course called "The United States and Africa" is designated as a "racial" topic. Is that because Africans south of the Sahara are black? Would "The United States and Europe" be categorized under "race"? What about "The History of Inter-American Relations"?

continued on next page

continued

The report concludes with a claim that "our findings in this study shed light on a source of Americans' increasing ignorance about their own history." We share the National Association of Scholars' concern over Americans' limited knowledge of "their own history" (not to speak of the history beyond our borders). It is not clear, however, that Americans knew more about the past before historians began to broaden and deepen their focus; the report assumes this rather than demonstrates it.

Many Americans once "knew" about the Civil War because they had watched *Gone with the Wind*. They might have "known" that George Washington's character was rooted in a tale about a cherry tree. They knew very little about the roles of their own ancestors in shaping the American landscape, literal and cultural. Our students learn many of the same things that their predecessors were taught, but they also know aspects of our past that help them to understand themselves and their families as makers, and not just students, of history.

James Grossman is executive director of the American Historical Association. Elaine Carey is vice president for the Teaching Division of the association and chair of the history department at St. John's University, in New York.

"THE OBSESSION WITH SOCIAL HISTORY" BY RICHARD PELLS

The National Association of Scholars recently released a report excoriating the teaching of American history at the University of Texas at Austin and, to a lesser extent, at Texas A&M University at College Station.

The report argues that there is an almost monomaniacal preoccupation in American-history courses with the issues of race, class, gender, and ethnicity. Meanwhile, it argues, not enough attention is being paid to the history of American politics, economics, and culture, and the military.

The report has caused considerable fury among University of Texas historians, and it has apparently incensed American historians at other universities as well. Its critics have accused the association's writers of being conservative assailants who don't know what they're talking about.

It's true that the NAS is a conservative organization. Yet being conservative does not by itself make an organization uninformed or invalidate its report.

I am neither a conservative nor a member of the association. But I am an American historian who taught at the University of Texas for 40 years, from 1971 to 2011. And based on my own experiences there, I believe the report's main arguments are largely correct.

These issues are by no means unique to Texas—they describe the situation at most history departments in America ever since the 1960s and 1970s. The obsession with social history originated in the 1960s, inspired by then-graduate students and young historians who wanted to concentrate on groups and classes that had been traditionally oppressed and whose history had been overlooked. For them, American history was too elitist; it needed instead to be taught and written about "from the bottom up."

Nevertheless, what has developed at the University of Texas over the past 20 years is an almost oppressive orthodoxy and a lack of intellectual diversity among the history faculty. The result is that (with a few notable exceptions, like the work of the presidential historian H. W. Brands) very few courses are taught or books written by the current faculty on the history of American government, economic development, or culture and the arts, or on America's strategic and tactical participation in wars, particularly in the 20th century. Indeed, the Texas department has not employed a military historian since the 1970s.

Those are all subjects of supreme importance in understanding the evolution and current state of America. One cannot expect either undergraduate or graduate students to fully comprehend the complexities of American history without serious and extensive consideration of such topics.

In short, to paraphrase the columnist George Will, academics and especially specialists in American history at Texas are in favor of diversity in everything but thought. This is not just an acerbic quotation, nor is the NAS report to be dismissed as a right-wing polemic. The crises of intellectual conformity that Will and the association are depicting are endemic to academic life all over the country.

Yet the University of Texas is facing special difficulties. The problem in Austin is that the history department, and UT in general, are in peril. Texas has an extremely conservative legislature, which has already intruded on how faculty teach and on defining "accountability," and has contemplated a host of other educational "reforms." At the same time, state support for the university has been severely reduced over the past several years.

I do not, nor do my former colleagues in the history department, think that the legislature or any other outside group should interfere with how to structure a curriculum, or apply financial pressure to force faculty members to teach certain courses in certain ways. Such interference would be a dangerous infringement on academic freedom.

Still, what University of Texas historians need to do is stop railing against the report and start re-examining their hiring practices. Historians, like all academics, tend to clone themselves when they employ new faculty members. They think that since my field is vital, we need more people teaching the same thing. But what American historians at UT really should do is expand their far-too-limited intellectual horizons.

That means abandoning their current political and intellectual biases, opening themselves up to new subjects and new ideas, and recruiting new sorts of faculty members. Only then will the history department fulfill the true mission of a great university by fostering debate and exploring alternative ways of understanding America's past and present.

I do not question that those faculty members who specialize only in the plight of women, African-Americans, Latinos, and Native Americans are in any way ignoring legitimate problems in American history from which those groups have long suffered. Moreover, academic historians before the 1960s ignored the experiences of those groups for far too many decades.

But I am arguing that the National Association of Scholars' report is not a document that should be sneered at or ignored. Rather, what the history department at the University of Texas needs (and what history departments all over the country could benefit

continued on next page

continued

from) is a willingness—in fact, an eagerness—to hire people who are pursuing different interests. And who don't simply replow the same topics, teach the same types of courses, and reinforce the same (as Orwell said about the ideologues of the 1930s) "smelly" orthodoxies.

If American historians at the University of Texas fail to open themselves up to different topics and different perspectives, they could face even more stringent meddling from the state Legislature. Even more important, they will be doing a disservice to their students, who deserve to encounter a variety of points of view, and then decide for themselves what they believe.

Richard Pells is professor of history emeritus at the University of Texas. He is the author of four books on modern American culture, most recently Modernist America: Art, Music, Movies, and the Globalization of American Culture (Yale University Press, 2011).

Respond to the following questions:

1. What appear to be the main findings of the report on the teaching of history published by The National Association of Scholars? What do the authors of the two articles claim has happened to historical subfields over the past twenty plus years?

2. What aspects of the report do Grossman and Carey find most objectionable and why? Why does Pells argue instead that there are legitimate criticisms made in the report?

3. What is your impression of the way history has been taught in your college or university? Does there seem to be a dominant subfield among faculty members in the history department at your school? How do different subfields and methodologies play a part in the courses you have taken? Would you say that you have developed an approach to history based on a particular subfield or perspective? How might this influence your research?

ACTIVITY: Understanding how historical subfields change over time (an introduction to historiography)

In Chapter Three, we will go into much more detail about historiography, the study of the discipline of history. Here, however, it is worth examining how subfields develop and change in relation to the interests and preoccupations of historians working at a particular time. As we saw in Chapter One, our awareness of and concerns in the present often not only influence what we research but also have an impact on the frameworks we work from as we broach different subject matters. The following examples will help you understand how and why interpretations of important historical moments rarely remain fixed and how historians working in particular subfields may broach them.

EXAMPLE 1: THE PLAGUE—READ THE FOLLOWING SELECTION FROM SLACK, PAUL. *PLAGUE: A VERY SHORT INTRODUCTION.* NEW YORK: OXFORD UNIVERSITY PRESS, 2012, 35–50

Chapter 3

Big Impacts: The Black Death

It has often been supposed that major epidemic disasters must not only have extraordinary causes of the kind discussed in the previous chapter, but also produce extraordinary and wholly unpredictable consequences. The severity of their impact in the past seems fully to justify their incorporation into what might be called "Great Disaster" interpretations of history, the contention that such crises changed the whole course of events, and that without them things would not have turned out as they did. It will already be evident that one purpose of this book is to draw attention to some of the limitations of such an approach to the complexities of historical causation. It leaves too much that is important out of account. It must be allowed, nonetheless, that there is something to be said for the Great Disaster argument in a limited number of instances. The arrival of smallpox in the Americas along with the Spanish conquistadors is one of them. Many factors determined the collapse of the Aztec and Inca empires in the 16th century, but no historian would deny smallpox a decisive role in what happened, both in the short and the longer term. In some periods and places, plague had similarly disastrous potential.

This chapter will concentrate on the second pandemic in Europe, and focus especially on the Black Death which initiated it, because the case for big impacts is most easily established there. The third pandemic had less decisive long-term effect. Where its impact on mortality was worst, in parts of India and China in the decades around 1900, it did not transform the demographic and economic *status quo*. As we shall see in Chapter 5, it created panics and aroused cultural responses more extreme than other causes of mortality crises at the time, such as cholera and famine. But in other respects, it was simply one more affliction keeping mortality high and living standards low. It did not alter the biological and social environment in either the short or the longer term.

The Plague of Justinian, at the start of the first pandemic in the 6th century, may have had larger effects, immediate and sometimes lasting, though the evidence is scattered and difficult to interpret. There are signs of abrupt population decline in parts of Gaul and England, of land being suddenly plentiful and tenants difficult to find in Egypt, and of peasants moving from poorer to richer land in several parts of Europe. Yet these were local phenomena which may not have been replicated elsewhere.

Large-scale arguments which have sometimes been advanced, to the effect that plague on its own weakened the military potential of Byzantium in the face of the armies of Persia and Islam, or that it caused the decline of the urban economies of the Roman Empire, have therefore been difficult to substantiate. "There was too much else going on," one historian comments, "for the pandemic to be accorded a leading role" in such large historic events.

The Black Death presents a much more formidable test case for Great Disaster theories of history, however; and there is plentiful evidence which allows plague to be set alongside everything else that was going on, so that its independent role in the outcomes can be assessed. The first two waves of plague, between 1347 and 1352 and then in the

continued on next page

continued

years around 1360, cut the population of Europe by roughly one-third, and it stayed low for a century afterwards. Labour suddenly became scarce and its price rose. In consequence, in much of Western Europe the balance of power between employers and workers, and between landlords and tenants, shifted to the advantage of the latter, and so did the distribution of wealth. Old agrarian institutions like serfdom and villeinage declined when customary labour services could no longer be enforced, and the status and living standards of the majority of the population materially improved. Sectors of international trade catering for an elite market and the industries which supplied them were depressed, while internal trade and local industry grew to meet the demands of local markets. In the later 14th and early 15th centuries, old social and economic relationships broke down and were reconstituted in new and enduring forms.

Other kinds of relationships, and the behaviour and attitudes of mind which underpinned them, may have been affected as profoundly. The initial shock of plague elicited extreme reactions like those common in other major disasters: a search for scapegoats, in this case the Jews, for example, and forms of religious enthusiasm intended to placate a hostile providence.

In the longer term, modes of piety and styles of artistic expression may have altered, both of them affected by shifts in patronage as wealth was redistributed and both perhaps responding to a new awareness of morbidity and mortality. There were many local variations in these outcomes, and none of them were wholly unprecedented. But plague in the later 14th century had an impact on every sphere of human activity, and it might well appear to have often been a prime mover, reshaping the course of European history.

Populations and Economies

The case is strongest in the area where sudden, severe, and prolonged high mortality might be expected to have an impact, that of economic and social relations. The usual ties that bound farmers to their land, tenants to lords, and artisans and apprentices to their masters, all became weaker when rents and the price of land fell, wages rose, and peasants, labourers, and even servants (female as well as male) had greater bargaining power and became more mobile. Matteo Villani was horrified by some of the consequences in Tuscany in 1363. "Serving girls and unskilled women with no experience in service" now demanded high wages, while artisans asked for three times their usual pay, and farm labourers all wanted "to work the best lands, and to abandon all others." Consumer expectations rose alongside living standards:

The common people, by reason of the abundance and superfluity that they found, would no longer work at their accustomed trades; they wanted the dearest and most delicate foods . . . while children and common women clad themselves in all the fair and costly garments of the illustrious who had died.

There were similar comments from an elite which felt threatened by rapid social change in England, where there is ample evidence of labourers moving to new lords and more fertile lands and of new employment opportunities opening up for women, and where the purchasing power of wages more than doubled between 1350 and 1450. The first of a series of ordinances trying to set a ceiling to high wages and prevent labour mobility in 1349 explicitly linked both phenomena to the death of "a great part of the population, and especially workers and servants" in the recent pestilence; and in 1363, dismay at "the outrageous and excessive apparel of many people, contrary to their estate and degree" prompted Parliament to pass the first English sumptuary law, designed to regulate dress and diet according to social status. Ordinary labourers and artisans were scarcely wearing silks, but they could now afford better woolens than before, and the English textile industry grew in response to new consumer demand.

The case for regarding plague as the prime mover of economic and social change in the later Middle Ages thus has contemporary comment and much other evidence to support it. It nevertheless has some weaknesses. The most obvious arise from conspicuous differences between the consequences of plague in different places. Much depended on pre-existing economic conditions which determined whether demographic recession and labour mobility led to prolonged depression, or instead provided a stimulus to economic growth. Within England, for example, the less productive arable regions of the Midlands were less well placed to benefit from new opportunities than parts of East Anglia, and smaller towns were quicker to adopt new trades and employ immigrants than large cities, including London. Something similar lay behind contrasts on a larger scale. In Italy, Sicily recovered more quickly from 14th-century plagues than Tuscany, despite the fact that Sicilian plague mortality had been higher. In the Middle East, commercial and agricultural productivity declined more rapidly after the Black Death than in Europe, and failed to recover at all during the 15th century.

Pre-existing structures of power might also produce diverse outcomes. One of the starkest contrasts was between Western Europe, where serfdom declined, and Eastern Europe, where lords were powerful enough to impose it on previously free populations. The Black Death did not dictate the decline of serfdom, and in some circumstances, the institution disappeared without any help from plague at all. Flanders and Holland were unusual in escaping the worst of plague in the mid-14th century, but serfdom had already withered away there in the course of the 12th and 13th.

Ultimate outcomes depended finally on the duration of the demographic recession, and hence on the many factors which might explain why some populations recovered more quickly than others. The rise in popular living standards was particularly pronounced in England because its population did not begin to increase again until the early 16th century, and even in 1600 it was still lower than it had been in 1300. In France, by contrast, demographic recovery began much earlier (in the south from the 1420s), and populations in parts of the western Mediterranean had generally returned to their pre–Black Death levels before 1550. It is no accident, therefore, that the first of many comments on the relative prosperity of the English as compared with the French peasantry, who ate no meat and only rye bread, comes from the 1470s. Similarly, when Italian visitors to England around 1500 thought the land uncultivated and its inhabitants lazy, they were reacting to the country's comparatively low population density. Contrasts of this kind were already separating some of the economies of north-western Europe from those of the south, despite shared experiences of plague.

It is not easy to explain why population remained low for long periods after the great epidemics of the later 14th century. Although recovery was quicker in some places than others, it was everywhere slower than Malthusian models would predict, given high wages and abundant cheap land. Mortality often remained high, especially in north-western Europe, where it may even have risen in the 15th century, elevated by diseases other than plague, whose outbreaks were more localized and generally less severe than before 1400. But fertility, which might have been expected to rise after mortality crises,

continued on next page

continued

also stayed low, and there has been much speculation about the possible reasons for that. In England, it has been suggested that the shortage of labour opened up employment opportunities for women and adolescents in trades and services, which delayed marriage and therefore the number of children born to each couple. Something similar may have been happening in parts of urbanized Tuscany, like Florence. There, it has been argued, the many people who enjoyed higher standards of living after the Black Death deliberately kept their fertility low, adjusting their decisions about marriage and family formation in order to maintain their new style of life.

In any event, it does not seem to have been plague, or at least plague on its own, which determined population trends in the 15th century, any more than it did in the 16th and 17th. At the end of the 16th century, despite continuing plague epidemics, European populations were rising again everywhere, and living standards for peasants and labourers, women as well as men, fell. The numbers of beggars and paupers increased, and there were famine conditions all over Europe in the 1590s. In the later 17th and early 18th centuries, populations were falling again, although plague was gradually disappearing from the continent altogether. They were depressed once again by rising mortality caused by other diseases and by changes in marital behaviour which affected fertility. After 1400, it would seem that plague never functioned as a lone historical actor in the great swings of demographic and economic fortunes across late medieval and early modern Europe.

If we are looking for explanations for long-term and large-scale economic and social change, therefore, it is impossible to attribute everything to plague. Too much else was involved in determining what were sometimes divergent outcomes. Yet this is not to suggest that the Black Death—an epidemic far more severe across the whole continent than any which followed—did not have a decisive effect in the short term. In parts of Europe, including England, populations had already been declining before 1348, and might have continued to do so if plague had not appeared, with results in the end similar to those which actually occurred. But the sudden and high mortality rates around 1350 greatly accelerated the pace of change, and in some places they may have initiated it.

In a searching analysis of the alternative models which have been employed to account for medieval economic change in England, John Hatcher and Mark Bailey conclude that none of them adequately explains why what occurred in the 14th century should have happened precisely when it did, and so quickly. Grand theories based on Adam Smith, Marx, or Malthus, about commercialization, or the evolution of class relations, or the balance between population and resources, are all found to be wanting, partly because they push plague too far into the background. Other factors determined the direction of historical change and its scale in any particular instance. Both depended on many things other than sickness and high mortality: on local circumstances and environments, and on the opportunities, inclinations, and relative power of different actors in the multitude of decisions which shaped economic and family relations. Nonetheless, the Black Death was responsible for the timing of change and the speed with which it occurred. In that sense, and in the short term, it was a prime mover of undeniable force.

Cultural Turns

Precisely the same conclusion can be applied to historical changes that accompanied or followed the onset of plague in areas beyond the economic and the social, in the realm of ideas. The Black Death had a great deal to do with their timing, and much less with their character, which depended on local circumstances and what had gone before. Historians have assumed, with good reason, that epidemic shocks as severe as those of the later 14th century must have had an impact on how people thought about their world and their place in it, and some have argued that there were wholesale changes in mentalities, amounting to turning points in contemporary culture. Unfortunately, changes in habits of mind across whole societies are in the nature of the case more difficult to pin down than changes in the social structure or the character and productivity of agriculture or industry. This is an area of historical inquiry where there has more often been rhetoric than scholarly precision, and yet it is one where being specific, as we shall see, pays dividends.

Some of the more extravagant assertions about the psychological impact of the Black Death need not detain us for long, therefore, although they have had a lasting influence. They originated with the first historical account of medieval plague across Europe, written by the German medical historian J. F. C. Hecker in 1832, at a time when cholera seemed about to recreate the horrors of the past. According to him, "the mental shock sustained by all nations during the prevalence of the Black Plague" was "without parallel and beyond description." It destroyed confidence in the future, undermined deference and conventional moral norms, produced extremes of religious enthusiasm and social and religious dissidence, turned everything upside down. In effect, Hecker was building on late-medieval interpretations of the great pestilence as an apocalyptic catastrophe; and he created what has been well described as a "Gothic" interpretation of plague which continues to colour many depictions of the later Middle Ages. Writing in 1893 about the Black Death in England, Cardinal Gasquet caught some of Hecker's tone. "The Black Death inflicted what can only be called a wound deep in the social body, and produced nothing less than a revolution of feeling and practice, especially of religious feeling and practice." It was "a turning point in the national life" and "the real close of the medieval period and the beginning of our modern age."

Such grandiose statements have a place among the enduring images of plague considered in Chapter 6 below, and they have helped to sustain popular interest in the topic as well as stimulating argument among historians. Whether one conceives of the later Middle Ages as an era of darkness, obsessed with sin and fears of death, or as one of intellectual renaissance and incipient enlightenment, however, probably depends on personal predilection, since a case can be made for either. Plagues, like other natural disasters, challenge established ways of thinking, and may prompt intellectual innovation as well as doubt and dismay, but that trite observation scarcely takes us very far. The extent of plague's impact on mentalities is better measured by taking a narrower view and focusing on parts of the historical terrain where sudden mortality can be shown to have had a tangible effect.

Fourteenth-century changes of fashion in architecture and art have provided fertile territory from this point of view. Here plague had an immediate impact, directly by depleting the ranks of skilled artists and craftsmen, indirectly by reducing the incomes of cultured patrons among the elite and increasing those of people less able, and perhaps less inclined, to fund expensive artistic innovation. The triumph of the "Perpendicular" style in English church architecture is an instructive case. Cheaper, because less labour-intensive, than its "Decorated" predecessor, it took hold from the 1350s and was

continued on next page

continued

the architectural orthodoxy for the next two hundred years. It might have caught on anyway, with or without plague, since there are earlier examples of it, as in the south transept of Gloucester Cathedral, which was finished by 1337, and probably in the cloister of old St Paul's in London, begun in 1332. But the consequences of the Black Death speeded the transition. It brought to a sudden close the great boom in cathedral and monastic building, which had been funded by the soaring agricultural profits of major ecclesiastical institutions in the 12th and 13th centuries. In its place, there was a proliferation of church-building on a less lavish scale, paid for by local communities. No fewer than three-quarters of the surviving medieval churches of England were built or rebuilt between 1350 and 1540, and in Perpendicular style.

Architectural fashions have less to tell us about modes of thought and feeling than other kinds of artistic expression, however. A classic study of painting in Florence and Siena in the 14th century takes us closer to mentalities, and into more controversial territory. In 1951, Millard Meiss claimed that there was a profound change of style and taste there after the Black Death. There was a reaction against the humanistic innovations of Duccio and Giotto and back to less naturalistic and more austere styles, redolent of a simpler spirituality and more suited to an era dominated by plague: "a darker realm of fearful, strenuous yet often uncertain piety, brightened only by mystical transports and visions of supernatural splendour." There is more than a hint of Gothic extravagance in that argument, and it has often been disputed. Some of the works fundamental to Meiss's case, including the frescoes depicting the "Triumph of Death" in the Camposanto at Pisa, probably pre-date the plague, for example. At the same time, it may well be the case that there was a reversion to more traditional styles when an enlightened elite of rich patrons, like the ecclesiastical authorities of Siena, were no longer able to afford the grandiose and innovative works they had funded in the past. The vast extension to the cathedral at Siena, begun in 1348, remains unfinished, a stark reminder of what a single munificent sponsor had once been able to contemplate.

What seems certain, however, is that Meiss's "darker realm" was not all-pervasive. If we place artistic and architectural endeavours in their proper context, alongside other forms of pious and charitable investment, we find novelty as well as conservatism. In England, the quality of manuscript illumination, wall paintings, and even monumental brasses may have declined after 1350, but there were alternative and large collective investments in much more than Perpendicular churches. New foundations after 1348 included scores of chantries, new colleges at Oxford and Cambridge, and new funds to support the poor, now deliberately targeted at the most "deserving" (not wandering beggars and vagrants). Many of these were designed primarily to provide prayers for the souls of the benefactors, and surviving wills display a similar concern with death and the afterlife. But alms and almshouses and university colleges also provided benefits for the living, and so did the many fraternities paid for by local subscriptions which by the 15th century sustained sociability and mutual aid in English parishes.

Lay piety turned in similar directions elsewhere in Western Europe after the plague. In Italy, testamentary bequests tended to focus on the family, often providing for memorials as well as prayers for the dead, but they also included bequests for dowries for girls from the deserving poor, and for the foundlings and orphans whose number multiplied in plague-time. The first European hospital exclusively for orphans was founded in Paris in 1363, and there was another in Florence early in the next century. There is no sign here of the breakdown of family ties and neighbourhood loyalties lamented by some of the contemporary chroniclers of epidemics. Neither can it be seen in the literature of the later 14th century, which included a remarkable group of Welsh poems expressing grief at the death of children during plagues. Rather, there is an evident concern to preserve the memory of the dead and equally to provide for the most vulnerable of those who survived.

Much of this evidence from testamentary and literary sources would support the view that plague helped to give death a more prominent place in popular mentalities. Such a shift of perception is suggested by the new forms of artistic and literary expression which have been used by many historians to demonstrate the pervasive appeal of macabre themes in the later Middle Ages. Although they mostly come from the 15th century and not the later 14th, and often from northern and not southern Europe, they illustrate a world with very different ways of thinking and feeling from our own. One example is the image of the "Dance of Death," the *danse macabre*. Its earliest known representation was on a mural in the cemetery of the Innocents in Paris, painted in 1424–5, and it was for centuries afterwards an iconic representation of the inevitability and unpredictability of mortality, striking rich and poor, virtuous and vicious, alike. The same message was driven home by the *transí* tombs of bishops and other notables, showing their corpses in various stages of decomposition, and by books on the *ars moriendi*, "the art of dying well," illustrated with exemplary death-bed scenes, which had earlier antecedents but flourished after 1408 and taught the literate how to prepare for their end. Some of these images seem grotesque to modern sensibilities in societies in which dying has become a more private affair, but in the context of their time, they are fully intelligible. They were ways of confronting realities, including the deaths of thousands in plague-time, and making them, to some degree, comprehensible.

The same might be said about two more dramatic phenomena, much more closely tied to the Black Death itself, which Hecker emphasized and which a great deal has been made of since: the pogroms inflicted on Jews, who were accused of spreading plague by poisoning wells and rivers, and the punishments which crowds of penitents, "flagellants," inflicted on themselves. Both of them prominent in 1348 and 1349, and both of them the result of apocalyptic interpretations of the Black Death as a sign that the Last Days of the world were at hand, they have sometimes been cited as instances of collective and almost psycho-pathological hysteria in critical circumstances. The pogroms were undeniably rapid and popular responses to rumours and scares, and horrific in their violence. Nearly a thousand Jews were burned in the Jewish cemetery at Strasbourg in 1349, and the large Jewish communities elsewhere in the Rhineland were almost wholly exterminated.

Yet these were massacres with some precedents behind them in the 1320s, and they were generally undertaken by due legal processes sanctioned by local authorities. Once magistrates began to have doubts about the evidence, and that came very quickly, persecution stopped. There were no more instances after 1352, except in 1360 in parts of Poland, which had scarcely been affected by plague earlier. There were to be similar scares about people deliberately spreading plague in later epidemics, when the scapegoats identified were often foreigners and other kinds of outsiders thought hostile to local populations. Less widespread than the earlier pogroms, and restrained by judicial processes, they scarcely amount to evidence of a mass hysteria typical of plague-time.

continued on next page

continued

The flagellant processions were as common as persecution of the Jews immediately after 1348, and they continued into the early 15th century. Marching along the roads across much of Europe proclaiming the need for repentance in the face of God's evident judgements, their participants scourged themselves as they went, "wearing hoods and beating themselves with whips until the blood flowed" according to a chronicle from Tournai. There had been similar movements earlier, one as early as 1260, but such autonomous expressions of religious enthusiasm without obvious official sanction in 1349–50 horrified ecclesiastical authorities. After that, the Church took them on board and exercised more control. When plague threatened Florence in 1399, there were similar crowded processions of the "Bianchi," who walked through the city and suburbs barefoot and dressed in white. One of the penitents participating was the great commercial tycoon Francesco Datini, the merchant of Prato, and his description of the occasion gives the impression, as his modern biographer remarks, of "a gigantic nine-days' picnic." There is no sign there of the hysteria there might possibly have been forty years earlier. It was a popular and pious outlet for stress, but it had become a wholly respectable affair.

These instances suggest that there was little that was wholly instinctive or irrational in popular responses to plague after 1348–9. Once the initial, apocalyptic shock of the Black Death had been absorbed and the challenges presented by epidemics become familiar, people adjusted their behaviour and adapted their ways of thinking so that they could accept them—not as something commonplace or everyday, but as inescapable facts of life. Plague was being accommodated.

Respond to the following questions:

1. Slack argues that the Black Death provides historians with an opportunity to evaluate "great disaster" theories in history and to assess interpretations of the impact of the second plague pandemic. What does he intend by this? How could a large devastating event, such as the plague, alter the course of history?

2. What are the stronger and weaker arguments for viewing the Black Death primarily as a source of tremendous social and economic change? According to Slack, what short- and long-term consequences did it ultimately have on shifts in population and employment? Why does Slack claim that grand economic theories, whether based on the Liberal ideas of Adam Smith or the class-based perspective of Karl Marx, are not sufficient to account for exactly why the fourteenth century was a time for such important economic change?

3. Slack points out that the Black Death helped generate the idea that the Middle Ages were filled with great tragedy and darkness. In fact, the term "Dark Ages" continues to circulate in part because of the widespread psychological and cultural impact of the plague. How did contemporaries respond to the plague in terms of religiosity and popular mentalities? How might historians account for shifts in intellectual thinking and cultural production that resulted from the pandemic? What kinds of cultural and intellectual evidence contribute to these viewpoints? How do economic or demographic sources differ from cultural ones?

EXAMPLE 2: THE FRENCH REVOLUTION—READ THE FOLLOWING
SELECTION FROM DOYLE, WILLIAM. *THE FRENCH REVOLUTION: A VERY
SHORT INTRODUCTION.* NEW YORK: OXFORD UNIVERSITY PRESS, 2001

Chapter 6

Where It Stands

"The whole business now seems over," wrote the English observer Arthur Young in Paris on 27 June 1789, "and the revolution complete." People would repeatedly make the same observation, usually more in hope than conviction, over the next ten years until Napoleon officially proclaimed the end of the Revolution in December 1799. Even then all he meant was the end of a series of spectacular events in France; he was to continue to export them for another sixteen years. Besides, the Revolution was not simply a meaningless sequence of upheavals. These conflicts were about principles and ideas which continued to clash throughout the nineteenth century, and would be reinvigorated by the triumphs of Marxist Communism in the twentieth. Thus it still seemed outrageous to many French intellectuals when, in 1978, the historian François Furet proclaimed, at the start of a celebrated essay, that "The French Revolution is finished" (*termínée*).

A Historical Challenge

What he meant was that the Revolution was now, or ought to be, a subject for historical enquiry as detached and dispassionate as that of medievalists studying (his example) the Merovingian kings. Whereas the history of the Revolution as it has been written in France for much of the twentieth century had been more a matter of commemoration than scholarly analysis, its legitimacy monopolized by a succession of Communists or fellow-travellers entrenched in the university hierarchy. Furet's attack was suffused with personal history. Though a Sorbonne graduate, he had always despised the university world, and had built a career in the rival *Ecole pratique des Hautes Etudes* (later EHESS). A Communist in youth, like so many others he was disillusioned by the Soviet invasion of Hungary in 1956, and renounced the party. And when he and a fellow apostate, Denis Richet, wrote a new history of the Revolution in 1965, they were unanimously denounced by leading specialists in the subject as intruders, not qualified in the subject, who, in offering an interpretation suggesting that it had "skidded off course," had traduced the Revolution's essential unity of purpose and direction. By 1978 Furet had abandoned this view, but not the enmities it had aroused. For the rest of his life (he died in 1997), he pressed home his attack, particularly during the debates of the bicentenary. As that year came to an end, he cheerfully proclaimed that he had won.

The Classic Interpretation

What had he defeated? He called it the "Jacobino-Marxist Vulgate." His opponents called it the "classic" interpretation of the Revolution. Its basis was (and is, since despite Furet's triumphalism it retains many adherents) the conviction that the Revolution was a force for progress. The fruit and vindication of the Enlightenment, it set out to emancipate not just the French, but humanity as a whole, from the grip of superstition, prejudice, routine, and unjustifiable social inequities by resolute and democratic political action. This was the "Jacobin" bedrock, differing little from the professions of countless clubbists in

continued on next page

continued

the 1790s. As a historical interpretation, it built on the work of nineteenth-century cus-
todians of revolutionary traditions, most famously perhaps Jules Michelet, that apocalyptic idolizer of "The People." Confident and complacent, the Jacobin perspective was
disturbed only by the terror, which it did not seek to defend except as a cruel necessity
and a reflex of national defence.

Around the turn of the twentieth century, this historiographical Jacobinism began
to acquire a new political overlay. From 1898 the great left-wing politician Jean Jaurès
began to produce a *Socialist History of the French Revolution* which emphasized its economic and social dimensions and introduced an element of Marxist analysis. Marx himself had written little directly on the Revolution, but it was easy enough to fit a movement
which had begun with an attack on nobles and feudalism into a theory of history that emphasized class struggle and the conflict between capitalism and feudalism. The French
Revolution from this viewpoint was the key moment in modern history, when the capitalist bourgeoisie overthrew the old feudal nobility. The fundamental questions about it
were therefore economic and social. At the very moment when Jaurès was writing, a
fierce young professional historian, Albert Mathiez, was beginning a lifelong campaign
to rehabilitate Robespierre, under whose terroristic rule clear "anticipations" of later socialist ideals had appeared. Mathiez set out to stamp his own viewpoint on the entire historiography of the Revolution, and his native vigour was redoubled from 1917 by the example and inspiration of the Bolshevik Revolution in Russia, which seemed to revive the
lost promise of 1794. Robespierre's Republic of Virtue would live again in Lenin's Soviet
Union. Mathiez only belonged briefly to the Communist Party, but he established a parallel historical party of his own in the form of a "Society of Robespierrist Studies." Its journal, the *Annales historiques de la Révolution française,* is still the main French-language
periodical devoted to the Revolution. Apart from the years of Vichy, when it was silenced,
from the death of Mathiez in 1932 until the advent of Furet this society and its members
dominated teaching and writing about the Revolution in France, and its successive leading figures occupied the chair of the History of the Revolution at the Sorbonne. When
Furet launched his polemics, the incumbent of this apostolic succession was the lifelong Communist Albert Soboul (d. 1982), against whose convictions the waters of what he
naturally called "revisionism" broke in vain.

Revisionism

But revisionism had not begun with Furet. It originated in the English-speaking world in
the 1950s—in England with Alfred Cobban, in the USA with George V. Taylor. Although
many of the great minds of nineteenth-century anglophone culture had been fascinated
by the French Revolution and Napoleon, interest lapsed during the first half of the twentieth century. The handful of historians still attracted to the subject worked little in France
and achieved almost no recognition there. After the Second World War, however, as Western democracy appeared threatened by Marxists both domestic and foreign, it seemed
urgent to rescue the great episodes of modem history from tendentious distortions. Both
Cobban and Taylor chose to confront what they called the French "orthodoxies" head-on.
It was a myth. Cobban claimed, that the revolutionaries of 1789 were the spokesmen of
capitalism: the deputies who destroyed the ancien régime were office-holders and land-
owners. In any case. Taylor argued, most pre-revolutionary wealth was non-capitalist,
and such capitalism as there was had no interest in the destruction of the old order. That

destruction, indeed, so far from sweeping away the obstacles holding back a thrusting capitalist bourgeoisie, proved an economic disaster and drove everyone with money to invest in the security of land. Taking their cue from the vast range of questions raised by these critiques, throughout the 1960s and 1970s a new generation of scholars from English-speaking countries invaded the French archives to test the new hypotheses. By the 1980s they had largely demolished the empirical basis and the intellectual coherence of the "classic" interpretation of the Revolution's origins.

Initially the French maintained their traditional disdain for the "Anglo-Saxons," dismissing Taylor and Cobban as cold warriors who had read too much Burke and wished only to disparage the Revolution as a continuing threat to the hegemony of the Western bourgeoisie. But when Furet and Richet challenged the classic interpretation from within the introverted world of French culture, the Robespierrists were forced onto the defensive. Furet, who had no problems with the English language, had by the early 1970s begun to incorporate the findings and arguments of the foreigners into his own interpretations; as well as those of a compatriot long neglected in France but always taken seriously by English speakers, Alexis de Tocqueville (d. 1859). Tocqueville saw the Revolution as the advent of democracy and equality but not of liberty. Napoleon and his nephew, whom this aristocrat of old stock hated, had shown how dictatorship could be established with democratic support, since the Revolution had swept away all the institutions which, in impeding the relentless growth of state power, had kept the spirit of liberty alive. These insights persuaded Furet that the Revolution had not after all skidded off course into terror. The potential for terror had been inherent right from the start, from the moment when national sovereignty was proclaimed and no recognition given to the legitimacy of conflicting interests within the national community. For all its libertarian rhetoric, the Revolution had no more been disposed to tolerate opposition than the old monarchy, and the origins of modern totalitarianism would be found in the years between 1789 and 1794.

Post-revisionism

This was more than revisionism. The approach of Cobban, Taylor, and those who came after them has largely been empirical, undermining the sweeping social and economic claims of the classic interpretation with new evidence, but seldom seeking to establish new grand overviews. The most they claimed was that the Revolution could be more convincingly explained in terms of politics, contingency, and perhaps even accident. This is largely the approach adopted in earlier chapters of this book. Such suggestions did not satisfy bolder minds. As Furet began to depict a Revolution in the grip of attitudes and convictions which propelled it inevitably towards terror, others, mostly in America, sought wider explanations for revolutionary behaviour in cultural terms. They saw a number of "discourses" emerging from the political conflict between 1770 and 1789, which laid the foundation for much of the uncompromising language and arguments of the revolutionaries. Borrowing from the speculations of the German left-wing philosopher Jürgen Habermas, they argued that in the generation before the Revolution public opinion escaped from the king's control, and that in the process respect and reverence for the monarchy ebbed away. Furet found these interpretative trends even more congenial than those of early revisionism, and spent increasing amounts of time in America and at conferences abroad, where yet another generation of young scholars committed to the cultural approach treated the triumphs of revisionism as yesterday's battles.

continued on next page

continued

By 1987, these trends were crystallizing into a new orthodoxy, and were being labelled as post-revisionism.

The Bicentenary

Whatever might be said against the classic interpretation, it was at least coherent and comprehensible. By contrast, the "linguistic turn" of post-revisionism, increasingly influenced by philosophers and literary theorists, produced much abstruse material that could barely be understood outside specialist circles. When, therefore, the Socialist president of France decreed, some years in advance, that the revolutionary bicentenary of 1989 must be celebrated, he entrusted the academic side of the festivities to the still well-entrenched defenders of what Soboul had called, just before he died, "our good old orthodoxy." Soboul's successor at the Sorbonne, Michel Vovelle, was given a worldwide mission of coordinating academic commemoration. He worked so hard at it that eventually doctors instructed him to stop. But the learned bicentenary proved just as unmanageable as the more public one. While both Vovelle and Furet toured colloquia in every continent, they never appeared together on the same platform, and Furet and his cohorts boycotted the biggest conference of the year organized by Vovelle in Paris. This was scarcely the attitude of scholarly detachment for which Furet had seemed to be calling in 1978. As a subject arousing sectarian passions, the Revolution was clearly far from finished, even for those claiming it was.

The bicentenary, in fact, released a torrent of vituperative publishing, most of it denouncing one aspect or another of the Revolution and its legacy. Particularly vocal in France were defenders of the Vendée rebels, the most persistent contemporary French enemies of the Revolution, and in consequence victims of the most savage repression. The heroism of devout peasant guerillas, long derided as superstitious fanatics, was now lovingly chronicled. Catholic clergy reminded their flocks of when modern impiety had begun. In the English-speaking world, meanwhile, while hundreds of learned gatherings picked over the debris of a generation of scholarly clashes, and publishers and the media felt obliged to mark the bicentenary in one way or another, the sensation of the year was the publication of Simon Schama's *Citizens*, a vast "chronicle" of the Revolution which ignored the historical debate almost entirely in the interests of telling a colourful and lurid story. The overall message was the folly of undertaking revolutions (one fortunately lost on the East Europeans who were at that moment defying Soviet satellite regimes). Yet there was an intellectual stance behind Schama's Dickensian narrative, and it was basically the same as Furet's. The terror, declared the most famous sentence in the book, was merely 1789 with a higher body count; and "violence . . . was not just an unfortunate side effect . . . it was the Revolution's source of collective energy. It was what made the Revolution revolutionary." Significantly, Schama's tale ended abruptly in 1794 with the fall of Robespierre and the end of the terror.

One of the favourite mantras of the Revolution's classic interpreters was taken from Georges Clemenceau, the statesman of the Third Republic who gloried in the achievements of the First. The Revolution, he declared, was a *bloc*. It had to be accepted in its totality, terror and all. It could not be disaggregated. Revisionism, with its emphasis on the contingent, the accidental, and the reality of choices facing those involved, suggested otherwise—as had the young Furet when he and Richet spoke of the Revolution skidding off course. Only by approaching events as contemporaries had to, without an awareness of horrors to come, could regicide, dechristianization, and the guillotine be prevented from throwing their shadows over what preceded them, as they did over everything that followed. Post-revisionists, however, turned against this approach. In emphasizing the cultural constraints that determined what history's actors could or could not think or do, they opened the way to a determinism not unlike that of the economic and social factors emphasized by the classic historians in their Marxist-inspired heyday. And in insisting that terror was inherent in the Revolution from the start, Furet made it the central issue by which to judge the movement's entire significance. For post-revisionists of all stamps, in fact, the Revolution was as much a *bloc* as it was for those they claimed to have vanquished.

It was, of course, a different sort of *bloc*. And while the post-revisionist emphasis on the centrality of terror encouraged blanket denunciations not only of the Revolution but also of the very attempt to commemorate it, there were also plenty of celebrations throughout France, as Mitterrand intended, of two hundred years of human rights. Vovelle, for his part, while reiterating his commitment to left-wing values traceable back to Jacobinism, refused to accept that there had been any sort of contest with Furet, observing meekly that scholarly enquiry was open to all viewpoints. But, apart from a few hard-line Communists, the adherents of the once-hegemonic classic tradition emerged from the bicentenary chastened. In the 1990s, the *Annales historiques de la Révolution française* began gingerly to open its pages to non-members of the Robespierrist studies circle, and to review their books for purposes other than denunciation. The chair of Mathiez, Soboul, and Vovelle is now occupied by a historian of the Vendée. And although since the death of Furet new sympathetic analyses of Jacobinism have begun to appear, they have been anxious to deny that terror was part of its mainstream. The heaviest blows, however, were not delivered by scholarly revisionists or post-revisionists. They came from the spectacular collapse of Soviet Communism, and the repressive attempts of its Chinese variant, just a few weeks before 14 July 1989, to shore up its authority against students calling for liberty and singing the *Marseillaise*.

The End of a Dream?

Awareness of the full repressive record of Soviet Communism had been growing at least since Krushchev had begun to denounce Stalin in 1956. But so long as the Soviet Union continued apparently flourishing and powerful, it could be argued that its Marxist ideology worked and that its bloody past had been a worthwhile price to pay to secure popular democracy. Similar arguments had been used to justify terror in 1793–4, and by later pro-Jacobin historians. When the rule of Gorbachev revealed the whole Soviet edifice to be unviable, and incapable of sustaining its sister-republics in Eastern Europe, this delusion collapsed. A regime invested for seventy years with all the hopes and dreams repeatedly frustrated since the fall of Robespierre had proved scarcely more successful, and at far heavier human cost, than the prototype which it and its friends held in reverence. The Chinese, whose historical loyalties were similar, had no answer to their own domestic critics other than to shoot or imprison them. If such regimes were the true heirs of the French Revolution, then Tocqueville and Furet were right in their perception that its significance lay not in the enhancement of liberty but in the promotion of state power. Faith in the benevolent potential of a rationalizing state was the first, and perhaps the last, illusion of the Enlightenment; and in this sense the French Revolution, and all the others that followed over two hundred years, were its authentic heirs. The illusion

continued on next page

continued

died whilst historians in the West squabbled about how, or even whether, to mark the Revolution's second centenary.

But of course totalitarian peoples' democracy was not the only legacy of ways of thinking that first triumphed in the 1790s. François Mitterrand's decision to celebrate the rights of man at the bicentenary was more than a doomed attempt to dissociate the memory of the Revolution from the terror. It was also a recognition that the ideology of human rights was, if anything, more important than it had ever been. Regimes of tyranny and massacre have no monopoly in the heritage of the Revolution. Citizens of modern constitutional democracies whose civil and political rights are guaranteed, and whose life chances are equal before the law, can find much in it to celebrate. The ambition of the French Revolution was so comprehensive that almost anyone living since can find something there to admire as well as to deplore. Nor are all the battles it launched yet over. If the collapse of Communism can be seen as defeat for Jacobins, the European Union looks very like a Girondin project to bring the liberal benefits of 1789 to Europe as a whole. In turn, this aspiration meets most resistance from national reflexes first fully aroused by the challenges emanating from revolutionary France. "The barest enumeration of some of the principal consequences of 1789," wrote an eminent literary critic in 1987, even before the full symbolic significance of the bicentennial year had emerged, enforce the realisation that the world as we know it today . . . is the composite of reflexes, political assumptions and structures, rhetorical postulates, bred by the French Revolution. More than arguably, for it entails subsequent, so often mimetic revolutionary movements and struggles across the rest of the planet, the French Revolution is the pivotal historical–social date after that of the foundation of Christianity . . . Time itself, the cycle of lived history, was deemed to have begun a second time . . . 1789 continues to be now.

G. Steiner, "Aspects of Counter-Revolution," in G. Best (ed.)

The Permanent Revolution

The last word, however, should perhaps be left to the author with whom this book began. "That, my dear Algy," says Ernest Worthing, "is the whole truth pure and simple." "The truth," his friend replies, "is rarely pure and never simple."

Respond to the following questions:

1. Doyle states that classic interpretations of the French Revolution perceived it as a "force for progress" (p. 99). Explain. Why did social and economic historians claim that it ushered in a better era? How did orthodox and revisionist historians connect the Revolution to the history of capitalism? Why might their arguments have been based more on political evidence and less on the tradition of social history?

2. How did the "linguistic turn" again change accounts of the French Revolution? What influence did the celebration of the bicentenary have on scholarly production on the Revolution? What is the relationship between the collapse of the Soviet Union and challenges to state authority in China to the legacy of the Revolution?

3. What does the example of the French Revolution suggest to you about how historical meaning changes based on previous interpretations and contemporary concerns?

4. Do you tend to see the world more from a political, economic, or social point of view? How might your own mentalities enter into your historical research?

CHAPTER THREE

Doing Historical Research and Writing a Historiographical Essay

Workbook Exercises

What is a historiographical essay? It is an essay that discusses how historians have treated a particular topic over time and reviews methods, approaches, and arguments. In some disciplines the essay is called a literature review. The task can be divided into three stages—research, analysis, and writing. In this section, you will find exercises to help you at each stage: you will learn how to find your way around your library, get to know your librarians, find relevant and useful sources, evaluate them, and, ultimately, write a historiographical essay or section on your own topic.

❶ Research: getting started

Your instructor may have assigned a topic, or you may have chosen it. Once you have your topic, your research begins. You will want to go to your library, learn something about the topic, and find relevant sources. This first stage has three exercises: mapping your college library, locating specialized scholarly reference sources, and finding usable secondary sources.

Mapping your library

You may have avoided the library until now, since so much material is available through the Internet. You may even have written some successful papers based solely on online data. But for a historical research paper at the college or university level, you will discover that your library has much to offer. First, get to know the layout of your library and make friends with your librarians. Once you have the lay of the land, you will find it easier and faster to find what you want. Librarians are always ready to help you. They can save you a lot of time and frustration and will help ensure you have appropriate sources.

ACTIVITY: Mapping your library

You can do this assignment alone, but it will be more fun if you do it in a small group of two or three classmates. That way, you can compare notes and learn from each other. You might want to draw a map, be it ever so rough, to help you remember where to locate particular items. Here are some of the locations you will want to map out. You may want to add others, depending on what your library has to offer and what you discover as you walk around. If some of the items listed below are not in your library, just skip them.

_____Circulation desk (where you check out books)

_____Reference desk (where you can find a librarian to answer questions)

_____A/V desk (is there a separate desk for checking out audiovisual items, like DVDs?)

_____Reference stacks (encyclopedias and other reference sources that typically cannot be checked out of the library)

_____Current periodicals (includes individual magazines, newspapers, journals)

_____Bound periodicals (older individual magazines and journals are sent out to be bound. For example, all *Time* magazines for January to June 1995 might be bound together as a book and found elsewhere in your library. This practice is nearly obsolete as materials move online, but most libraries have decades worth of bound periodicals, and some, such as popular magazines, are worth leafing through in the flesh rather than online to get a sense of the advertisements and layout.)

_____Current newspapers

_____Music CDs

_____DVDs and VHSs

_____Writing/tutoring center

_____Information literacy instruction classrooms

_____Computer pods for general work

_____Computer pods dedicated to library searches

_____If your library has a librarian who is assigned specifically to the discipline of history, then find out who that person is, introduce yourself, and ask for his or her name, e-mail address, and telephone extension. This librarian will be delighted that you are a serious student and will be all the more willing to help you with your research.

_____If your library has a librarian whose responsibility it is to organize information literacy instruction, get to know that person too and ask for his or her contact information. You may want to sign up for some courses to develop your study skills.

ACTIVITY: Where are the history books?

Below is a list of general topics that will help you navigate the library to find where books on particular subjects can be found. Locate three books on each topic. If you have not had instruction on searching your college catalog and research databases, now is the time to sign up for a session.

_____The Nanking Massacre

_____The Reconstruction of the American South

_____Zimbabwe

_____Gold rushes

_____Sparta

_____Your topic

To do this exercise, first go to your library's online catalog to find the call numbers for books on these topics. Call numbers help you locate books in the stacks. Type in the general subjects as "keywords." Check to make sure that the hits you find refer to books, not DVDs, and click on the titles to obtain more information that will confirm that the books are historical treatments of the topics, as opposed, say, to literary treatments. Then make a note of the call numbers and walk to the stacks to find the books. As you peruse the shelves to find your books, you will also locate other titles that may appeal to you. Sometimes some of your best finds will be located like this, serendipitously. That is one of the advantages of walking through the stacks. If it would help you to understand the rationale behind the call numbers, do ask a librarian.

Locating specialized scholarly reference sources for your topic

Because students frequently head to Wikipedia for their initial information on a topic, here is a word of caution. A wiki is a document that can be collaboratively authored by many individuals and constantly changed. Because anyone can add information, and because bylines are unusual, you have no idea whether the writers are well informed. Wikipedia offers the following description:

"Wikipedia is written collaboratively by largely anonymous Internet volunteers who write without pay. Anyone with Internet access can write and make changes to Wikipedia articles (except in certain cases where editing is restricted to prevent disruption or vandalism). Users can contribute anonymously, under a pseudonym, or with their real identity, if they choose."[1]

Wikipedia might offer the best, most cogent explanation of a historical concept that you have been able to find. It might be correct, or it might be misleading. So by all means use Wikipedia to grasp a general sense of your topic and check the bibliography, but then move on to more reliable sources, such as your college or university's online encyclopedias, most likely *Encyclopaedia Britannica* or *Grolier Encyclopedia*. These sources are meant to give you an overall grasp of your topic *before* you start more focused research.

Sitting in your library right now, however, are specialized print encyclopedias with lengthy entries, written by scholarly experts, for example, *The Encyclopedia of the Holocaust*. These entries often provide a list of sources for further exploration, saving you considerable time. Just remember that, as a general rule, you do not cite encyclopedias (or dictionaries) in college-level papers. Finally, you would also do well to consult collective historical works, for example *The Cambridge Ancient History,* in the initial stages of your research.

ACTIVITY: Historical encyclopedias

_____ASK one of the librarians you became acquainted with while doing the mapping exercise for a relevant scholarly encyclopedia on your topic. This is not a do-it-yourself moment. A librarian will be able to save you from wasting valuable time.

[1.] Wikipedia, "About Wikipedia," http://en.wikipedia.org/wiki/Wikipedia:About/.

_____FIND an encyclopedia article on your topic. While reading through the article, you will likely see subheadings on aspects of your topic and recurring key terms. While taking notes in this preliminary stage of your research, be sure to note relevant terms. You will use them in your search for secondary sources. Since you cannot typically check out a reference book, a good entry is worth photocopying. (But do not mistake photocopying for research—more about that in Chapter Five.)

Locating scholarly secondary sources

If you have been assigned a historiographical essay, your instructor may have stipulated the number of sources you need and perhaps other restrictions. Let's say you need to find three monographs (historical study by a single author of a specific topic) published by a university or reliable trade press since 1970 plus three scholarly articles.

ACTIVITY: Find monographs (scholarly books)

_____Search the name of an author you found in the recommended further reading section in your historical encyclopedia or perhaps a textbook. (Most textbooks offer a list of suggestions for further reading at the end of the relevant chapter).

_____Search using one or more of the keywords you found in the encyclopedic articles.

Simple versus advanced search: Most catalog systems offer a "simple search" with one textbox in which to type your search words, but if you click on "advanced search" you will see several textboxes and often the choice of "and" or "or" between the textboxes. Choose "and" if you want results that include the words you typed into both textboxes. Choose "or" if you want one or the other (although you often get too many hits this way). If you get too many hits (more than one thousand), remember to put quotation marks around an exact phrase, for example, "Nanking Massacre" or "Kennedy Assassination." Note spelling variations. "Nanking" is also spelled "Nanjing." Search under both spellings.

_____Use the keywords associated with your search that pop up with your "hits," that is your list of book titles, by clicking on the titles to discover more information about them.

_____Use the subject terms that pop up with your hits.

(Subjects are useful but you can't guess them. They are created by the specialists who classify books. If you find a good book, look at the full online catalog description. Each book is usually categorized under more than one subject heading. For example, a book on the Nanking Massacre might list this as a subject: "Nanking Massacre, Nanjing, Jiangsu Sheng, China, 1937." Click on the subject heading and you'll find more books on that subject.)

_____If you cannot find enough books in your own college library, see whether your library belongs to a larger, multiple-college system that you can search online. If your library subscribes to it, you can also search WorldCat. Be sure to give yourself enough time to order books through WorldCat via interlibrary loan. Check with your librarian about delivery times.

_____If you still cannot find books, TALK TO A LIBRARIAN. Finding books is sometimes more of an art than a science. Don't give up too soon. Ask first.

_____Eliminate books published before 1970 (or whatever year your instructor suggests).

_____If your books are not published by an academic or university press, check to make sure that they are published by a reliable trade press.

How can you be sure you have located a scholarly monograph? If your book is published by a university press or a reliable trade press, you can be quite confident. If in doubt, check to see whether you can answer at least two of the following three questions positively.

Does the book have footnotes or endnotes?

Does the book have a bibliography? (Sadly, economic pressures sometimes exclude this component.)

Does the book have an index?

ACTIVITY: Find scholarly articles

How are you supposed to know which articles are "scholarly" and which are not? Use your college library research databases, such as JSTOR or Project Muse. These databases include only scholarly articles, that is, they were peer reviewed, which means that they were critiqued by other scholars in the field before they were accepted for publication. Your college library may have different databases. As always, check with a librarian.

_____On JSTOR, click on "advanced search." This will enable you to limit your search as instructed.

_____In the appropriate fields, type in your keywords (you should have a list by now).

_____In the appropriate fields, limit your search by date (when the article was published, so again, after 1970 or the date set by your instructor).

_____Check the "articles" box to be sure your hits include only articles.

_____Scroll through the disciplines and click on "History."

_____Click on "search."

_____The first ten articles that JSTOR presents are not necessarily the best related to your search. Be discriminating. Read carefully the introduction to each article on line to be sure it fits your needs. Print it only when you are confident that it is relevant. Most articles are more than thirty pages long. You do not want to use up your print allocation needlessly.

ACTIVITY: Find book reviews

You are about to discover a secret. A well-written book review is like having a seasoned guide on a hike through the woods. When a university press publishes a new book, scholarly journal editors ask scholars in the field to read the book and then write a review. Much like a movie review, it covers the basic scope of the book and delivers an opinion (thumbs-up or thumbs-down), but the best reviewers also ask: does this book offer something new? To answer this question, writers frequently mention what previous scholars have said about the subject before this new book appeared. **This is historiography**. Pay close attention to the books they discuss in addition to the book they are reviewing and what they are saying about them.

_____Go to JSTOR online. In Advanced Search, type the author's name in the first box and choose "author" from the drop-down menu to the right of the box. Type the title in the second box and choose "item title" from the drop-down menu to the right of the box.

_____Choose "reviews."

_____Choose "History" from the disciplines.

_____Click on "search."

It can take up to two years for scholarly reviews to appear after a book has been published. In addition, some journals have a "moving wall"; that is, the latest issues are not available online. You may well find reviews of recently published books on the freely available online academic service H-Net. Look up http://www.h-net.org/reviews/home.php/. Above all, do not give up too soon. Ask your instructor or your librarian for assistance if you cannot find a review for a book. Be sure to obtain more than one review of a scholarly monograph. Reviewers generally have different perspectives on the same book. Their views, and their comments, depend heavily on their own academic specialization and their methodological and philosophical standpoints. You will want to read different opinions.

ACTIVITY: Find a hard copy of a scholarly journal

Why? Because it will help you understand what you are finding online. Articles and book reviews are not floating separately in space. They are packaged in a specific way that you can only see in hard copy. And you are about to discover where you might find historiographical essays on your very topic.

_____Find the _American Historical Review_ in recent periodicals, where the newest, individual issues are located. This scholarly journal covers all geographical areas of world history.

_____Look at the table of contents and find one of the following: "Review Essay," "Featured Reviews," and/or "_AHR_ Roundtable" or "_AHR_ Exchange" or "_AHR_ Conversations." Either photocopy the table of contents or make a note of the author/titles/date of publication.

Each of these types of articles typically offers historiography. "Review Essays" are, by nature, historiographical essays. They offer a review of the literature about a certain topic. Even if it is not your topic, take a look at how one of these is written. "Featured Reviews" are longer-than-average book reviews that often feature a brief historiographical discussion of the topic. And finally, if you find an *AHR* Roundtable (or Exchange or Conversation) on your topic, you are lucky indeed. These features include an introductory essay or section on the historiography of the topic, followed by several articles or sections by experts giving their points of view. If you find one of these on your topic, you have struck historiographical gold. Read carefully, take notes, look for sources, and carefully track how these sources are discussed. For example, is one book or article noted as the "first" or "best" on the topic? Is a book or article noted as a game-changer, a publication that changed the way historians viewed that topic? This is the stuff of historiography.

Each subfield of history has its own leading journals, and you would do well to become acquainted with the key journals in the subfield of your topic. You can find the titles of journals using the browsing options on JSTOR and Project Muse. Titles are generally self-explanatory, so you will find and recognize them easily. For example, take a look at the following titles:

- *Hispanic American Historical Review*

- *Gender and History*

- *Journal of Women's History*

- *Journal of the History of Childhood and Youth*

- *International Journal of Middle East Studies*

ACTIVITY: Group discussion

_____Collect your books and articles and get together with a group from your class to talk about your findings. How useful are these sources to you? What kinds of sources did other students find? How did they find them?

❷ Analyzing sources

Once you have your sources, you need to annotate them, that is, take notes of the relevant material for your historiographical essay (or the historiographical section of your research paper). This seems like a daunting task at first. You need to break it down into manageable parts. Annotations help you decide whether a book or article is really useful for your purposes.

ACTIVITY: Scan a monograph

You do not have to read every word of your monograph to acquire a good grasp of its contents. We hope this comes as a pleasant surprise. In this section you will learn to scan intelligently and save yourself a lot of time. Your goal is to gather as much useful information as possible as quickly as possible. Sit down with one of your monographs. Examine each of the following items in order.

_____Write down the *entire* title. Does the title give you some hint of the book's contents?

Most monograph titles first include a short title, a colon, then a longer description, and sometimes a range of dates:

Pakistan: History and Politics, 1947–1971

Others are brief:

Murder of a Medici Princess

Do not assume a title will fit your needs unless you've taken a close look at the actual book. Students often miss the specific period covered by a book and discover too late that it will not be useful.

_____What other information can you get from the front cover?

- Is there an illustration? What is it? What kind of message does it convey? (A paperback will usually have an illustration; a hardback without a dust cover will not.)
- If the book has a dust cover, what does the inside front flap tell you?

_____What does the back cover tell you?

- Is there a succinct summary?
- Are there quotes from other scholars? Do their names and credentials give you any idea about the significance of the book you hold in your hand?
- Is there any information about the author? If there is a dust cover, check the inside back flap for information. Who is this person? What are his/her credentials? Again, a paperback will include this information; a hardback without a dust cover will not.

_____Without reading a word from inside the covers, you should now be able to draft a brief sentence about the book. Try it now. If your book is hardback without a dust cover, you cannot do this part of the exercise. Start with the table of contents.

_____Look at the table of contents. How is the book organized? What is its structure? Are there subsections; if so, what kind of issues do they cover? Is the book organized chronologically or thematically? Mention these elements only if they seem relevant.

_____Read the introduction. Students instinctively skip introductions. This is a big mistake. You save time here. In this section of the book the author explains why s/he wrote the book, how s/he grappled with previous scholarship, what theoretical perspectives shaped the research, and how s/he answered her research question. In other words, here is where you find the thesis (the answer to the research question). Read through the introduction and try to locate the following:

_____The historical problem that propelled him or her into writing the book (purpose: why s/he wrote the book).

_____The question that guided his or her research (research question).

_____The categories of analysis s/he uses (race, class, gender, generations).

_____What other historians have written on the topic (historiography or literature review).

_____The key primary sources used to find an answer to the question (evidence).

_____His or her response to the research question (thesis or argument, which often begins with the markers "I argue" or "I contend" or "I claim").

_____Read the conclusion. Here the author summarizes the key findings of the book and explains to you why the findings are important. S/he answers the "so what?" question. (What was at stake? What do we know now that we didn't know before, and why does it matter?)

_____Write a summary of the author's research question and answer, based only on the introduction and conclusion.

_____Skim each chapter.

_____Read the introduction and conclusion of each chapter. Look for each chapter's research question and answer (thesis).

_____Are there subheadings? How do they help structure chapter sections, guide your reading, and facilitate your understanding?

_____Are there quotations? Do they support the author's points?

_____Are there illustrations, charts, tables? Do they support the author's points?

ACTIVITY: Write a book annotation

An annotation is a brief description of a scholarly book that includes the scope of the book (subject, place, time period) and the primary points made by the author. Some instructors may ask you to submit an annotated bibliography of your sources. If so, your task is to demonstrate that these sources are useful to your topic. Write one now on the book you have just scanned.

EXAMPLE OF A STRONG ANNOTATION

Deutsch, Sarah. *Women and the City: Gender, Space, and Power in Boston, 1870–1940.* New York: Oxford University Press, 2000.

In this book, Sarah Deutsch, then an associate professor of history at the University of Arizona, argues that between the end of the Civil War and World War II, women drastically changed the city of Boston, from defining acceptable public behavior to the actual physical layout of the city. Tracing the activities not only of upper-class women, but of

continued on next page

continued

working-class and middle-class women, Deutsch contends that women were powerful agents in creating public spaces for themselves that did not exist at the start of the period. Although women never achieved total freedom or acceptance in public spaces, and not all women enjoyed the same level of freedom or power, Deutsch's findings change the way we understand the creation of the twentieth-century city. This book is useful for my paper on the New Woman in the 1910s because it offers me insight into what urban women were doing at that time in a major city.

EXAMPLE OF A WEAK ANNOTATION

Sarah Deutsch, *Women and the City* (Oxford University Press).

This book talks about women in Boston who lived in the city and were able to change the way the city was. The period is from 1870 to 1940. Women at this time were unable to be in public because of male spitting and other activities and during this time were able to make progress in terms of politics and also creating spaces in public for women. Since it covers the 1910s, the period I am looking at for New Women, this book will be useful for my paper.

Notice:

1. *The incomplete and incorrect title (use the Chicago Style for bibliography format):*
2. *The phrase "this book talks about" (books can't talk; also avoid "deals with");*
3. *The weak and grammatically poor summary;*
4. *The lack of identification of a thesis or argument; and*
5. *The incomplete summary and analysis. It is not enough to state that a book will be useful; you need to explain why.*

ACTIVITY: Anatomy of a scholarly article

Scholarly articles, like the ones you found on JSTOR, are actually close to what your history thesis or capstone paper will look like. By taking a scholarly article apart, you can see how it was put together. This exercise will help you read scholarly articles, which can be a bit daunting. It will also help you understand how to put together your own paper, which should have the same elements.

Like monographs, scholarly articles have been read and approved by a number of experts in the field before they were published ("peer reviewed"). All journals in JSTOR and ProjectMuse follow a peer-review process, so you can rely on their level of scholarship. Check with your librarians if you use other databases.

_____Find a scholarly article on your topic (see "Activity: Find Scholarly Article" above if you have not completed that activity).

_____How does the article begin? Does it begin with an anecdote, story, or "hook" of some kind to try to grab your interest? Does it start by posing a historical problem? Does it wade right into a historiographical debate? Or does it attract your attention in some other way? Your paper will need a similar introduction.

_____Find the author's research question. What is it? Write it down or underline it. Where does it appear?

_____Find the author's argument/thesis, that is, the answer to the research question. What is it? Write it down or underline it. Where does it appear? Both research question and answer/thesis should appear in the first quarter of the paper. Is it fuzzy? Confusing?

_____Does the author position his or her question/thesis in the context of what other historians have said about this topic? In other words, is there a historiographical section? If so, circle it. Where does it appear? Does it help make this research question/thesis seem important?

_____What sources does this author use? Are there quotes? Visual images? Graphs? Tables? If not, should there be? If so, do they seem necessary?

_____How does the article proceed? Chronologically? Thematically?

_____By the end of the article, were you convinced by the author's original point/thesis/argument, and has it been amply demonstrated? If not, why not?

ACTIVITY: Write an annotation of a scholarly article

Some of the questions above are irrelevant for some articles. Use your judgment to answer appropriate questions for the articles you have selected. Once you have the answers to these questions, you can write an annotation or an article review. Article annotations are similar to book annotations.

EXAMPLE OF A STRONG ARTICLE ANNOTATION

Wehrle, Edmund F. "'Aid Where It Is Needed Most': American Labor's Military–Industrial Complex." *Enterprise & Society* 12 (2011): 96–119.

Although it seems unlikely that labor unions and the military–industrial complex of the Cold War would have much in common, Wehrle argues that, in fact, labor leaders encouraged and used military spending to aid workers, such as urging that defense spending during the Korean War be aimed at areas that were suffering from the greatest unemployment. The AFL-CIO even became an active supporter of fallout shelter construction during the Cold War to enhance opportunities for American workers. One of the important arguments made by Wehrle in this article is that the military–industrial complex was not so powerful that it fit all resources to its own ends, but that even labor unions could harness the military–industrial complex to fit a more social vision of the democratic state. This article will be useful for my research paper on Civil Defense during the American Cold War because it shows that the encouragement to build bomb shelters came from several sources: not just the government or manufacturers of bomb shelters, but even labor unions.

EXAMPLE OF A WEAK ARTICLE ANNOTATION

Edmund Wehrle, "Aid Where It Is Needed Most," 12 (2011): 96–119.

This article talks about how labor unions during the Cold War were in favor of fallout shelters. It also talks about how defense spending was used to put workers back to work during the Korean War. This article will be useful because it mentions fallout shelters, which my paper is about.

Notice:

1. *The incomplete and incorrect title (use the Chicago Style for bibliography format);*
2. *The phrase "this article talks about" (articles can't talk; also avoid "deals with");*
3. *The weak summary;*
4. *The lack of identification of a thesis or argument; and*
5. *Incomplete summary and analysis. It is not enough to state that an article will be useful; you need to explain why.*

❸ Writing a historiographical essay

Now it is time for you to write a historiographical essay on your own topic. You have everything you need.

Examples of historiographical writing are provided at the end of this workbook chapter.

Your instructor will give you the technical specifications of your paper (for example, number of pages, font, margin dimensions) and any special instructions. Here, we give you a general format for a historiographical paper. Those of you who are writing a historiographical section for your final research paper will need to adjust to those instructions.

What will the historiographical essay look like? The content will consist of the following.

A. **YOUR TOPIC:** An introduction to the topic at hand that provides a historical context. What is your research question and why do you think it is important and interesting? What is the scope (event, place, time period)? Do not begin your paper with clichéd phrases such as "since the beginning of time" or "throughout history." You are not dealing with all of history. Introduce *your* topic in its relevant context. Look at the scholarly articles you found to get some ideas. The introduction should not exceed twenty percent of your allotted length. By the end of your introduction, you should have introduced your research question.

B. **HISTORIOGRAPHY:** The body of the paper will concern how historians have treated your topic over time. Most of the time, it is simplest to write chronologically.

Who was the first to write about your topic? You should know that by now based on the research you have done thus far on your topic. Who subsequently mentioned that first author and disagreed with him or her? Was there a general understanding of your topic thirty or fifty years ago that is now considered outdated? Your book reviews may tell you this. This is where any relevant historiographical essays, say from the *American Historical Review,* will come in handy. You now need to grapple with authors' arguments, approaches, frameworks, and evidence.

    i. Are some arguments more convincing than others?

    ii. Do certain approaches offer advantages over others?

    iii. Do authors build on the work of previous scholars and engage with each other's work?

    iv. Can you detect any biases, assumptions, or presuppositions held by authors? If so, discuss them.

C. CHICAGO STYLE CITATIONS (endnote or footnotes—ask your instructor).

D. CONCLUSION: Your conclusion depends on your assignment.

    v. Historiographical essay

       1. How have scholars contributed to changing the field?

    vi. Historiographical section of your research paper

       1. How will you approach your topic now that you know how other historians have treated it?

       2. What have historians left undone?

       3. What questions remain to be answered?

       4. What is your guiding research question?

④ Addendum

For those who like to look at models of how it should be done, we offer two examples here to inspire you:

    A. The historiographical section from the introduction to an article by Sarah Kinkel on naval reform in eighteenth-century Britain.

    B. The historiographical section of a research paper written by a college student.

A. EXAMPLE OF HISTORIOGRAPHY BY A PROFESSIONAL HISTORIAN

Kinkel, Sarah. "Disorder, Discipline, and Naval Reform in Mid-Eighteenth-Century Britain." *English Historical Review* **128, no. 535 (2013): 1451–82.**

Note: The article was published in a British journal and contains British spellings, punctuation, and citation conventions.

continued on next page

continued

Britain had very few naval successes to point to in the early years of the War of Jenkins' Ear (1739–48) and the War of the Austrian Succession (1742–8). The widely lauded success of Admiral Edward Vernon in capturing Porto Bello in November 1739 was followed by the abortive siege of St Augustine (1740), the destructive and counter-productive attacks on Cartagena (1741) and Cuba (1741), and the battles of La Guaira (1743) and Puerto Cabello (1743), all of which took place in the Spanish Caribbean and all of which resulted in either the defeat or withdrawal of British naval forces. These were followed by the Battle of Toulon (1744), during which the British Mediterranean fleet allowed blockaded French forces to escape, and the Battle of Negapatam (1744), by which France conquered the British colony of Madras in India. In contrast to these early disappointments, the naval engagements of the later years of the war included the capture of Louisburg (1745), decisive victories at the First and Second Battles of Finisterre (1747), a defeat at the Second Battle of Santiago de Cuba (1748), and a more limited victory at the Battle of Havana (1748). Britain's naval success was even more pronounced in the Seven Years War, which followed a decade later, in which the Navy supported the capture by British forces of French Canada, many Caribbean islands, areas of French Africa, French Indian ports and Spanish Manila, as well as achieving definitive victories on the seas in battles such as those at Quiberon Bay and Lagos (both 1759). Why, then, did Britain's Navy become more successful in the late 1740s?[1]

Historians attempting to explain this turnaround in British naval fortunes have given some attention to a series of reforms enacted by the Admiralty Board in the years 1745–9. Changes implemented during this time included modifications in dockyard infrastructure, revised systems of promotion and retirement, the introduction of the first naval uniform, new ship designs, and an increased emphasis on training. The Admiralty Board consisted of a combination of political figures and high-ranking sea officers. The principal members of the Board during these years were John Russell, fourth duke of Bedford; John Montagu, fourth earl of Sandwich; and Admiral George Anson. All three came into power at the Board in December 1744, with Bedford as First Lord of the Admiralty and head of the Board. When Bedford moved on to become Secretary of State for the Southern Department in 1748, Sandwich succeeded him; Anson succeeded Sandwich in 1751. A variety of other members of the Board, both sea officers and politicians, also came and went during these years. Although the Admiralty Board consisted of seven members at any given time, much of the historical literature has suggested that, in the words of Daniel Baugh, "the improvements of leadership at sea after 1744 came largely through the efforts of a single, dedicated officer," namely, George Anson.[2] "By the middle of the century," writes Clive Wilkinson, "George Anson had transformed the Navy, both as a fighting force and as a civil department of the State."[3] N.A.M. Rodger also argues that "the transformation in a dozen years from the humiliating failures of the early 1740s to the triumphs of the Seven Years' War" was the consequence of Anson's "rigorous devotion to high standards of training and conduct" and that Anson was "one of the key figures in the creation of a distinctive naval ethos . . . the ingrained assumption that a man's first duty was to the good of the Service." He concludes that "the Navy of the Seven Years' War was what Anson had made it, and the list of its virtues is to a great extent the list of his achievements."[4]

Historians have described these reforms as uncontroversial, in part because the reforms were essentially rational, and in part because they perceive the Navy itself to have been apolitical. They have taken the view that any officer of Anson's generation would have implemented these reforms, but he happened to be the first one in a position of power to do so. As Brian Lavery writes, "At forty-seven he was much younger than any of his recent predecessors, and able to view the problems with a fresh eye."[5] Anson's experience led him naturally to see that the Royal Navy was inefficient, factional and out of date and, consequently, the reforms were, G. S. Smith has asserted, no more than a matter of "common sense."[6] This account of unproblematic modernisation fits in with an understanding of the Navy as a point of consensus in eighteenth-century British society. Rodger describes the "strong, consistent and broad-based political support" which surrounded what John Brewer calls a "virtually incontestable shibboleth"; Jeremy Black argues that the Navy was "one of the few fields in which opposition criticism was not directed at the fundamental bases of government policy."[7] This consensus was based on the vision of the Navy as a bastion of liberty: unlike a professional standing army, a navy would be confined to the seas, could not enter civilians' homes, and therefore could not crush civilian liberties.

What is absent from these narratives is an awareness of the important roles played by the two other principal members of the Admiralty Board, the duke of Bedford and the earl of Sandwich, in developing the reform programme. Omitting the politicians from the narrative precludes a full understanding of the imperatives which made naval reform a priority; in particular, it obscures a crucial component of Britain's naval resurgence, that is the connection between these politicians' actions at the Admiralty Board and their other political projects. Undoubtedly Anson's experience as an officer contributed to his conception of how to remedy the perceived problems of the Navy, but experience is filtered through ideology: different individuals may perceive the same problems, but propose very different solutions. Indeed, some officers with just as much experience as Anson—such as the celebrated Admiral Vernon—opposed the majority of the Admiralty Board reforms, some of which also generated widespread discontent within the sea service at large. Contrary to the historians' consensus, the reforms were not uncontroversial within the service, nor were they apolitical: one element of the reforms—a recodification of court-martial law—spawned an intense parliamentary debate and a series of pamphlets and newspaper articles, in which opponents denounced the bill for initiating oriental despotism in Britain. Some claimed the bill was intended to "make [sea officers] the cut-throats of the state . . . to make them the Admiralty Janissaries."[8] Others compared sea officers to mamelukes. (The Janissaries were the household troops and bodyguards of the Ottoman sultans; the mamelukes were the slave soldiers of Egypt.) One Londoner remarked at the time that the "affairs of the Navy have lately much engaged the thought and conversation of this Town," adding that "matters have been carried on with much warmth."[9] Thus, though the naval reforms might seem to be of small interest in and of themselves, they had a much greater significance for contemporaries.

The naval reforms of the 1740s were linked to both imperial and constitutional debates. Observers viewed the attempted reforms in the context of the other actions and preoccupations of the political members of the Board and thus interpreted them through an ideological prism. Bedford and Sandwich were at least as influential in pushing the reform of the Navy as Anson; in fact, some of the reforms instituted during their terms as First Lord fell by the wayside during that of Anson. Bedford and Sandwich believed the primary flaws undermining the Navy's performance were disorder and disobedience;

continued on next page

continued

this disorder threatened the Navy's capacity to expand and secure an American empire. Their solution was to impose discipline and hierarchy, and thereby to create order and enable success. Discipline and hierarchy were the same tools that Bedford, Sandwich and their associates would deploy during the next three decades when faced with disorder in either imperial or domestic society. In contrast, resistance to the naval reforms came overwhelmingly from the "patriot" opposition. The patriots valued liberty and civic participation; they resisted the expansion of ministerial power because of the corrupting consequences it was believed to have for political virtue. Their interpretation of Britain's naval failures lay in the restraints that the long-serving Prime Minister, Robert Walpole, had placed on the Navy; success would come once the Navy was permitted to fight aggressively, under a free and virtuous leadership. According to these patriots, the sea service did not need to be changed; it only needed to be unleashed. Creating a naval force bound by discipline and strict hierarchy both infringed on the liberties of those in the service and created an extraordinarily dangerous weapon in the hands of ministers: a professional military capable of subverting the constitution. For them, naval reform did indeed raise the spectre of despotism.

The naval reforms of the 1740s created, for the first time, a professionalised naval force. The Admiralty Board did not simply attempt to oil the wheels of the service, as it were; they intended to create a new culture of naval service, the "distinctive naval ethos" referred to by Rodger. This new ethos was, however, politically controversial: the importance of unquestioning obedience was not a universally accepted value. It was also divisive because the subordination of individuals (including those with honourable personal reputations) to ministerial authority was seen as emblematic of other wider concerns over the decay of British society and the country's political future. Thus, the naval reforms provide a window into the early stages of wider socio-political tensions which would harden and escalate during the following decades. These tensions were sometimes still inchoate and the lines of debate were not yet defined, but their existence suggests that there were deeper roots to the arguments over disorder, empire, obedience and the constitution which shook the Anglo-imperial world in the 1760s and 1770s. Only by contextualising the reforms within the political worldview of the members of the Admiralty Board—and that of their opponents—can we truly understand the contemporary implications of the alterations in naval culture that occurred during this period.

NOTES

* I am grateful to the Duke of Bedford for his permission to use the archives at Woburn Abbey; all material cited from these papers appears by kind permission of the Duke of Bedford and the Trustees of the Bedford Estate. The research for this article was supported by the Smith Richardson Foundation and the MacMillan Center, John F. Enders Fellowship, and Georg W. Leitner Program in International and Comparative Political Economy of Yale University. I would also like to thank the EHR's anonymous readers for their extremely helpful comments and suggestions.

1. By "success" I mean the extent to which the British Navy was able to achieve its own priorities, which included the ability to force decisive battles and the ability to protect trade against foreign predators. The French and Spanish navies had other priorities which did not include forcing decisive battles, and in any comparison they should be judged based on their ability to achieve their own priorities rather than those of another power. Over the course of the eighteenth century, the British Navy increasingly succeeded in forcing decisive battles, blockading enemy fleets, and protecting British trade. Privateers from the French privateering hub of Saint-Malo captured 858 ships in the

wars of 1695–1713, but only forty-one in those of 1756–63, for example. Though privateering once again became a concern during the American Revolutionary War, the Admiralty convoy system also improved during the century and, by the time of the French Revolutionary Wars, could organise convoys protecting up to a thousand ships; as a consequence, during those wars, the number of British merchant ships actually increased: P. Crowhurst, *The Defence of British Trade, 1689–1815* (Folkestone, 1977), pp. 28, 71–80.

2. D. Baugh, *British Naval Administration in the Age of Walpole* (Princeton, NJ, 1965), p. 504.

3. C. Wilkinson, *The British Navy and the State in the Eighteenth Century* (Woodbridge, 2004), p. 211.

4. N. A. M. Rodger, *The Wooden World: An Anatomy of the Georgian Navy* (New York, 1996), p. 31.

5. B. Lavery, *The Ship of the Line* (2 vols., Annapolis, MD, 1983), i. 90; N. A. M. Rodger, *The Command of the Ocean: A Naval History of Britain 1649–1815* (New York, 2004); Sir John Barrow, *The Life of George, Lord Anson, Admiral of the Fleet, Vice-Admiral of Great Britain, and First Lord Commissioner of the Admiralty, previous to, and during, the Seven Years' War* (London, 1839); W. V. Anson, *The Life of Admiral Lord Anson, the Father of the British Navy, 1697–1762* (London, 1912).

6. G. S. Graham, "The Naval Defence of British North America, 1739–1763," *Transactions of the Royal Historical Society*, 4th ser., xxx (1948), p. 108.

7. Rodger, *Command of the Ocean*, pp. 178, 577; J. Brewer, *The Sinews of Power: War, Money, and the English State, 1688–1783* (Cambridge, MA, 1988), p. 33; J. Black, "Introduction," in J. Black and P. Woodfine, eds., *The British Navy and the Use of Naval Power in the Eighteenth Century* (Leicester, 1988), p. 3.

8. Seaman [Augustus Hervey], *A Detection of the Considerations on the Navy-Bill* (London, 1749), p. 15; [Cobbett's] P[arliamentary] H[istory] (36 vols., London, 1806–20), xiv. 542, 550 (John Perceval, second earl of Egmont, Debate in the Commons on the Bill for subjecting Half-Pay Naval Officers to Martial Law, 1 Feb. 1749).

9. Stafford, Staffordshire Record Office, D1798/HMDrakeford/22, J. Ayscough to Richard Drakeford, 11 Mar. 1749.

B. EXAMPLE OF HISTORIOGRAPHY BY A COLLEGE STUDENT

THESIS TITLE: The Northern Noose: Racial Discrimination in Housing and Martin Luther King Jr.'s Chicago Campaign, 1966

HISTORIOGRAPHY SECTION:

The Civil Rights Movement of the mid-twentieth century is one of the most studied periods in the history of the United States. It has received both mass popular and scholarly attention in the decades which have followed it. However, the focus of this attention has been uneven over the years, with certain stories being thoroughly examined and others being left relatively ignored. This paper's focus is pointed towards the latter, namely Martin Luther King's time in Chicago (a campaign which would come to be known as the Chicago Freedom Movement). While materials on Southern campaigns, such as the Montgomery Bus Boycott and protests in Birmingham, are abundant, the same cannot

continued

be said for King's time in Chicago, a fact noted by David J. Garrow, a well-known biog-rapher of King and Civil Rights historian, in *Chicago 1966: Open Housing Marches, Summit Negotiations, And Operation Breadbasket* (1989). In that book's introduction, Garrow wrote: "The Chicago Freedom Movement of 1966 was as significant a campaign as any that was mounted during the black freedom struggle of the 1950's and 1960's, but now, almost twenty-five years later, it is neither among the best remembered nor most celebrated."[2] Historians seem to have neglected the Chicago movement.

Vincent Gordon Harding, a prominent African American historian and religious scholar, wrote of the "amnesia" which plagues the study of this time in King's life in a 1987 article.[3] He believes that this period in the Civil Rights Movement is too difficult for many Americans to focus on. Hardened by the realities of economic racism, splits within the Civil Rights Movement, and the escalating war in Vietnam, King's writings and speeches took on a new "harshness."[4] King believed the only way to address the issues of those in the ghettos and those who suffered was a "radical redistribution of economic and political power" in America.[5] The image which this presents, of radicalization and extremeness, is one which is difficult for both the public and scholars to reconcile with the King of the 1950's and early 1960's. Both scholars and the public have chosen to view King through the "narrow civil rights frame" and ignore the coarse battle against poverty and greed which characterized his activities from 1966 onwards.[6] The ignorance which exists five decades later is important to examine because it helps to highlight many of the social and cultural obstacles which King would have faced in 1966 and the last few years of his life.

One of the most comprehensive studies to date on this issue is James R. Ralph's *Northern Protest: Martin Luther King Jr., Chicago, and the Civil Rights Movement* (1993). The book, lauded by William Grimshaw as "a significant contribution" to the field, focuses on the African American community in Chicago and their response to King's campaign.[7] Ralph writes that King never really had the support of the majority of Chicago's African Americans. Many African Americans in Chicago did not want to work with southern-ers who they did not believe had their interests at stake. Activists reported that African American Chicagoans, ". . . told us to go back down South where we came from."[8] While the city remained one of the most segregated in the country, 30 percent of its African Americans citizens were considered middle class.[9] People pointed to statistics such as these and claimed that progress was being made in Chicago, even if it was gradual.

While competing views exist on the cause of the Chicago campaign's failure, nearly all scholars who write about it agree that it was indeed a failure. The Chicago Freedom Movement was able to obtain written agreements from the city, but they ultimately came on the city's and Mayor Richard Daley's terms and proved to be little more than prom-ises. The evolving study of this topic presents a number of opportunities for a better un-derstanding of the reasons behind Martin Luther King's failures in Chicago. Through all of these sources, a clearer picture of the city which King encountered in 1966 develops. Firsthand accounts testify to the prominent divisions within the city's civil rights orga-nizations, including an evolving rift within the African American community, not only in Chicago but across the country. King had lost the support of many of these people, who believed his campaigns of non-violence were not extreme enough to address their situ-ation or anger. And then there were outside groups, notably Northern whites, who had once been close allies of the Civil Rights Movement. However, the changing environment of the nation and the perceived radicalization of the Civil Rights struggle had changed these groups from allies to antagonists.

NOTES

2. David J. Garrow, ed. *Chicago 1966: Open Housing Marches, Summit Negotiations, and Operation Breadbasket* (New York: Carlson Publishing Inc., 1989), ix.

3. Vincent Gordon Harding, "Beyond Amnesia: Martin Luther King Jr., and the Future of America", *The Journal of American History* 74, no. 2 (1987): 468–76.

4. Harding, "Beyond Amnesia," 474.

5. Ibid., 473.

6. Wesley Hogan, review of *From Civil Rights to Human Rights: Martin Luther King Jr. and the Struggle for Economic Justice*, by Thomas F. Jackson, *Reviews in American History* 35, no. 4 (2007): 642.

7. William Grimshaw, review of *Northern Protest: Martin Luther King Jr., Chicago, and the Civil Rights Movement*, by James R. Ralph, *The Journal of American History* 81, no. 4 (1995): 1836.

8. James R. Ralph, *Northern Protest: Martin Luther King Jr., Chicago, and the Civil Rights Movement*, (Cambridge, MA: Harvard University Press, 1993), 45.

9. Ralph, *Northern Protest*, 44.

Working with Primary Sources
Workbook Exercises

Chapter Four defined primary sources and suggested where to find them. This section will direct you to find specific kinds of primary sources and begin the task of analysis. In this workbook chapter we will use actual scholarly articles to (1) see how historians use primary sources, (2) discover how to use citations as an "address" to locate sources, and (3) find and analyze similar sources. Here it becomes clear that the first purpose of footnotes or endnotes is not to prevent plagiarism, but to help other scholars track down relevant sources.

The first set of examples comes from an article by Nick Cullather, "The Foreign Policy of the Calorie," *American Historical Review* 112, no. 2 (April 2007): 337–64. The *American Historical Review* is the premier history journal published in the United States and can be found in most college and university digital holdings through *JSTOR*. This article was chosen for its global reach, and because the author employed a wide variety of sources to argue that the seemingly neutral, scientific definition of the calorie naturalizes what are really social, cultural, and political meanings and uses. For the sake of clarity and brevity, the citations have been edited.

① Using film as a primary source

It is a time-honored strategy to begin a scholarly article (or thesis) with an anecdote designed to entice the reader. On the very first page (p. 337) Cullather cites from a popular documentary film *Super Size Me* (2004). This scholar uses the interviews recorded in this theatrically released film as evidence that although most Americans have only a hazy understanding of the scientific definition of a calorie, calories are nevertheless freighted with power: they are "not good," they are "something you should count," they must be listed on the side of a cereal box. The filmmaker had a different use for these quotes, but they also supported Cullather's thesis that such hazy understanding is both the consequence and the source of government power to define and monitor caloric information. Thus these quotes work in a similar fashion to oral history for Cullather because they come directly from historical actors in the time and place he is studying, which stretches into the present:

> The ninth-graders had fully absorbed the governmentality of the calorie; they understood that it patterns food with particular obligations, aesthetic and hygienic norms, and techniques of management. Knowing too much about an indicator's original purpose, or what it actually records, might only diminish its authority.[1]

[1.] Nick Cullather, "The Foreign Policy of the Calorie," *The American Historical Review* 112, no. 2 (April 2007): 337.

FIGURE 4.1. *Super Size Me* (2004) Movie Poster. ROADSIDE / GOLDWYN / THE KOBAL COLLECTION.

Documentaries and even fictional films can be used by historians, if they are used cautiously. Chapter Four refers to *Casablanca*, 1942, distributed by Warner Brothers, Los Angeles. It is a love story set in Morocco against the backdrop of then-raging World War II. Could you use it as evidence of conditions in Africa during the World War II? No, but you could use it to describe the culture of the American home front. Like America itself before Pearl Harbor, Rick, the fictional, self-interested bar owner, appears only interested in making a profit, but ends up sacrificing the love of his life for the Allied cause.

ACTIVITY: Using film as a primary source

Choose one documentary film that you have seen plus one fictional film and complete the following for each film:

A. Cite the film using Cullather's citation style:

[1] *Super Size Me*, 2005, distributed by Samuel Goldwyn Films, Los Angeles.

_____Why are the date, production company, and place important to know?

_____Where can you find trustworthy information about the production credits for your chosen films?

B. Consider the content:
_____What is the film about?

_____Is it a remake of an earlier film or based on a source or event that happened long before the film was made?

FIGURE 4.2. *Casablanca* (1942) Movie Poster. WARNER BROS / THE KOBAL COLLECTION.

_____Is there anything about the conditions under which the film was made (wartime, for example) that might influence the final product?

_____Do these circumstances change the way a historian can interpret the film?

_____Was this a major theatrical release seen by large audiences or a small independent film seen by relatively few people?

C. Consider film reviews as part of your research.

_____First, find a film review published in a major news source, such as *The New York Times* or the *Times* (London), and printed just after the first release of the film.

_____Then find a review from a popular film review website, such as *Rotten Tomatoes* (http://www.rottentomatoes.com/).

_____Consider both reviews. Which is more helpful to the historian? How can they both be used?

D. Consider how the film might be used by a historian.

_____Create a historical research question that one of your films might be able to address.

_____What are the benefits and limits of using films in a history thesis? Could a history thesis be sustained solely through the use of films as primary sources?

② Using maps and data as primary sources

Cullather cites a map produced by the United Nations World Food Programme to demonstrate how the apparently scientific definition of the calorie can be loaded with political meanings that distort its neutrality. Here is the footnote for the map:

⁶ World Food Programme, Interactive Hunger Map, http://www.wfp.org/country_brief/hunger_map/map/hungermap_popup/map_popup.html (accessed February 20, 2007).

A student interested in seeing this map would type in the URL, only to find disappointment. The page is missing. After all, the map was cited some years ago (why the "accessed" date is important). However, if the resourceful student typed "World Food Programme" into a search engine, she would discover that the map was updated in 2013 and does the same work that Cullather notes: "the outlines of the caloric deficit align with national frontiers; hungry nations are marked in bright red, while cooler shades blue and green indicate progressive degrees of satiety."[2]

FIGURE 4.3.   World Food Programme World Hunger Map 2014 edition. © World Food Programme, 2014.

What is wrong with this map? First, Cullather argues, it indicates that entire countries can be defined as well-fed or malnourished, when in fact such conditions are localized and would presumably produce a different map; second, this map implicitly suggests that the well-fed countries could, and perhaps should, share with the malnourished; and third, the map concludes that food "has a standard value that can be tabulated as easily

_____

2. Ibid., 339.

as currency or petroleum."[3] This map uses the seemingly neutral measurement of the calorie in a distorted fashion that has real-world implications for foreign policy.

ACTIVITY: Maps and data

Historians are concerned with change over time, but we are often challenged to explain change over *time* as well as *space*. Choose one of the images from the "Gallery" page of the Stanford Spatial History Project: https://web.stanford.edu/group/spatialhistory/cgi-bin/site/gallery.php/. This site has a global reach, from the spatial history of the arrest of Italian Jews during World War II to prostitution arrests in Philadelphia during World War I, but it is primarily twentieth century. Many of the maps are interactive and/or animated. Examine the map of your choosing, and answer the following:

_____What research question was this map designed to answer?

_____What kind of information did it reveal that could not have been made visible through words alone?

Try your hand at creating a simple map based on your own research question using Google Maps Engines (https://mapsengine.google.com/map/). Create a research question that might benefit from a map. Keep it simple; perhaps just knowing the distance between two points might help answer a question about the conditions facing a marching army or a traveling wagon of goods.

_____Choose "Create New Map" and go to "Base Map" to choose what kind of map would work best for your question. For the examples above, you might want to choose a map that illustrates the terrain. For a political question, you might want to choose a map that shows borders (this tool does limit you to twenty-first-century political borders, but it is global).

_____Choose at least two points. Type the name of the places you would like to mark in the search box. Click on the icon that looks like a ruler to measure the distance between points.

_____You can build layers into your map, each with a different set of data. See the "Help" function for specific instructions. For example, type in the name of current business and find those locations. You can import photos for each of your data points. It becomes really useful if you have data in a spreadsheet, for example, census information that includes location as well as information on income, purchases, household composition, occupation, etc.

_____Click on the folder icon to save and to print your map.

❸ Newspapers and popular journals as primary sources

Students are often surprised at the number of newspapers and popular journals (not scholarly journals) that are cited by professional historians, although, of course, only

---

[3.] Ibid.

those working after the invention of the printing press can profitably use these kinds of primary materials. For many students, this will be the richest, and frankly easiest, category to mine for primary source data. Cullather used a number of these sources to write the following passage:

> The work of rendering food into hard figures began just after breakfast on Monday, March 23, 1896, when Wilbur O. Atwater sealed a graduate student into an airtight chamber in the basement of Judd Hall on the Wesleyan University campus. This apparatus was described by the press as resembling a meat locker, a room "about as large as an ordinary convict's cell" . . . It recorded his food intake and labor output in units of thermal energy.[4]

Consider the sources in this footnote, which is the citation for the quote above. (It was the seventh citation in the article). All of these sources are likely to be available to students through their college or university library's digital subscription database. In other words, students need just a laptop to locate the different kinds of sources listed below.

[7] "The Wesleyan Calorimeter," *New York Times,* April 5, 1896, 5; "Occupant of the Wesleyan Cage Changed," *Chicago Daily Tribune,* March 24, 1896, 10; "The Human Body," *Los Angeles Times*, May 3, 1896, 22; "Conservation of Energy in the Human Body," *Scientific American,* August 5, 1899, 85; "Almost a Hero," *Boston Daily Globe,* March 22, 1896, 1.

ACTIVITY: Newspapers and popular journals

This activity asks you to track down each of the individual articles in the citation above. It will not suffice to just find the journal or the newspaper, but you are tasked to find the articles in full-text, as if you needed them for your own research. Printing out each article is the best way to demonstrate that you were successful.

_____Google the articles. Were you able to find full-text versions for free, or were you asked to pay for them? Do not pay for them.

_____Go to your library's online site. If there is a search box, experiment with typing in the title of the article.

_____If that did not work, type in the title of the journal itself, for example, *Chicago Daily News.*

_____If that did not work, go to your library's journals database. There will be an alphabetical list of all the journals they can access through their multiple subscriptions. See whether you can find the titles of the journals listed in the footnote.

_____If you wanted to cut to the chase, you could have begun this exercise by consulting a librarian. The authors of this volume strongly recommend that you make your librarian your research partner, and this includes assistance with the exercises in this book.

Create a historical research question that might be answered using newspapers or popular journals, and then do the following.

[4.] Ibid., 340.

_____Find and print three articles from newspapers or popular journals (remember, not scholarly journals and articles that were published at the time of the historical event you are investigating).

_____Briefly describe how each article addresses the research question.

_____Cite each of your three articles, modeling your citations after the format used by Cullather above.

❹ **Primary printed sources**

Cullather used a printed collection of letters relevant to the League of Nations in his consideration of foreign policy and the calorie. Cullather noted that American Raymond B. Fosdick "sought to 'humanize' the Versailles system by displacing balance-of-power politics with 'a systematic approach to international problems where everybody has everything to gain and nothing to lose.'"[5] This is what his footnote looks like:

> [35] Raymond B. Fosdick, _Letters on the League of Nations: From the Files of Raymond B. Fosdick_ (Princeton, NJ, 1966), 9, 22.

As you can see, it looks like a normal book, and it is. Printed, collected letters are quite valuable to the historian because not only are they typed and thus legible and almost always have a biographical sketch and introductions to letters written by a knowledgeable editor, but also they are easy to obtain. If a volume you wish to see is not on the shelf of your own library, it can be delivered via your consortium of libraries or through interlibrary loan.

ACTIVITY: Using primary printed sources

Use your institution's library to find a primary printed source. It is not always easy to limit a keyword search to primary printed sources, so for our purposes here, type the word "letters" into your keyword search. Your results should include several bound collections of letters from prominent historical figures: Cicero, Thomas Jefferson, Sigmund Freud, etc. Choose one example of a bound collection of letters, find it on the shelf, and take it down to examine it. Then answer the following questions.

_____Who is the editor of the volume? What connection does this scholar have to the author of the letters? Why is he or she qualified to collect and possibly edit the letters?

_____Are the letters edited and how so? Is this a complete volume of all the known letters of this person? Are the letters themselves complete, or have parts of them been modified by the editor or perhaps censored when they were written?

_____Does the collection provide a biographical sketch of the letter writer? How would this be helpful?

_____How are the letters themselves organized? Are there introductions to each section?

_____Choose one letter and analyze it for content:

[5.] Ibid., 355.

_____Who is the letter writer, and why is he or she significant?

_____When was this letter written? What were the relevant circumstances of the letter writer at the time? (Age, place, employment, family, context such as war, peace, childbirth, travel, etc.)

_____Who is the recipient of the letter, and what is the relation of the letter writer to the recipient?

_____Create a historical research question that this letter might address. How could it be helpful? What does it evidence?

⑤ Documents or photographs from an archive

Archival materials run the gamut from handwritten letters, to declarations, telegrams, scrapbooks, rare books, newspaper clippings files, and often photographs. The newspaper accounts cited earlier in this workbook chapter indicate that the "airtight chamber" at Wesleyan University was "about as large as a convict's cell." To make it clearer, on page 343 of his article, Cullather provides a photograph of the chamber that he found in the Wesleyan University Archives:

FIGURE 4.4. Atwater–Rosa Respiration Calorimeter: "An instrument as delicate and sensitive as the nerves of the human body." Atwater's experiments with men sealed inside the respiration calorimeter captivated the national press. Wesleyan University Library, Special Collections & Archives.

Cullather used print-based archival materials as well, including material from a collection of primary documents housed at the Rockefeller Archive Center. Here is his citation for those materials:

[39] See, for instance, Norman Borlaug's 1970 Nobel Prize citation, Rockefeller Foundation Papers, RG 6.7, series 4, subseries 6, box 88, Rockefeller Archive Center, Tarrytown, New York.

If a student believed that this collection housed at the Rockefeller Archive Center looked useful for his own research, he would go online to see whether this collection was digitized and available online. The Center is online at http://www.rockarch.org/. But like most archives, only a few select documents are available in full text. If after checking with the Center and discovering that the documents he seeks are not available in any other form and that he has permission to use the archive and an appointment to do so, this student would be on his way to the archive with an address for the specific document he seeks. A mental map would look like this:

Town: Tarrytown, New York
Archive: Rockefeller Archive Center
Collection: Rockefeller Foundation Papers
Series: 4
Subseries: 6
Box: 88
File: RG 7
Paper: Norman Borlaug's 1970 Nobel Prize citation.

The citation is a trail of breadcrumbs that the student can use to find his way back to the source.

ACTIVITY: Transcribing a handwritten primary source document

As elementary schools cease teaching cursive, younger generations are unable to read handwritten documents even in their native tongue. This is a skill required by the historian; typewritten letters have only been possible since the late nineteenth century, and handwritten letters in cursive were common into the late twentieth century. In this exercise, you will assist the Smithsonian Institution while learning how to read and assess a handwritten document.

_____Register at the Smithsonian Digital Volunteers: Transcription Center more than seventy-five thousand documents wait to be transcribed. Read the brief online training.

_____Choose a document to transcribe. When you are finished, send it on for peer review and then to a trained Smithsonian staff member who may accept it or send it back for editing.

_____What did you find most difficult about reading historic handwriting?

_____What meanings can you glean from a handwritten letter that you cannot get from an email or even a typed document?

FIGURE 4.5. Vintage Handwriting Sample. © Roman Pavlik | Dreamstime.com.

❻ When secondary becomes primary

One of Cullather's arguments is that seemingly neutral scientific data about nutrition were used to justify imperialism. Peoples who were believed to be weak because of incorrect diet would require Western oversight until their poor dietary habits could be corrected. To illustrate these ideas, Cullather mines publications from the period that were originally published as scholarship or medical news. One of the publications below, *The Lancet*, is a prestigious medical journal still published today. In 1937, it represented medical scholarship. In 2007, when Cullather's article was published, he was using it as a primary source to unpack the cultural assumptions believed to be scientific at the time. Dal, mentioned in the quote below, is a dish made of beans, peas, or lentils, typically eaten with rice, which then creates a complete protein. Today it is considered quite nutritious. Here is what Cullather found to be the belief about dal in the 1930s:

> European nutritionists uniformly disparaged rice, while dal, according to McCarrison, had a nutritive factor so low as to be "toxic." These lessons were absorbed into the school curriculum, and Indian students were counseled that "rice is not very nourishing," while dal induced "paralysis of the legs."[6]

[6.] Ibid., 359.

Cullather's sources for this information are scholarly medical journals published in the 1930s:

[46] Robert McCarrison, "The Nutritive Value of Wheat, Paddy, and Certain Other Food-Grains," *Indian Journal of Medical Research* 14, no. 3 (1927): 631–39; Dagmar Curjel Wilson and E. M. Widdowson, "Nutrition and Diet in Northern India," *The Lancet* 233 (December 18, 1937): 1445–48; W. R. Akroyd, *The Nutritive Value of Indian Foods and the Planning of Satisfactory Diets* (Delhi, 1937); John Wallace Megaw, *The First Laws of Health: A Health Reader for Indian Schools* (Bombay, 1924), 12–13.

ACTIVITY: Etiquette manuals

For topics in the nineteenth and twentieth centuries, these kinds of sources are relatively easy to locate and often extremely useful. And they are often fun to read. Examples include etiquette manuals, diet books, career guides, and even historical scholarship itself. As you write your historiographies, you will discover that even history has a history. But this exercise will be limited to a subset of advice books: the etiquette manual.

_____Use your institution's online library catalog to look for "etiquette books" and limit your search to books published before 1950.

_____Find one interesting book and pull it from the shelf. What kind of etiquette book is it? (For men? Women? Business?)

_____Read the introduction and a sample chapter. What can this book tell you about the time and place in which it was published?

_____Why do you think it was published? Why was it written? Why would there be a market for this book at this time and place? Is it prescriptive or descriptive?

⑦ Quoting a primary source found in a secondary source

It is tempting to just want to lift a good quote from a secondary source rather than track down the original source in all the ways just illustrated. It can be a lot of work. It is true that on rare occasions, established scholars do this very thing. The following example of an established scholar using a quote he found in another secondary source is from Kenneth Lipartito's "When Women Were Switches: Technology, Work, and Gender in the Telephone Industry, 1890–1920," which appeared on page 1084 in the *American Historical Review* in October 1994. Here is the passage from the article itself:

> By hiring employees of "good character," telephone firms were seeking workers who could deal with customers "on an equal plane," as one manager put it.[25]

And here is the citation for the passage above:

[25] P. M. Grant, "The Selection and Training of Operators," *Southwestern Telephone News* (August 1908): 2, as quoted in Norwood, *Labor's Flaming Youth*, 41.

Note how the author gives all of the bibliographical information for the primary source and the secondary source, which is abbreviated here because he had cited it in full in a previous citation. The full citation for the secondary source he used is Stephen Norwood, *Labor's Flaming Youth: Telephone Operators and Worker Militancy, 1878–1923* (Urbana, IL, 1990).

The only legitimate reason for quoting from a quote found in a secondary source is that it is impossible for the student to get the original source. This may be because the only copy is in an archive hundreds of miles away or perhaps because it is a quote from an interview that only the author of the secondary source can access. As stated, it is tempting to do this, especially because you now know how to decode the citations, but resist. Go find the original source for yourself. And please do not suggest that you did find the primary source by neglecting to mention the secondary source in your footnote or endnote. This is bad faith, and scholarship can only move forward in an atmosphere of trust and good faith. Cite all of your primary sources, fully and properly.

CHAPTER FIVE

Ensuring a Successful Research Outcome
Workbook Exercises

❶ Using and evaluating websites

As with all your research, you need to evaluate the reliability of the evidence you find on websites. Just as you use your judgment in selecting your scholarly printed sources, so too you need to exercise caution in selecting materials online. In recent years, governments around the world have urged the owners of popular search engines and social media sites to control some of the material that they allow to be published in an effort to ensure that no harm comes to those who use the sites. In some countries, governments overtly control the information their populations have access to. In general, however, there are no gatekeepers to the Internet. Anyone can publish anything, and the quality of information you find online varies enormously. You cannot automatically rely on the information you find there.

ACTIVITY: How much can I rely on the information in this website?

When evaluating a website, you may be swayed by the sophistication of illustrations, an elegant search function, the nature and quality of hyperlinks, and navigability. These elements are important and certainly might influence your assessment of site aesthetics and ease of use, but you need another set of criteria to determine reliability. What does the URL tell you about the origin of the information? Can you find the names of authors, contributors, sponsors, and publishers? What are their credentials? How is the site funded? Does it provide contact information? Does the site provide information relating to the sources of its information; in other words, can you verify the information you find there? How does knowledge about the intended audience affect your assessment? Does the site present information in a balanced way? How are you able to detect bias and verify accuracy? Is the information current, and does that matter? Currency may be important; you will at least want to know that the individuals who provide the content of the website are keeping it up to date. These questions enable us to make a quick assessment of any website to determine its usability. Completing an item check list will facilitate your task and enable you to keep a record of the sites you have evaluated for future reference.

Example One: African Diaspora in the Indian Ocean World. If you wanted to write a research paper on some aspect of the African Diaspora, your first step would likely be to go to your favorite search engine and type in "African Diaspora." We have done likewise and found a large number of websites, from which we have selected one to discuss with you.

FIGURE 5.1. The African Diaspora in the Indian Ocean World webpage from the Schomburg Center for Research in Black Culture at the New York Public Library; http://exhibitions.nypl.org/africansindianocean/index2.php/. Used by permission of the New York Public Library.

CHECK LIST FOR WEBSITE EVALUATION

1. Name of site:
2. URL of main page and subpages:
3. Name and contact information of author(s):
4. Credentials of author(s):
5. Name of publisher or sponsoring institution:
6. Accuracy/verifiability:
7. Intended audience:
8. Point of view/bias:
9. Source of funding:
10. Date of most recent update:
11. Your overall evaluation:

Here you have a colorful, inviting webpage with hyperlinks that introduce you to essays about African dispersal in the Arabian Peninsula, the Persian Gulf, Southeast Asia, and other regions. You also find an introductory essay by Dr. Omar H. Ali. If you scroll to the bottom of the page, you will see a copyright date of 2011 and the name of the Schomburg Center for Research in Black Culture. Above the copyright you will see the link word "about." Click on it and you will be taken to a separate page that shows you the name of all the individuals associated with the content of the African Diaspora in the Indian Ocean World, including contact information for enquiries. There you find Dr. Ali's name as the responsible scholar and you learn that he is associate professor of African American and African Diaspora Studies. If you wanted to learn more about his credentials, you could simple "Google" him to locate his faculty webpage and discover, among other things, that he is a professor-researcher at the University of North Carolina, Greensboro, that he earned his Ph.D. at Columbia University, and that he is a well published and highly awarded scholar. His credentials are strong. Returning to the site, you find you have links to maps, images, videos, and a bibliography of secondary sources, all of which you can explore at will. All this information confirms that you have a reliable source for the information on the webpage.

Returning again to the initial site, note the links in the right-hand corner to the Schomburg Center for Research in Black Culture and the New York Public Library. Click on the Schomburg Center. You now find yourself at the center's main webpage, which you see is published by the New York Public Library, a fact that is also indicated in the URL.

FIGURE 5.2. The New York Public Library Website for the Schomburg Center for Research in Black Culture; http://www.nypl.org/about/locations/schomburg/. Used by permission of the New York Public Library.

If you scroll around the page, you learn that the Schomburg Center is a research unit of the New York Public Library with a particular mission to study the African Diaspora, African American history, and African experiences. Look for a link that connects you to the Center's educational projects, which run the gamut from research fellowships to programs for the general public. You can explore the many options that this website makes available to you. Indeed, it will take you a long time to exhaust the possibilities on offer. For an example, click on "Digital Schomburg" and discover rich options of hyperlinks connecting you to online sources of images, books, articles, and primary sources, all of which allow you to verify the information contained in the essays. You will also find online exhibitions about the African Diaspora that are more wide ranging than the one on the Indian Ocean World, which has been less extensively researched. Please note that the primary sources are all provided with their full citations. This is an important point; not all websites are so thorough. Under a link that lists site credits you will find the names of the individuals responsible for the information within the exhibits. Scholars are listed along with their institutional affiliations. You will want to check the credentials of these experts through a web search.

Finally, you need to try to find out the source of funding for the site and determine whether there might be any indication of bias. Can you find a link that might help you find this type of information? Look for a link that says "Support Schomburg" or "Donate Now" or "Help us Continue Our Work." If you find some such phrase, you will discover information about the source of funding for the center, which comes from a mix of government, corporate, and philanthropic organizations, as well as the general public. You have enough information to know that the information presented within this site is verifiable and that there are no obvious biases other than the activist stance presented on the site home page that "The Schomburg Center fights against those who try to distort or ignore black history." Because professional historians seek to combat distortion and ignorance, this activist stance can hardly be perceived as bias. We suggest that this site is reliable. It is also a site that makes it easy for you to do your work of evaluation.

Example Two: Lewis and Clark Expedition. For our second example, we have chosen the topic of the Lewis and Clark expedition and located in our online search the website *Discovering Lewis & Clark*. Here, too, you have an attractive site to begin investigating. Spend some time browsing its offerings to gather your first general impression. How easy is it to navigate the pages to locate information? What do you think is the target audience for this site--general public, students, scholars, or all three? Then begin collecting your information. Do the articles provide the bylines of their authors? Do the authors provide endnotes and bibliographies? Can you find primary sources on the site? Have the organizers included full citations for extracts from the sources so that you can verify them? Click on the "credits" link and you will find a long list of individuals and institutions involved with the project. Can you locate their credentials? Do you learn anything about the site's mission, its funding and sponsorship? Do you see anything that leads you to think that the site offers one

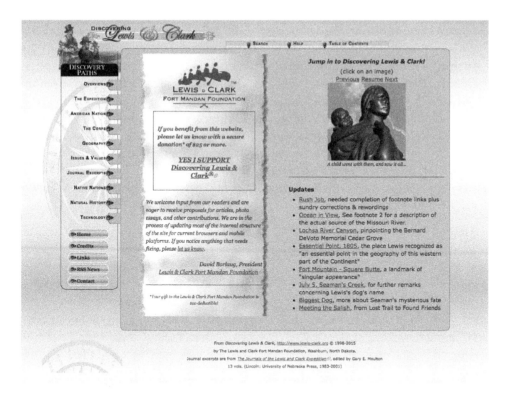

FIGURE 5.3. Discovering Lewis and Clark Website; http://www.lewis-clark.org/. Used by permission of the Lewis & Clark, Fort Mandan Foundation.

particular perspective? Does the website give you contact information? How can you tell whether it is regularly updated? We suggest that this site is a useful place to learn about the Lewis and Clark expedition before you begin your scholarly research. Can you explain why?

Finally, we want to offer a word of caution. In your searches, you will come across examples of websites that initially appear to meet the criteria on our checklist but are inappropriate, misleading, and potentially even harmful sites. They have a reputable appearance. They frequently incorporate abstracts from current news reports with links to highly regarded organizations, such as broadcasting companies like the Public Broadcasting Corporation, news agencies such as Reuters, a polling organization such as Gallup, or an independent foundation such as the Pew Charitable Trust, to give just some examples. Inclusion of the names of such well-known organizations is designed to lend an air of respectability. The site may contain the jacket covers of published books and articles on a wide spectrum of topics. It may describe itself as an independent foundation, a research institute, an educational organization, or a publishing house. It may also list some laudable goals, which sound well and good to you until you take your check list and begin your assessment. As always, check to see who is responsible for the site. Does the site list a board of directors or other governing body? What can you find out about them? Who are the key donors? Check the book titles and articles. Who wrote them? Who published them? Some individuals call themselves historians when they have no credentials as historians. They write books and articles they call history, even including the paraphernalia of the discipline, for example, endnotes and bibliographies; but they intentionally misconstrue arguments and employ quotations out of context. If the books are all published by the owners of the website, does that give you cause for concern? Might the website exist for the promotion of one particular viewpoint? Is that necessarily a bad thing? If you cannot satisfy yourself as to the credentials of the authors and organizers through an independent search, then you will need to proceed cautiously.

ACTIVITY: Evaluating websites

Using the checklist provided on page 204, evaluate the following two websites and determine whether you would be able to rely on them for a research project on a topic relating to genocide.

-Yale University Genocide Studies Program: http://www.yale.edu/gsp/links/index .html/

FIGURE 5.4. Website of the Genocide Studies Program at Yale University; http://gsp.yale.edu/. Used by permission of the Genocide Studies Program.

-Prevent Genocide International: http://www.preventgenocide.org/

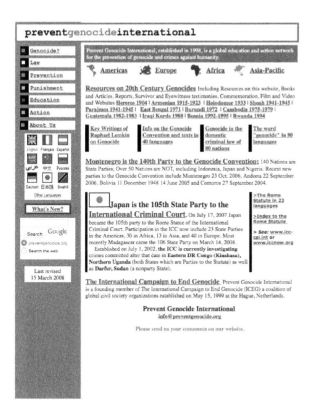

FIGURE 5.5. Prevent Genocide International website; http://www.preventgenocide.org/.

② Analyzing primary sources

Primary sources provide historians with the evidence to interpret the past, and analysis of a primary source is almost certainly among the written assignments you will be required to complete during your college career. Just because sources speak to us from the past does not mean that they are free of bias or misleading information. Indeed, you can expect sources to express the opinions of the individuals who produce them. Approach them with a critical eye, question them, and compare the viewpoints expressed by different people about the same event. Indeed, you are likely to detect bias only by comparing viewpoints. In addition to posing the standard questions—who, what, when, where, why, and how—you will also want to ask what those people hoped to gain and who they were trying to influence as they composed their texts. We expect that the majority of your sources will be written documents, but your basic questions remain the same regardless of the type of source you have—written documents, artwork, maps, films, music, political cartoons, government propaganda posters, and more. That said, each type of source will raise additional questions of its own. For example, in addition to knowing when and where a composer wrote a particular symphony, you would definitely want to know when and where it was first performed and by which orchestra. You would also want to know whether the work was commissioned, by whom, and what kind of relationship the composer enjoyed with the commissioner.

ACTIVITY: Using a primary source worksheet

We recommend that you use both a worksheet with a checklist of information that you need to acquire and a basic format for mining the document for themes, arguments, and supporting quotes. You can make the task as simple or as sophisticated as you need for your purposes. Read your document through once to get a general sense of it and then read it a second time and complete the worksheet. Once you have finished this task you will find it relatively easy to draft a primary document analysis. If you complete the worksheet for the key primary documents you plan to use for your research paper, you will be able to compare the viewpoints of your various actors and gather a wealth of evidence for a nuanced argument. The questions you ask of the document depend on your overall research question. The number of claims and questions depend on the length and content of the source.

PRIMARY SOURCE WORKSHEET

Author:

Title:

Full citation:

Author's identity:

Date and place of document:

Intended audience:

Intended purpose:

Brief summary:

Historical context:

Perspective/possible bias:

Key claims (in your own words) and supporting evidence (quotes)

    Claim 1:

      Evidence 1:

    Claim 2:

      Evidence 2:

    Claim 3:

      Evidence 3:

Questions the document raises in your mind, for which you need additional evidence

    Q1:

    Q2:

    Q3:

Example One: Late-Nineteenth-Century Imperialism in France. Historians frequently refer to the late nineteenth and early twentieth centuries as the age of imperialism. Western European powers and the United States colonized much of the rest of the world, controlling trade relations and exercising control over billions of people. Pro-imperialists justified expansion by claiming superiority in political, economic, technological, moral, cultural, and racial terms. The following text provides justification for expansion from French politician Jules Ferry (1832–1893), interspersed with comments from other politicians sitting in the French National Assembly.

Jules Ferry

READ   **SPEECH BEFORE THE FRENCH CHAMBER OF DEPUTIES, 1883**

From Overfield, James H. *Sources of Twentieth-Century Global History*. Boston: Houghton Mifflin Harcourt, 2002, 8–10.

M. Jules Ferry. . . . It is as strenuous for me as for you, but I believe that there is some benefit in summarizing and condensing, in the form of arguments, the principles, the motives, and the various interests by which a policy of colonial expansion may be justified; it goes without saying that I will try to remain reasonable, moderate, and never lose sight of the major continental interests which are the primary concern of this country. What I wish to say . . . is that . . . the policy of colonial expansion is a political and economic system; I wish to say that one can relate this system to three orders of ideas: economic ideas, ideas of civilization in its highest sense, and ideas of politics and patriotism.

   In the area of economics, I will allow myself to place before you, with the support of some figures, the considerations which justify a policy of colonial expansion from the point of view of that need, felt more and more strongly by the industrial populations of Europe and particularly those of our own rich and hard working country: the need for export markets. . . . I will formulate only in a general way what each of you, in the different parts of France, is in a position to confirm. Yes, what is lacking for our great industry, drawn irrevocably on to the path of exportation by the . . . treaties of 1860,[1] what it lacks more and more is export markets. Why? Because next door to us Germany is surrounded by barriers, because beyond the ocean, the United States of America has become protectionist, protectionist in the most extreme sense, because not only have these great markets, I will not say closed but shrunk, and thus become more difficult of access for our industrial products, but also these great states are beginning to pour products not seen heretofore onto our own markets. . . . It is not necessary to pursue this demonstration any farther. . . .

   . . . Gentlemen, there is a second point, a second order of ideas to which I have to give equal attention, but as quickly as possible, believe me; it is the humanitarian and civilizing side of the question. On this point the honorable M. Camille Pelletan[2] has jeered in his own refined and clever manner; he jeers, he condemns, and he says "What is this civilization which you impose with cannon-balls? What is it but another form of barbarism? Don't these populations, these inferior races, have the same rights as you? Aren't they masters of their own houses? Have they called upon you? You come to them against their will, you offer them violence, but not civilization." There, gentlemen, is the thesis; I do not hesitate to say that this is not politics, nor is it history: it is political metaphysics. ("Ah, Ah" *on far left*.)[3]

continued on next page

continued

. . . Gentlemen, I must speak from a higher and more truthful plane. It must be stated openly that, in effect, superior races have rights over inferior races. (*Movement on many benches on the far left.*)

M. Jules Maigne.[4] Oh! You dare to say this in the country which has proclaimed the rights of man!

M. de Guilloutet. This is a justification of slavery and the slave trade!

M. Jules Ferry. If M. Maigne is right, if the declaration of the rights of man was written for the blacks of equatorial Africa, then by what right do you impose regular commerce upon them? They have not called upon you.

M. Raoul Duval. We do not want to impose anything upon them. It is you who wish to do so! . . .

M. Jules Ferry. I repeat that superior races have a right, because they have a duty. They have the duty to civilize inferior races. . . .

That is what I have to answer M. Pelletan in regard to the second point upon which he touched.

He then touched upon a third point, more delicate, more serious, and upon which I ask your permission to express myself quite frankly. It is the political side of the question. . . .

"It is a system," he says, "which consists of seeking out compensations in the Orient with a circumspect and peaceful seclusion which is actually imposed upon us in Europe."

I would like to explain myself in regard to this. I do not like this word "compensation," and, in effect, not here but elsewhere it has often been used in a treacherous way. If what is being said or insinuated is that a republican minister could possibly believe that there are in any part of the world compensations for the disasters which we have experienced,[5] an injury is being inflicted . . . and an injury undeserved by that government. (*Applause at the center and left.*) I will ward off this injury with all the force of my patriotism! (*New applause and bravos from the same benches.*)

Gentlemen, there are certain considerations which merit the attention of all patriots. The conditions of naval warfare have been profoundly altered. ("Very true! Very true!")

At this time, as you know, a warship cannot carry more than fourteen days' worth of coal, no matter how perfectly it is organized, and a ship which is out of coal is a derelict on the surface of the sea, abandoned to the first person who comes along. Thence the necessity of having on the oceans provision stations, shelters, ports for defense and revictualing. (*Applause at the center and left. Various interruptions.*) And it is for this that we needed Tunisia, for this that we needed Saigon and the Mekong Delta, for this that we need Madagascar, that we are at Diégo-Suarez and Vohemar[6] and will never leave them! (*Applause from a great number of benches.*) Gentlemen, in Europe as it is today, in this competition of so many rivals which we see growing around us, some by perfecting their military or maritime forces, others by the prodigious development of an ever growing population; in a Europe, or rather in a universe of this sort, a policy of peaceful seclusion or abstention is simply the highway to decadence! Nations are great in our times only by means of the activities which they develop; it is not simply "by the peaceful shining forth of institutions" that they are great at this hour. . . .

The Republican Party has shown that it is quite aware that one cannot impose upon France a political ideal conforming to that of nations like independent Belgium and the Swiss Republic; that something else is needed for France: that she cannot be merely a free country, that she must also be a great country, exercising all of her rightful influence over the destiny of Europe, that she ought to propagate this influence throughout the world and carry everywhere that she can her language, her customs, her flag, her arms, and her genius. (*Applause at center and left.*)

NOTES

1. These agreements with Great Britain lowered tariffs between the two nations.

2. Pelletan (1815–1846) was a radical republican politician and an ardent patriot.

3. Going back to a tradition begun in the legislative assemblies of the French Revolution, democrats sat on the left, moderates in the center, and conservatives and monarchists on the right. By the 1880s, the "left" also included socialists.

4. Maigne and the speakers who follow, Guilloutet and Duval, were members of the Chamber of Deputies.

5. The reference is to France's defeat by Prussia and other German states in the Franco-Prussian War of 1870–1871.

6. Madagascar port cities.

PRIMARY SOURCE WORKSHEET

Author: Jules Ferry

Title: "Speech before the French Chamber of Deputies, 1883"

Full citation: Overfield, James H. *Sources of Twentieth-Century Global History*. Boston: Houghton Mifflin Harcourt, 2002, 8–10.

Author's identity: Politician, deputy in French National Assembly, Minister of Foreign Affairs

Date and place of document: 1883, Paris

Intended audience: Other deputies in National Assembly and general public

Intended purpose: Justify his views on French imperialism; influence his colleagues' perspectives, and shape public opinion

Brief summary: Ferry offers several justifications for French imperialism based on economics, military might, culture, and nationalism. In his view, France has a need, a duty, and a right to expand to secure its trading position in the world, extend its civilizing influences to perceived lesser nations, and promote its greatness.

Historical context: late-nineteenth-century western European and U.S. imperialist expansion and competition; paradox of imperialism and expansion of human rights in Europe

Perspective/possible bias? Staunch defense of French imperialism, interspersed with criticisms from anti-imperialist deputies in the Assembly

Key claims (in your own words) and supporting evidence (quotes)

   Claim 1: Some of Ferry's concerns related to competition from other imperial nations. If France did not expand its trade, it would lose markets and prestige. France needed export markets as Germany and the United States had raised tariff barriers to imports while exporting to France.

   Evidence 1: Germany "surrounded by barriers," the U.S. "has become protectionist, protectionist in the most extreme sense," and both countries "pour products not seen heretofore onto our own markets." (p. 9)

continued on next page

continued

Claim 2: To maintain its ability to wage war on the high seas in the age of steam power, France needed to expand its navy and acquire coaling stations, that is, ports around the world where it could take on fuel, do repairs, and reprovision.

> **Evidence 2:** "The conditions of naval warfare have been profoundly altered. . . . And it is for this that we needed Tunisia, for this that we needed Saigon and the Mekong Delta, for this that we need Madagascar, that we are at Diego-Suarez and Vohemar" (p. 10).

Claim 3: Ferry's justifications were cloaked in the language of humanitarianism and spreading civilization but his perceptions of rights and duty in this respect were grounded in racism.

> **Evidence 3:** "Superior races have rights over inferior races;" "duty to civilize inferior races" (p. 9).

Claim 4: Ferry displayed a sense of patriotic hyperbole in his view of the greatness of France, perhaps to help win over his detractors.

> **Evidence 4:** It was not enough for France to be "a free country"; she must also be "a great country." She had the right to influence the future of Europe and the world and should "carry everywhere that she can her language, her customs, her flag, her arms, and her genius" (p. 10).

Questions the document raises in your mind, for which you need additional evidence:

Q1: To what extent were Ferry's justifications similar to those presented by imperialists in other nations?

Q2: Ferry's arguments clearly won the day, but who were the anti-imperialists, what were their arguments, and how much influence did they have?

Q3: How did anticolonialism develop in the various French colonies?

Example Two: Early-Twentieth-Century Feminism in Egypt. Feminism in the early twentieth century was not an idea that only women in Western Europe shared. Women, and some men, around the world recognized that women should have more rights, particularly to education, independent control of their finances, and suffrage. In the following extract, Bahithat al-Badiya (a pseudonym, 1886-1918), a teacher, discusses some of the discrimination that Egyptian women faced and offers her solutions.

Bahithat al-Badiya

READ   **A LECTURE IN THE CLUB OF THE UMMA PARTY, 1909**

From Overfield, James H. *Sources of Twentieth-Century Global History*. Boston: Houghton Mifflin Harcourt, 2002, 52–55.

Men say when we become educated we shall push them out of work and abandon the role for which God has created us. But, isn't it rather men who have pushed women out of work? Before, women used to spin and to weave cloth for clothes for themselves and their children, but men invented machines for spinning and weaving and put women out of work. In the past, women sewed clothes for themselves and their households but men invented the sewing machine. . . . Then men took up the profession of tailoring and began to make clothes for our men and children. Before women winnowed the wheat and ground flour on grinding stones for the bread they used to make with their own hands, sifting flour and kneading dough. Then men established bakeries employing men. They gave us rest but at the same time pushed us out of work. . . .

The question of monopolizing the workplace comes down to individual freedom. One man wishes to become a doctor, another a merchant. Is it right to tell a doctor he must quit his profession and become a merchant or vice versa? No. Each has the freedom to do as he wishes. . . . Work at home now does not occupy more than half the day. We must pursue an education in order to occupy the other half of the day but that is what men wish to prevent us from doing under the pretext of taking their jobs away. . . .

The division of labor is merely a human creation. We still witness people like the Nubians[1] whose men sew clothes for themselves and the household while the women work in the fields. Some women even climb palm trees to harvest the dates. Women in villages in both Upper and Lower Egypt help their men till the land and plant crops. Some women do the fertilizing, haul crops, lead animals, draw water for irrigation, and other chores. You may have observed that women in the villages work as hard as the strongest men and we see that their children are strong and healthy.

Specialised work for each sex is a matter of convention. It is not mandatory. We women are now unable to do hard work because we have not been accustomed to it. . . . After long centuries of enslavement by men, our minds rusted and our bodies weakened. Is it right that they accuse us of being created weaker than them in mind and body?

◇◇

Men criticize the way we dress in the street. They have a point because we have exceeded the bounds of custom and propriety. We claim we are veiling but we are neither properly covered nor unveiled. I do not advocate a return to the veils of our grandmother because it can rightly be called being buried alive, not *hijab*,[2] correct covering. The woman used to spend her whole life within the walls of her house not going out into the street except when she was carried to her grave. I do not, on the other hand, advocate unveiling, like Europeans, and mixing with men, because they can be harmful to us. . . .

If we had been raised from childhood to go unveiled and if our men were ready for it I would approve of unveiling for those who want it. But the nation is not ready for it now. Some of our prudent women do not fear to mix with men, but we have to place limits on those who are less prudent because we are quick to imitate and seldom find our authenticity in the veil. . . .

If the change that some women have made in the *izar*[3] is in order to shed it when they go out that would be all right if these women would only uncover their faces but keep their hair and figures concealed. I think the most appropriate way to dress outside is to cover the head and wear a coat with long sleeves which touches the ground the way the European women do. I am told this is the way women in Istanbul[4] dress when they go out shopping. . . .

◇◇

On the subject of customs and veiling I would like to remind you of something that causes us great unhappiness—the question of engagement and marriage. Most sensible people in Egypt believe it is necessary for fiancés to meet and speak with each other before their marriage. It is wise and the Prophet[5] himself, peace be upon him and his followers, did not do otherwise. . . .

continued on next page

continued

By not allowing men to see their prospective wives following their engagement we cause Egyptian men to seek European women in marriage. They marry European servants and working class women thinking they would be happy with them rather than daughters of pashas and beys[6] hidden away in "a box of chance." If we do not solve this problem we shall become subject to occupation by women of the West. We shall suffer double occupation, one by men and the other by women. The second will be worse than the first because the first occurred against our will but we shall have invited the second by our own actions. . . . Most Egyptian men who have married European women suffer from the foreign habits and extravagance of their wives. The European woman thinks she is of a superior race to the Egyptian and bosses her husband around after marriage. When the European woman marries an Egyptian she becomes a spend-thrift while she would be thrifty if she were married to a westerner. . . .

◇◇

Our beliefs and actions have been a great cause of the lesser respect that men accord us. How can a sensible man respect a woman who believes in magic, superstition, and the blessing of the dead and who allows women peddlars and washerwomen, or even devils, to have authority over her? Can he respect a woman who speaks only about the clothes of her neighbor and the jewellery of her friend and the furniture of a bride? This is added to the notion imprinted in a man's mind that woman is weaker and less intelligent than he is. . . .

We shall advance when we give up idleness. The work of most of us at home is lounging on cushions all day or going out to visit other women. . . . Being given over to idleness or luxury has given us weak constitutions and pale complexions. We have to find work to do at home. At a first glance one can see that the working classes have better health and more energy and more intelligent children. The children of the middle and lower classes are, almost all of them, in good health and have a strong constitution, while most of the children of the elite are sick or frail and prone to illness despite the care lavished on them by their parents. . . .

Now I shall turn to the path we should follow. If I had the right to legislate I would decree:

1. Teaching girls the Quran and the correct Sunna.[7]

2. Primary and secondary school education for girls, and compulsory preparatory school education for all.

3. Instruction for girls on the theory and practice of home economics, health, first aid, and childcare.

4. Setting a quota for females in medicine and education so they can serve the women of Egypt.

5. Allowing women to study any other advanced subjects they wish without restriction.

6. Upbringing for girls from infancy stressing patience, honesty, work and other virtues.

7. Adhering to the *Sharia*[8] concerning betrothal and marriage, and not permitting any woman and man to marry without first meeting each other in the presence of the father or male relative of the bride.

8. Adopting the veil and outdoor dress of the Turkish women of Istanbul.

9. Maintaining the best interests of the country and dispensing with foreign goods and people as much as possible.

10. Make it encumbent upon our brothers, the men of Egypt, to implement this program.

NOTES

[1] A Negroid people who inhabit the region in southern Egypt and northern Sudan between the Nile and the Red Sea.

[2] *Hijab* in Arabic literally means "veil" or "partition"; it also means adherence to certain standards of modest dress for women.

[3] A loose-fitting shawl, usually made of white calico.

[4] The largest city in Turkey and the seat of Ottoman government.

[5] Islam's greatest prophet and founder, Muhammad lived from 570 to 632 C.E. God's revelations to him comprise Islam's most holy book, the Quran, or Koran.

[6] Courtesy titles for Egyptian gentlemen of high rank.

[7] *Sunna* refers to the customs and traditions of the Islamic community.

[8] Literally, the "right path," or Islamic law.

PRIMARY SOURCE WORKSHEET

Author: Bahithat al-Badiya (pen name)

Title: "A Lecture in the Club of the Umma Party, 1909"

Full citation: Overfield, James H. *Sources of Twentieth-Century Global History*. Boston: Houghton Mifflin Harcourt, 2002, 52–55.

Author's identity: School teacher, early Egyptian feminist

Date and place of document: Cairo, 1909

Intended audience: Educated Egyptian women and male politicians

Intended purpose: Raise awareness about the status of women in Egypt

Brief summary: Bahithat al-Badiya answers male critiques about women in the workplace and offers her own critiques about cultural conventions that cause unhappiness among women and prevent their social advancement. She offers a ten-point plan to improve education for girls, marriage conditions, and dress, arguing that she would legislate the changes if she had the power.

Historical context: Worldwide feminist movement; Egypt under British semicolonial rule.

Perspective/possible bias? Feminist perspective, arguing for rights of women in Egyptian society; likely to be disregarded by many Egyptian men.

Key claims (in your own words) and supporting evidence (quotes):

Claim 1: Men argue that educated women who take jobs in the marketplace will cause unemployment among men; but Bahithat al-Badiya argues that men have caused unemployment among women by inventing machinery that took women's traditional work away from them.

continued on next page

continued

Evidence 1: "Isn't it rather men who have pushed women out of work? . . . Men invented machines for spinning and weaving and put women out of work . . . men took up the profession of tailoring . . . men established bakeries employing men" (p. 52–53).

Claim 2: She makes a concession to men who criticize women's dress as she herself believes that women dress inappropriately. She is not against unveiling, but recommends the modest Istanbul-style dress.

Evidence 2: "They have a point because we have exceeded the bounds of custom and propriety." "I think the most appropriate way to dress outside is to cover the head and wear a coat with long sleeves which touches the ground the way European women do. I am told this is the way women in Istanbul dress when they go out shopping" (p. 53).

Claim 3: She criticizes the custom that does not allow a couple to meet before they get married, arguing that this has led some Egyptian men to marry foreign women.

Evidence 3: "By not allowing men to see their prospective wives following their engagement we cause Egyptian men to seek European women in marriage" (p. 54).

Claim 4: She offers a ten-point plan that she would legislate if she had the power. These points include dress and marriage but her emphasis is on education, from primary through university and even medical education.

Evidence 4: "Setting a quota for females in medicine and education so they can serve the women of Egypt."

Questions the document raises in your mind, for which you need additional evidence:

Q1: What was the educational system in Egypt in the early twentieth century? What was the percentage of boys and girls that attended primary school, secondary school, university?

Q2: How unusual was Bahithat al-Badiya? What was her social position? Which other women wrote and lectured? How had they acquired their education? Was she part of a general feminist movement?

Q3: What impact did she have?

ACTIVITY: Analyzing a primary document

- Use the worksheet to analyze the following document.

Following the defeat of the Ottoman Empire in World War I, former subjects of the empire in its Arab domains expected to achieve self-rule, as had former subjects in Europe. They were disappointed when they were decreed to be mandates under British or French control. In July 1919, Syrian nationalists organized a congress in which they argued against imperial domination and stipulated their wishes for an independent future.

THE RESOLUTION OF THE GENERAL SYRIAN CONGRESS AT DAMASCUS PROCLAIMS ARAB SOVEREIGNTY OVER GREATER SYRIA, JULY 2, 1919

From Khater, Akram Fouad. *Sources in the History of the Modern Middle East*, Second edition. Boston: Wadsworth, 2011, 158-160.

We, the undersigned, members of the General Syrian Congress meeting in Damascus on Wednesday, July 2nd, 1919, made up of representatives from the three Zones, viz., the Southern, Eastern, and Western, provided with credentials and authorizations by the inhabitants of our various districts, Moslems, Christians, and Jews, have agreed upon the following statement of the desires of the people of the country who have elected us to present them to the American Section of the International Commission; the fifth article was passed by a very large majority; all the other articles were accepted unanimously:—

1. We ask absolutely complete political independence for Syria within these boundaries. The Taurus System on the North; Rafah and a line running from Al Jauf to the south of the Syrian and the Hejazian line to Akaba on the south; the Euphrates and Khabur Rivers and a line extending east of Abu Kamal to the east of Al Jauf on the east; and the Mediterranean on the West.

2. We ask that the Government of this Syrian country should be a democratic civil constitutional Monarchy on broad decentralization principles, safeguarding the rights of minorities, and that the King be the Emir Feisal, who carried on a glorious struggle in the cause of our liberation and merited our full confidence and entire reliance.

3. Considering the fact that the Arabs inhabiting the Syrian area are not naturally less gifted than other more advanced races and that they are by no means less developed than the Bulgarians, Serbians, Greeks, and Roumanians at the beginning of their independence, we protest against Article 22 of the Covenant of the League of Nations placing us among the nations in their middle stage of development which stand in need of a mandatory power.

4. In the event of the rejection by the Peace Conference of this just protest for certain considerations that we may not understand, we, relying on the declarations of President Wilson that his object in waging war was to put an end to the ambition of conquest and colonization, can only regard the mandate mentioned in the Covenant of the League of Nations as equivalent to the rendering of economical and technical assistance that does not prejudice our complete independence. And desiring that our country should not fall a prey to colonization and believing that the American Nation is farthest from any thought of colonization and has no political ambition in our country, we will seek the technical and economical assistance from the United States of America, provided that such assistance does not exceed 20 years.

5. In the event of America not finding herself in a position to accept our desire for assistance, we will seek this assistance from Great Britain, also provided that such assistance does not infringe the complete independence and unity of our country and that the duration of such assistance does not exceed that mentioned in the previous article.

6. We do not acknowledge any right claimed by the French Government in any part whatever of our Syrian country and refuse that she should assist us or have a hand in our country under any circumstances and in any place.

continued on next page

continued

7. We oppose the pretentions of the Zionists to create a Jewish commonwealth in the southern part of Syria, known as Palestine, and oppose Zionist migration to any part of our country; for we do not acknowledge their title but consider them a grave peril to our people from the national, economical, and political points of view. Our Jewish compatriots shall enjoy our common rights and assume the common responsibilities.

8. We ask that there should be no separation of the southern part of Syria, known as Palestine, nor of the littoral western zone, which includes Lebanon, from the Syrian country. We desire that the unity of the country should be guaranteed against partition under whatever circumstances.

9. We ask complete independence for emancipated Mesopotamia and that there should be no economical barriers between the two countries.

10. The fundamental principles laid down by President Wilson in condemnation of secret treaties impel us to protest most emphatically against any treaty that stipulates the partition of our Syrian country and against any private engagement aiming at the establishment of Zionism in the southern part of Syria; therefore we ask the complete annulment of these conventions and agreements.

The noble principles enunciated by President Wilson strengthen our confidence that our desires emanating from the depths of our hearts, shall be the decisive factor in determining our future; and that President Wilson and the free American people will be our supporters for the realization of our hopes, thereby proving their sincerity and noble sympathy with the aspiration of the weaker nations in general and our Arab people in particular. We also have the fullest confidence that the Peace Conference will realize that we would not have risen against the Turks, with whom we had participated in all civil, political, and representative privileges, but for their violation of our national rights, and so will grant us our desires in full in order that our political rights may not be less after the war than they were before, since we have shed so much blood in the cause of our liberty and independence.

We request to be allowed to send a delegation to represent us at the Peace Conference to defend our rights and secure the realization of our aspirations.

ACTIVITY: Analyze one of your own sources

- Use the worksheet to analyze a document that you plan to use for your own research paper.

❸ Crafting an initial thesis statement

A successful thesis statement does not merely provide an answer to your research question. It also explains its significance. It answers the question *so what*? That is, it explains the broader impact of your work. Sometimes, even experienced researchers are able to craft a strong answer to the *so what* question only toward the end of their writing; but they craft an initial answer, and so can you. We call this a working thesis statement. You answer your question and make a specific argument that can be supported by evidence, knowing that your argument could be disputed by other researchers who use different sources.

Example One: French Imperialism. Let us say that your topic is French imperialism in the late nineteenth century. Your research question is: "How did French politicians justify French expansionism in the final quarter of the nineteenth century?" Jules Ferry's speech is a key source, and you have additional sources that support his pro-imperialist stance. What is your initial working thesis? Remember that you need to go beyond a basic statement of fact to incorporate some explanatory potential and an indication of what motivated actors or what resulted from their actions.

Possible working thesis:
Concern about economic competition from Germany and the United States in the 1880s inclined some French politicians to the idea that France might lose its prestige among imperial nations, a possibility that goaded them to justify expansion on the grounds that their efforts would have a beneficial humanitarian impact in their colonies that would resound to the glory of France.

This argument explains what motivated French politicians to justify imperialism (international competition and loss of prestige on the world stage) and what they expected to result from French expansion (benefits to colonies and national glory). It also hints at larger global picture (the *so what?*)—national identity in an imperial age. Your reader expects you to develop all these elements and provide evidence to support them.

The following assertions are not arguments:
- This paper explains French justification for imperialism. (purpose)
- French politicians justified imperialism on economic, military, and cultural grounds. (statement of fact)
- French politicians were racists. (overgeneralized opinion)

Example Two: Egyptian Feminism. Consider the following attempts to develop a working thesis statement about women and education in early-twentieth-century Egypt.

1. Most girls did not go to school in the early-twentieth century.

   A statement so vague that it is meaningless.

2. Men were not interested in supporting education for girls in early-twentieth-century Egypt.

   This statement is a generalized, unfounded opinion. We cannot possibly include all men in our argument, and we could surely find evidence that some men did support the idea of female education.

3. Education for girls was a major demand of feminists in early-twentieth-century Egypt.

   This sentence offers a statement of fact that can be defended but has little substance to recommend it as a working thesis statement.

4. Egyptian feminists put forward proposals to develop education for girls as a means to the social advancement of women in the early-twentieth century.

   This fourth effort is more specific than the third inasmuch as it offers an explanation for why feminists promoted the idea of female education, but it lacks motivating factors and consequences, and gives the reader little sense of the type of evidence that the author plans to offer in her research paper.

5. Frustrated by the encroachments of men in women's work and by the general lack of opportunities for women outside the home, many Egyptian feminists promoted the idea of education for girls, particularly medical education, as a way to improve their general well-being, social status, and economic standing; however, with no political clout, they remained reliant on men to legislate female education.

This last effort is a solid working thesis incorporating specific ideas that the author will develop in its support. It also offers possibilities for a structural outline. The reader knows what to expect from this thesis.

ACTIVITY: Crafting an initial thesis statement

- From the worksheet you used to analyze the resolution of the Syrian National Congress, craft an initial thesis statement.
- Craft an initial thesis statement for your own research project.
- For both exercises, bring together a group of peer reviewers to compare and critique your thesis statements.

❹ Sample research prospectus

Your initial research is done. You have narrowed down your topic, located secondary and primary sources, completed your annotations (Chapter Three Workbook) and worksheets, and drafted your initial thesis statement. It is now time for you to put all your work together in your research prospectus. Completing this task will give you a great sense of achievement. In the following text, we provide an example of a strong student research prospectus that you can use as a model.

EXAMPLE OF STUDENT RESEARCH PROSPECTUS

Note: The student who prepared this prospectus initially planned a broad examination of the free black population of the Capital Region of New York (the cities of Albany, Troy, and Rensselaer) in the decades leading up to the American Civil War, focusing on its anti-slavery activism. He believed he had the time and the resources to complete it. He soon realized that the scope of the project was too broad. He also discovered that several of the library guides he had used to identify sources did not accurately reflect what the archives held. As a consequence, his project transitioned to be a demographic survey of Albany's African American community and an analysis of how the messages of Albany's black abolitionists aligned with the national black abolitionist movement and spoke to the needs of Albany's black community. He understood that his experience was representative of the research process historians go through. His project stayed true to his intent, an examination of Albany's African American community and the role of black abolitionists in that community, but it left some parts of the initial project out and shifted in new directions, such as incorporation of the demographic aspect as a central part of the thesis project. His experience serves to remind us all that research and ideas always change. It is the rare project that ends as it begins.

Working Title: Forging Freedom in Fraternity and Friction: The New York Capital Region's Antebellum African-American Community, 1827–1865.

Initial Research Questions: How did New York Capital Region's black community organize and participate in anti-slavery politics, how did its members interact with the colonization movement, and how do their activities correlate to historiographical interpretations of abolitionism?

Working Thesis: By organizing on national, state, and local levels to struggle against racism, political oppression, and public indifference or hostility, the Capital Region's black community worked to win the rights of freedom for their southern brethren and citizenship for all black Americans.

New York's Capital Region developed as a nexus of commerce and industrial enterprise during the antebellum era. Centered on the cities of Albany, Troy, and Rensselaer, the region drew to it the forces of political change, commercial innovation, economic diversification, and cultural renewal. In this urban context of rapid change, members of the African American community sought to capitalize on the fruits of statewide emancipation and forge for themselves a place as free and equal citizens in New York. To do this, free black elites in the Capital Region aligned with national anti-slavery organizations, particularly those founded by other prominent free blacks. In addition, the Capital Region's black population created local associations focused on anti-slavery activism, evangelization, and improving social conditions. Free blacks defined themselves through community-building and abolitionism and, like a select few of their white colleagues, saw the attainment of civic equality for blacks as the ultimate goal of abolitionism.

This project does not offer a new interpretation of abolitionism. Rather, it is a microcosmic test of what established scholarship says free black urban communities looked like and experienced during the antebellum period. Other avenues of exploration that need to be fleshed out include collaboration between communities of African descent in the Atlantic world and the relationship that the Capital Region's community had with the colonization movement that was designed to transport freed blacks to Africa.

Purpose and Rationale: The purpose of this project is to illuminate the role that the Capital Region's black community played in the abolitionist movement on a national, state, and local level. Much work has been done on emancipation in New York State and the experiences of African Americans in New York City during the antebellum period. The Capital Region's community, however, has been neglected. This project seeks to reconstruct the Capital Region's African American community to see how these men and women addressed issues of slavery and prejudice and whether or not their experiences align with those of free African Americans elsewhere across the North. By illuminating the role that New York Capital Region's blacks played in the abolitionist movement as a whole, I hope to expand upon current understandings of the meanings, methods, and ideologies of black abolitionism in the antebellum period.

The project has a secondary purpose beyond its strictly academic one. My research is funded by an AmeriCorps Summer Scholar fellowship designed to promote the work of Albany's Underground Railroad History Project, Inc. In order to further the educational goals and mission of the Underground Railroad History Project, this research will be used to create resources for Albany's public schools to use for black history education.

continued on next page

continued

In addition, research and resources used for this project will be compiled into a database for broader public access.

Methodological Approach: I shall approach this topic as a social historian. Using social history will allow me to engage in an in-depth analysis of the African American community, focusing on their political activities, social organizations, labor, and religious life. I will use this summer to read the secondary literature concerning free black entrepreneurship, political activity, social organization, and religious life in the North during the antebellum period. This will establish the framework in which I will situate my analysis and find points of difference between the experiences of Northern free blacks as compared to New York's Capital Region.

Research into the Capital Region's free black population raises questions about how such a project can be accomplished when there are few written records pertaining to it. To compensate for this lack, the project will combine analysis of written texts with demographic information culled from federal and state census records, church records of births, baptisms, and deaths, tax records, and municipal and state laws pertaining to free blacks, as well as newspapers, published proceedings of state and national Negro conventions, and manuscript collections relevant to my topic. The archival resources of the Capital Region, including the New York State Museum, the Albany Institute of History and Art, the Rensselaer Historical Society, and the Albany Historical Society provide the resources needed to complete this project.

Brief Historiography: Scholars have shown that free blacks across the United States used print culture and organized events to fight against racial oppression. Erica Ball, in *To Live an Antislavery Life*, asserts that Northern blacks used the spoken and written word to create a culture focused on privately and publicly living "an antislavery life."[1] She contends that instructive literature sought to teach young and aspiring middle-class blacks how to live, work, and behave in a manner that would readily identify them as capable individuals worthy of freedom and committed to the end of slavery. As John Ernest makes clear in *A Nation within a Nation*, urban areas were the most practical locations for free blacks to organize.[2] Turning inward to resist white restrictions, they attempted to shape their own identities, undermine white oppression, and create the kind of civil, social, and political organizations to which they would have access.

New York's Capital Region has evidence of such activities. Elizabeth Wick's address to the African Female Benevolent Society of Troy in 1834 stands out as an early example of a black woman using the spoken word to call on all African Americans, men and women, to join the crusade against slavery and prejudice.[3] The proceedings of Troy's 1847 Negro Convention indicate how organizing activities, print culture, and ideas about freedom influenced the abolitionist movement.[4] For example, a discussion about land for freed slaves at that convention suggests that black antebellum activists looked beyond emancipation for the goals of their crusade. It also calls into question the definition of abolitionist.

For his part, historian Andrew Delbanco, in his article "The Abolitionist Imagination," defines abolitionists as uncompromising moralists who saw "a heinous evil" in slavery and sought to destroy it "not tomorrow, not next year" but immediately.[5] Delbanco claims that the reservations of American intellectuals such as Hawthorne and Melville about the movement indicate that many Americans, especially American intellectuals, were reluctant to tie themselves to a movement that called for the immediate end of slavery without discussion or compromise.[6] Consequently, Delbanco's abolitionists are radical and un-yielding men and women who eschewed compromise in their moralist crusade. Delbanco asserts that it was the unwillingness of the abolitionists to compromise on the issue of slavery that drove Southerners to become increasingly radicalized in their own defense of slavery and thus secede from the Union.[7]

Placing the impetus for civil war with abolitionists means that the black abolitionists I study are the men and women who plunged the United States into the Civil War. Thinking about abolitionists under Delbanco's schema is significant because it transforms abolitionists from reformers into rash radicals myopically and aggressively attacking slavery without heed to the consequences of such agitation, that is, civil war. Consequently, such an interpretation casts the black abolitionists of New York's Capital Region as vitriolic and irrational beings who pursued an unrealistic goal and who had no vision or plan for what the end of slavery would mean for the United States.

In response to Delbanco, Manisha Sinha qualifies the definition of abolitionists in a different way. Rather than looking to the political aspects of the abolitionist movement, Sinha focuses on abolitionist ideology. She asserts that the true abolitionists were those committed not only to the end of slavery, but also to black civic equality.[8] This argument is substantiated by the work of John Ernest, who identifies the struggle to create a community identity and promote African American rights as integral, though often overlooked, aspects of the abolitionist, and particularly the black abolitionist, movement. Again, the emphasis on land redistribution in the proceedings of the 1847 Negro Convention and Elizabeth Wick's call for all blacks to support abolitionism substantiates Sinha and Ernest's schema and repudiates Delbanco's assertion that abolitionists were just irrational radicals.

I will complete most of my research this summer through the Summer Service Scholars program, which will fund my research and allow me to develop my projects for the Underground Railroad History Project, Inc. I plan to read more deeply in the secondary literature concerning free black entrepreneurship, political activity, social organization, and religious life in the North during the antebellum period. This will establish the framework in which I will situate my analysis and find points of difference between the experiences of Northern free blacks across the Free States as compared to New York's Capital Region.

Annotated Bibliography:
Primary Sources

Bell, Howard Hollman. *Minutes of the Proceedings of the National Negro Conventions, 1830–1864*. New York: Arno Press, 1969.

The companion book to Bell's *A Survey of the Negro Convention Movement* (1969), this book provides published transcriptions that detail the debates of prominent black and white abolitionists at Negro conventions from the 1830s through the end of the Civil War. My interest focuses on the convention that occurred in Troy in 1847. While this convention is closest to the geographical area of my thesis, the prominent members of Albany's abolitionist community participated in nearly all of the conventions from 1847 to 1864. These published proceedings also give insight into the activities of black abolitionists and their relationship with the abolition movement in general. Bell also provides analysis of the convention movement in each of the decades in which they occurred, up to the movement's end in the 1860s.

continued on next page

continued

Office of the Secretary of the State of New York, *Census of the State of New York for 1845: Containing an Enumeration of the Inhabitants of the State, with other Statistical Information, in Pursuance of Chapter Third of the First Part of the Revised Statutes, and of the Act Amending the Same, Passed on the 7th Day of May, 1845.* Albany: Carroll and Cook, 1846.

This is just one of the census records that I plan to use. Detailing the incomes, religious affiliations, economic activities, occupations, and ages of the colored community of Albany County during the antebellum period, the census records from New York, both state and national, provide an invaluable demographic resource and primary source. While I have to face the problems of fallibility in nineteenth century record-keeping, this information allows an approach for a social historian to reconstruct Albany's black community through historical demography.

Rock, John S., George L. Ruffin, and William Howard Day. "Proceedings of the National convention of colored men, held in the city of Syracuse, N.Y., October 4, 5, 6, and 7, 1864; with the bill of wrongs and rights, and the address to the American people." Boston: J. S. Rock and G. L. Ruffin, 1864. *From Slavery to Freedom: The African American Pamphlet Collection, 1822-1909,* Library of Congress. http://memory.loc.gov/cgi-bin/query/ D?rbaapcbib:4:./temp/~ammem_n6ll::@@@mdb=aap,rbaapcbib,aaodyssey,bbpix, rbpebib,gmd,mcc,afcesnbib,mesnbib,llstbib.

While this convention took place in Syracuse, prominent members of Albany's abolitionist and free black communities attended and participated in the debates. As this convention occurred toward the end of the period that I analyze, it is an invaluable source because it encapsulates what free blacks across the United States, especially key players in Albany, were thinking as emancipation unfolded on a national scale. This source is accessible through the Library of Congress's website and is therefore within usable reach despite the fact that the majority of this collection is located in D.C.

Wick, Elizabeth. "Address before the African Female Benevolent Society of Troy." In *Pamphlets of Protest: An Anthology of Early African American Protest Literature, 1790–1860,* edited by Richard Newman, Patrick Rael, and Phillip Lapsansky, 114–121. New York and London: Routledge, 2001.

Elizabeth Wick, a prominent educated free black woman from Troy, New York, delivered a speech before the African Female Benevolent Society attacking a rival black female charity organization in Troy, praising the efforts of Society members for helping the local community, and calling on all African American people, men and women, to join the crusade against slavery and prejudice. Wick's speech raises many questions. First, why were there two female African charity organizations in Troy? Second, who belonged to them and how were they able to organize, especially as black women in antebellum Albany? What was their impact on the community they served? How did they interact with leading black abolitionists in the area such as Stephen Myers? This source indicates that the African American communities in Albany, Troy, and Rensselaer were active not only in anti-slavery activities, but also in general philanthropic and reform movements as well. Such activity implies that African American women were just as involved in their communities as men.

Secondary Sources

Ball, Erica L. *To Live an Antislavery Life: Personal Politics and the Antebellum Black Middle Class*. Athens, GA: University of Georgia Press, 2012.

Ball's work is an in-depth study of the politics and print culture of the black middle class in antebellum America. Ball emphasizes the centrality of ideas on respectability and how the desire among black middle-class families to live model lives based upon the ideas of prudence, moderation, and temperance represented a personal desire among them to legitimize their freedom. In addition, Ball challenges the idea that the black middle class targeted didactic literature at lower-class blacks. Rather, she argues that middle-class blacks were writing to each other and rising blacks, instructing members of the lower echelon of the middle class on what constituted proper behavior. This book will be invaluable to me since Albany's black middle-class population was comprised of men and women who would have been involved in this discourse of respectability. I found Ball's book through a session with a research librarian.

David Brion Davis, *Inhuman Bondage: The Rise and Fall of Slavery in the New World*. Oxford: Oxford University Press, 2006.

Davis's work is a synthesis of historical scholarship on slavery and abolitionism in the Atlantic world. He takes prevailing arguments in the historiography of slavery and abolitionism and assesses the arguments and their merits in an overarching narrative. This project deals with that narrative and with abolitionism in general. Davis's work, as the master narrative of slavery and abolitionism, establishes the foundational knowledge needed to complete this project.

Carpenter, Daniel, ed. *The Abolitionist Imagination*. Cambridge, MA: Harvard University Press, 2012.

The Abolitionist Imagination is a published compilation of lectures given on the topic of the abolitionist movement as a component of the Alex de Tocqueville Lectures on American Political Studies at Harvard University. The format of the book presents Andrew Delbanco's lecture-article, *The Abolitionist Imagination,* and is followed by commentaries on Delbanco's approach to abolitionism from the other contributors. Written within the context of the 150th Anniversary of the Emancipation Proclamation, this book offers a current introduction to the historiographical questions that drive the leading historians of antebellum and Civil War African American history and will help frame my investigation of the African American experience and anti-slavery activism during the antebellum period. Delbanco defines abolitionists as people who perceive the world divided into the dichotomy of good versus evil. In the case of antebellum American abolitionists, this evil was primarily slavery and abolitionists wanted it completely eradicated. Because of the rigidity of the abolitionists, Delbanco views them as the catalyst of the American Civil War. He pinpoints their vociferous call for the immediate end of slavery as the reason Southerners could not differentiate the anti-slavery Lincoln from abolitionists during

continued on next page

continued

and after the election of 1860. The other contributors in this book largely disagree with Delbanco. Primarily, John Stauffer and Manisha Sinha deconstruct Delbanco's argument that abolitionists caused the Civil War by detailing the aggressiveness of pro-slavery Southerners and their use of government power to protect slavery's existence and expansion. Stauffer and Sinha contend that abolitionists did not take a middle ground because there was no centrist position to take, especially after the 1830s saw the growth of pro-slavery fervor among Southern intellectuals and political leaders.

Ernest, John. *A Nation within a Nation: Organizing African-American Communities before the Civil War*. Chicago: Ivan R. Dee, 2011.

John Ernest explores the creation of African American fraternal and community organizations throughout the North in the decades prior to the American Civil War. His work examines how African Americans used these community organizations to create their own cultural space and separate communal identity. Ernest's work connects with Erica Ball's study of African American print culture, *To Live an Antislavery Life*, since both examine how African Americans used the organs of their own community organizations to promote an antislavery agenda and find support among each other. Even if Ernest does not address Upstate New York, his work provides needed background and context about African American community-building in the antebellum period.

Gellman, David Nathaniel. *Emancipating New York: The Politics of Slavery and Freedom, 1777–1827*. Baton Rouge: Louisiana State University Press, 2006.

Focusing on the political struggle for emancipation in New York State, Gellman's account takes on the political debates between New York leaders as well as examining public opinion and public discourse on emancipation and its implications. Gellman's work details the way that New York's (white) public approached the issue of slavery and African American freedom in the fifty years before this project's exploration of the African American community in the Capital Region. His work provides context to these debates and outlines how and why New York decided to emancipate its slaves in 1827.

McDaniel, W. Caleb. The *Problem of Democracy in the Age of Slavery: Garrisonian Abolitionists and Transatlantic Reform*. Baton Rouge: Louisiana State University Press, 2013.

McDaniel explores the Garrisonian movement and its efforts to use moral suasion to bring about a legislative end to slavery. McDaniel analyzes the Garrisonian movement in an international light and focuses on the evolution of the Garrisonian ideology through Reconstruction. Many Garrisonian abolitionists worked closely with black abolitionists throughout the antebellum period. Since many of Garrison's followers had an affinity with black abolitionists in New York, this book unpacks the philosophy and perspective of Garrison's followers during the antebellum period and serves to help differentiate between Garrison and black abolitionists.

Quarles, Benjamin. *Black Abolitionists*. New York: Oxford University Press, 1969.

Quarles's book is the foundational text for the study of black abolitionists in the antebellum United States. While historiography has developed since this book was published, I feel it is important to know what the historian who began working with black abolitionism has to say. Quarles argues that free Northern blacks were unique to the abolition move-ment because they not only spearheaded it, but also "felt that the fight against slavery was the black man's fight" (viii). While black abolitionists believed in the basic equality of all human beings and saw slavery as a threat to American democracy, like many white anti-slavery Americans, black abolitionists were the preeminent symbol of the struggle, especially since many were former slaves themselves. This text is important to my re-search since it not only provides introductory background information about black abo-litionism, but also established the historiographic questions that have shaped its study.

Polgar, Paul J. "'Whenever They Judge it Expedient': The Politics of Partisanship and Free Black Voting Rights in Early National New York." *American Nineteenth Century History.* 12, no. 1 (2011): 1–23.

Paul Polgar argues that the disenfranchisement of African American men in New York between 1800 and 1830 was a result of party politics rather than a blatantly exclusionary practice based upon race. He uses New York state as a case study to prove that not only was black disenfranchisement in New York a product of party politics, but also that the entire process of black disenfranchisement in the antebellum North stemmed from the rivalries created by the first and second party systems. In defending this claim, Polgar refutes the established narrative that places racial theories of whiteness at the center of white enfranchisement and black disenfranchisement. This case study deals with New York at the beginning of my period and has allowed me to ask how prominent members of Albany's African American community reacted to their disenfranchisement and what it meant to them as political and economic actors in the wider Albany community.

Stauffer, John. *The Black Hearts of Men: Radical Abolitionists and the Transformation of Race.* Cambridge, MA, and London, 2002.

Stauffer's book is an analysis of the lives of Gerrit Smith, James McCune Smith, Frederick Douglass, and John Brown and how these four men, two of them black and two of them white, attempted to redefine the meaning of race in the nineteenth century. Stauffer argues that Smith, McCune Smith, Douglass, and Brown wanted to deconstruct the American view of the superiority of whiteness by demonstrating the common human-ity between whites and blacks. Stauffer frames their crusade to deconstruct nineteenth century racial theory as an effort to give white men "black hearts." This book is useful since Smith, McCune Smith, Douglass, and Brown interacted with each other the most when they all lived in upstate New York. Stauffer's four-person biography serves as a useful introduction to the abolitionist community in New York and the major players who influenced abolitionist work.

Verter, Bradford. "Interracial Festivity and Power in Antebellum New York: The Case of Pinkster." *Journal of Urban History* 28, no. 4 (2002): 398–428.

This article examines the 1811 City of Albany ordinance that banned the celebration of the Dutch Pentecostal holiday known as Pinkster. This holiday had developed as a multiracial extravaganza that enabled poor white laborers and African Americans to express their frustration and discontent with the Dutch aristocracy and Yankee elites who controlled

continued on next page

continued

Albany's politics and economy. While this event occurred before the time-frame of my own topic, it provides a very detailed outline of African American history in Albany in the early nineteenth century. It also raises further questions concerning how long Pinkster was celebrated in Albany after it was banned in 1811 and what a continuation of those celebrations tell us about African American political and cultural resistance and expression in antebellum Albany.

NOTES

1. Erica Ball, *To Live an Antislavery Life, Personal Politics and the Antebellum Black Middle Class* (Athens, GA: University of Georgia Press, 2012).

2. John Ernest, *A Nation within A Nation: Organizing African American Communities before the Civil War* (Chicago: Ivan R. Dee, 2011).

3. Elizabeth Wicks, "Address Delivered Before the African Female Benevolent Society of Troy," 1834, in *Pamphlets of Protest: An Anthology of Early African American Protest Literature, 1790–1860*, eds. Richard Newman, Patrick Rael, and Phillip Lapsansky (New York and London: Routledge, 2001).

4. "Proceedings of the National Convention of Colored People and their Friends, Held in Troy, NY on the 6th, 7th, 8th, and 9th October, 1847," (Troy, NY: Steam Press of J. C. Kneeland and Co., 1847), in *Minutes of the Proceedings of the National Negro Conventions, 1830–1864* (New York: Arno Press, 1969), 6. The term "Negro Convention movement" was used by the reformers and abolitionists themselves to describe their activities. It does not mean that all members of the movement were black, nor is it meant to be a derogatory term. I am using this terminology because it is the way that the people I am studying identified themselves.

5. Andrew Delbanco, "The Abolitionists Imagination," in *The Abolitionist Imagination*, ed. Daniel Carpenter (Cambridge, MA: Harvard University Press, 2012), 23.

6. Ibid., 35–37, 39, 43.

7. Ibid., 44–45.

8. Manisha Sinha, "Did the Abolitionists Cause the Civil War?," in *The Abolitionist Imagination*, 94.

CHAPTER SIX

How Do Historians Write?

Workbook Exercises

❶ Avoiding plagiarism

Many instances of plagiarism occur unintentionally as a result of careless note-taking, hesitant paraphrasing, doubts about using quotations, and lack of knowledge about the rules relating to the citation of sources. Test your knowledge about plagiarism in the following quizzes.

QUIZ 1

1. The published ideas of historians and other scholars are theirs alone and may not be used by others in the development of their own scholarship.	True or false
2. A good way to guard against plagiarism when taking notes is to close your book before summarizing what you have just read in your own words.	True or false
3. If you wish to quote from a source, you must make absolutely sure that you copy the quote exactly, insert the quote within quotation marks, and note down the full citation, including page number.	True or false
4. You should not quote passages that simply provide factual information.	True or false
5. You cannot be accused of plagiarism if you do not know your college's policy on plagiarism.	True or false
6. To paraphrase effectively, you should use the thesaurus option in your word-processing program to replace an author's key words with synonyms.	True or false
7. You paraphrase a paragraph from a website and do not cite the site. Is this plagiarism?	Yes or no

continued on next page

continued

8. You paraphrase a key argument from a journal article but do not cite the article. Is this plagiarism?	Yes or no
9. A friend gives you an essay he wrote for a class the previous year. He says you can use it as the basis for one of your assignments in a different class. You copy some sections and make sure you include the original sources. Is this plagiarism?	Yes or no

Answers to Quiz One

1. False. Historians build on the work of other scholars to enrich our knowledge.

2. True. Keep your book open only to ensure that you copy quotes correctly.

3. True. You need full information to indicate the source of your quote in an endnote.

4. True. Use quotes to support your arguments rather than provide facts.

5. False. You need to study the rules and apply them.

6. False. Instead, think about the ideas expressed and convey them in your own words.

7. Yes. You must indicate the source of all your information, including web sites.

8. Yes. You must indicate the source of your information.

9. Yes. You copied ideas and words from your friend.

QUIZ 2

Read this extract from a published text then read the following excerpts from a research paper and decide whether the excerpts constitute plagiarism.

> "The heritage of women's history in China legitimizes women as the subject of historical research without in any way requiring a feminist critical stance. Thus, viewing women's history as a feminist project is not an automatic move for Chinese historians of women's history."

—Hershatter, Gail, and Wang Zheng, "Chinese History: A Useful Category of Gender Analysis," *American Historical Review* 113, no. 5 (2008): 1404–21, extract on 1419.

1. Gail Hershatter and Wang Zheng argued that women constituted a legitimate subject of historical study in China; they noted, however, that Chinese historians did not necessarily adopt a feminist theoretical framework.[1] [1] Gail Hershatter and Wang Zheng, "Chinese History: A Useful Category of Gender Analysis," *American Historical Review* 113, no. 5 (2008): 1404–21.	Yes or no

2. Women constitute a legitimate subject of historical study in China even though Chinese historians do not necessarily adopt a feminist standpoint.	Yes or no
3. Traditions of women's history in China justify historical research into women but do not require a feminist critical stance.[1] [1] Gail Hershatter and Wang Zheng, "Chinese History: A Useful Category of Gender Analysis," *American Historical Review* 113, no. 5 (2008): 1404–21.	Yes or no

Answers to Quiz Two

1. No. The sentence acknowledges the source of the idea by mentioning the authors, is appropriately paraphrased, and provides a citation.

2. Yes. The sentence is appropriately paraphrased but lacks a citation.

3. Yes. Although the sentence provides a citation, it is inadequately paraphrased, merely using synonyms to substitute for several original words, and fails to provide quotation marks for the words "feminist critical stance."

ACTIVITY: Correct the following citations using the examples of citation conventions in Chapter Six

A. Bibliography

1. Penny M. Von Eschen, 2004. Satchmo blows up the world, jazz ambassadors play the cold war. Cambridge. Mass. Harvard University Press.

2. Vinayak Chaturvedi, editor. "Mapping Subaltern Studies and the Postcolonial," (2000) London, Verso, 2000.

3. David Rieff. "Liberal Imperialism," In Bacevich, Andrew. The Imperial Tense: prospects and problems of an American empire (2003), 10–28. Chicago, Ivan R. Dee.

4. Nazan Maksudyan, "Modernization of Welfare or Further Depriving? State Provisions for Foundlings in the Late Ottoman Empire." Journal of the History of Childhood and Youth 23 (2009); 361–92.

B. Endnotes

1. Linda Colley. Britons: Forging the Nation, 1770–1837. New Haven, Yale University Press, 1992.

2. David Crouch. *Earl Gilbert Marshal and his Mortal Enemies*, Historical Research 87, 237, 393–403, 2014.

3. Price, Alan. (1991) "Edith Wharton at War With The American Red Cross: The End of Noblesse Oblige." Women's Studies 20, 121–31.

4. Leonard, Thomas C. When News is Not Enough: American Media and Armenian Deaths. In Jay Winter, editor, America and the Armenian Genocide of 1915. Cambridge University Press, U.K., 2003.

❷ Writing strong paragraphs

A strong paragraph focuses on one idea that is connected to and supports your thesis statement and the overarching argument of a section of your paper. It begins with a topic sentence that alerts the reader to that idea and makes or is followed by a claim about the idea, offers evidence (including quotes and paraphrases) to support the claim. It clarifies actors and explains their actions, providing enough background information for the reader to follow your narrative and your argument. Finally, it closes with a sentence that interprets the significance of the evidence, that is, brings meaning for your reader. As you construct your paragraph, try to be sure that your sentences are connected logically and transition smoothly.

ACTIVITY: Use the checklist to compare and contrast the following paragraphs about the dissolution of the monasteries in England in the 1530s

---

CHECKLIST

- ❏ Does the paragraph contain a strong topic sentence?
- ❏ Does the paragraph make a claim?
- ❏ Are the actors clearly identified?
- ❏ Are their actions explained? Are cause and effect established?
- ❏ Does the paragraph provide enough context (background information) for the reader to understand actions and consequences?
- ❏ Do the sentences flow logically with smooth transitions?
- ❏ Does the paragraph include a sense of time?
- ❏ Does the paragraph have an appropriate conclusion?
- ❏ Is the source of information appropriately cited?

PARAGRAPH ONE

When Henry was unable to get a divorce from his wife, he no longer followed the Pope. Cromwell continued Wolsey's reforms. His men went to every monastery and convent, interviewed the monks and nuns, and took notes about their wealth. Cromwell published accounts of corruption, greed, and promiscuity in the monasteries. There were rebellions against reform in the north of England, supported by some monks. Henry put them down and dissolved the monasteries. He destroyed them and took their wealth.

PARAGRAPH TWO

As religious communities in England were already in decline at the beginning of the sixteenth century, the great monasteries could not withstand the offensive launched by Henry VIII. When Henry failed in his diplomatic efforts to gain consent from the Pope for a divorce from his first wife, Catherine of Aragon, he broke with Rome.[1] He authorized his first minister Thomas Cromwell to resume a program of religious reform initiated by Cromwell's former mentor, Cardinal Wolsey, in the 1520s. Cromwell's men visited every monastery and convent in England and Wales, interviewed the monks and nuns about their lifestyles, reviewed accounts, and recorded landholdings, income, and financial assets. Soon after the visits began in 1535, Cromwell published spurious accounts of corruption, greed, and promiscuity within the monasteries. At the same time, popular rebellions against religious reform broke out in the north of England. Although most of the religious communities were not involved, some of them supported the rebels, materially and financially. Perceiving the monasteries as both a threat to his power and a source of funds for his ailing treasury, Henry consequently demanded dissolution rather than reform. He confiscated the considerable wealth of the monasteries and ordered their destruction. By 1540, the monasteries had been dissolved.

NOTE

[1] G. W. Bernard, *The King's Reformation: Henry VIII and the Remaking of the English Church* (New Haven, CT: Yale University Press, 2005).

Both paragraphs contain the same basic facts; however, whereas the first paragraph fails to meet any of the criteria on the checklist, the second paragraph meets them all. In a paragraph about the dissolution of monasteries, a sentence about Henry VIII's divorce constitutes an important piece of information but is not a strong initial sentence because it does not introduce the topic of the paragraph. The monasteries are the topic, not the king or his divorce. The second paragraph does offer a strong topic sentence and also makes a small claim. Note that the second paragraph is twice as long as the first, but it contains no extraneous information. The additional length is required to provide context, identify actors (your readers need to know who Henry, Thomas Cromwell, and Wolsey were) and explain *why* they did what they did and *how* they did it. Remember, the bare facts are not enough; you need to establish the causes of actions and their consequences. The second paragraph also includes words and phrases that offer transitions between sentences. For example, the first word "as" connects from a previous (unshown) paragraph. Phrases such as "soon after the visits began," "at the same time," and "consequently" move the narrative along in time. Dates in the second paragraph also clarify chronological development. The second paragraph offers an appropriate conclusion, connecting with the topic sentence. Finally, it is appropriately cited.

ACTIVITY: Revise the following paragraph so it meets the criteria in the checklist

Jews migrated from Europe to the Ottoman Empire after the Ottoman conquest of Byzantium. Conditions for Jews were more attractive. Jews were persecuted in the Byzantine Empire. They were also persecuted in the states of Europe. They were expelled from Spain. They migrated to areas already settled by Jews since the first century CE. They prospered in the great commercial centers of Istanbul, Edirne, and Salonika. Historians dispute the exact numbers.[1] They agree they represented sizable communities comparable to those in the Baltic states. Avigdor Levy argues that these Jewish population movements from central and western Europe to the Ottoman Empire represented "the most important demographic change in the structure of the Jewish diaspora" in the early modern era.[2] Stanford Shaw maintains that the size and wealth of the Ottoman Jewish community made them "not only the largest but also the most prosperous Jewish community in the world."[3]

NOTES

[1] Avigdor Levy, *The Sephardim in the Ottoman Empire* (Princeton: The Darwin Press, 1992); Stanford J. Shaw, *The Jews of the Ottoman Empire and the Turkish Republic* (New York: New York University Press, 1991).

[2] Levy, *The Sephardim*, 12.

[3] Shaw, *The Jews of the Ottoman Empire*, 36.

③ Integrating quotations

Overreliance on quotes suggests that you have not done the hard work of analysis. Experienced historians use quotations judiciously and integrate them carefully into their writing.

ACTIVITY: Use the checklist to compare and contrast the following paragraphs, constructed from the primary source worksheets in Chapter Five. Explain which paragraph makes a more effective use of quotations and why

CHECKLIST

- ❏ Does the author use quotes judiciously or does she rely too heavily on them?
- ❏ Does the author quote mostly from secondary or primary sources?
- ❏ Does the author use quotes to support evidence or to substitute her own words?

❑   Does the author integrate quotes into her text or simply drop them in the paragraph?

❑   Has the author done the work of analysis or has she left the reader to try to make sense of the quotes?

PARAGRAPH ONE

Jules Ferry argued that "the policy of colonial expansion is a political and economic system" that was related to three ideas.[1] He said that France needed export markets because "Germany is surrounded by barriers, because beyond the ocean, the United States of America has become protectionist, protectionist in the most extreme sense . . ."[2] He also said that there was a "humanitarian and civilizing side of the question" and "superior races have rights over inferior races."[3] The opposition was incensed. "Oh! You dare to say this in the country which has proclaimed the rights of man!"[4] Another point he made was that France should seek "compensations for the disasters which we have experienced."[5] And conditions of naval warfare have created "the necessity of having on the oceans provision stations, shelters, ports for defense and revictualing."[6] Finally, he said that France "must also be a great country, exercising all of her rightful influence over the destiny of Europe, that she ought to propagate this influence throughout the world and carry everywhere that she can her language, her customs, her flag, her arms, and her genius."[7]

NOTES

[1.] Jules Ferry, "Speech before the French Chamber of Deputies, 1883," in *Sources of Twentieth-Century Global History* ed. James H. Overfield (Boston: Houghton Mifflin Harcourt, 2002), 8.

[2.] Ibid., 9.

[3.] Ibid., 9.

[4.] Ibid., 9

[5.] Ibid., 9.

[6.] Ibid., 10.

[7.] Ibid., 10.

PARAGRAPH TWO

Jules Ferry, a major architect of French colonial expansion, defended his pro-imperialist stance in a key speech in the French Assembly on July 28, 1883, justifying his policy on economic, cultural, political, and patriotic grounds.[1] He argued that France had a need, a right, and a duty to expand in order to secure its trading position in the world, extend its civilizing influences to perceived lesser nations, safeguard its navy, and promote its greatness. Ferry's concerns about the French economy related to competition from other imperial nations. Germany and the United States had resorted to protectionism

continued on next page

continued

by raising tariffs against French products even as France continued to import from both countries. To protect itself against serious trade imbalances, France was obliged to expand by seeking new markets. In establishing colonies abroad, continued Ferry, France would also restore its prestige on the international stage after recent political and military setbacks. Its recent acquisition of strategic ports would protect its navy by providing refuelling and provisioning points. France's duty to civilize other nations provided an additional rationalization for expansion; however, Ferry's comment that "superior races have rights over inferior races" provoked outrage from his opponents who maintained that he brazenly disregarded French traditions of rights and equality proclaimed in the French Revolution.[2] Finally, Ferry defended his policy with a remarkable call to patriotism, maintaining that France, gendered female, would become a great country as she exported her influence through "her language, her customs, her flag, her arms, and her genius."[3] This rousing appeal to national pride and expansion won applause from politicians on the left and center of the political spectrum, but those on the right remained silent.

NOTES

[1] Jules Ferry, "Speech before the French Chamber of Deputies, 1883," in *Sources of Twentieth-Century Global History*, ed. James H. Overfield (Boston: Houghton Mifflin Harcourt, 2002), 8–10.

[2] Ibid., 9.

[3] Ibid., 10.

Paragraph One is an example of an overly cautious use of a primary source in which the author commits all the faults of failing to appropriately integrate quotes. He relies too heavily on quotes, uses them to substitute for his own words, simply drops a whole sentence as a quote in the middle of his paragraph, and includes quotes in his introductory and concluding sentences. His paragraph contains no topic sentence that would alert his readers to the subject he plans to discuss, and he makes no arguments. He has not done the work of paraphrase and analysis; instead he leaves his readers to guess at the point of the paragraph and the meaning of the quotes. It seems that he has simply read through the source once, highlighted phrases and sentences, and then cobbled them all together in a list of issues without taking care to offer a cohesive narrative with strong transitions between sentences. His approach has also resulted in an overly long list of endnotes. In contrast, paragraph two offers a strong paragraph developed from the primary source worksheet in Chapter Five.

ACTIVITY: Revise the following paragraph so that it meets the checklist criteria

Bahithat al-Badiya countered men's arguments by saying they were at fault. "Isn't it rather men who have pushed women out of work?" she wrote. She wrote that "men invented machines for spinning and weaving and put women out of work." She said that "men took up the profession of tailoring" and that they "established bakeries employing men." As far as clothing was concerned, she had her own ideas. "I think the most appropriate way to dress outside is to cover the head and wear a coat with long sleeves which touches the ground the way European women do." She offered her solutions. They focused mainly on improved education.

❹ Revising your writing: correcting grammar and syntax

Common grammatical errors, unwieldy sentences, and repetitious material mar your work and impair the ability of readers to follow your argument. This exercise is designed to help you recognize and correct such problems.

ACTIVITY: Revise the following paragraph

Grammatical errors are numbered for ease of recognition. Most of the errors listed in Chapter Six of the manual are incorporated here, although not in the order presented there.

In the late fourteenth century, the Ming Dynasty ushered in a period of stability in China. There was (1) still a threat from the Mongols. The Ming maintained strong defenses to the north and began a new program of building. Zhu Di, which (2) became emperor in 1403, ordered the construction of a vast imperial city in Beijing. It represented a new center of power which (3) housed a centralized bureaucracy responsible for administering an immense territory incorporating some two hundred million inhabitants. The Ming Dynasty was (4) stable. It goes without saying that (5) stability allowed trade to flourish. Wealthy urban Europeans constituted an appreciative market for Chinese products, particularly silks and porcelains, which were much in demand in Europe, and Chinese traders exported there (6) goods from prosperous port cities along the southern coast. The merchants' (7) were paid with (8) silver mined in Spanish possessions in south America. This (9) attracted large amounts (10) of European traders and missionaries that (11) were confined to port city's (12). The Portuguese were the first to establish a trading enclave along the coast at Macao. It's (13) modest origins belied its significance. The foreigners (14) reports contained glowing descriptions of the wealth and splendor of Chinese cities. Zhu Di's reign saw the considerable explorations of General Zheng. He sailed across the South China Sea and the Indian Ocean. Zheng's sailing vessels dwarfed those of European explorers, which would've (15) carried far less (16) men. But most (17) were sceptical about contacts with the outside world. Subsequent Chinese emperors halted Chinese expeditions. Fearing that traders would unduly influence Chinese society, the foreigners (18) were stuck (19) in port cities. They (20) saw little that impressed them from outside China.

❺ Formal peer review

Your professor has likely assigned peer partners. When you have completed your first draft, it is time for a formal review. The following template, checklist, and example will help you provide a written review for your peer partner. Remember, your comments should be helpful. Choose your words carefully. Begin and end your review with positive comments.

TEMPLATE

Objective: To help improve your classmate's paper by pointing out strengths and weaknesses that may not be apparent to the author.

Procedure: Exchange papers with your review partner. Read the paper twice, once to get an overview and a second time to read more carefully and provide constructive criticism for the author to use when revising. Answer the questions below, then complete the checklist. Using the criteria and your notes to the questions, develop a two-page response to the paper that will help the author revise. You want to determine whether the paper is clear, coherent, organized, and analytical. Because the paper you are reviewing is a first draft, do not be too concerned about sentence-level issues unless errors in grammar or punctuation appear so frequently that they interfere with your understanding of the text.

Organization

1. Is the paper well organized? Does it have a strong introduction and conclusion? Do the subheads clarify the sections of the text? Is the order of presentation of information logical. Has the author crafted strong paragraphs with clear topic sentences and smooth transitions?

Analysis

2. What is the thesis or overarching argument? Has the author formulated a thesis that she can support? Do you understand it? Is the historiographic section well developed?

3. Is the argument clear and convincing? Does the author provide adequate analysis (not just narrative, description, and summary) to convince you? Does he provide answers to the "how" and "why" questions that offer explanatory potential, or does he simply provide a chronological narrative that lacks analysis? How does the author use sources to support his arguments? Does his use of quotes and examples support the argument?

Context

4. Is the paper well contextualized? Does the author provide enough background information to help you understand the argument and its significance?

Readability/Use of English

5. How readable is the draft? Is the narrative coherent and cohesive? Does it flow smoothly and logically? What, if anything is missing? Comment on grammatical errors only if they seem excessive.

Bibliography and Endnotes

6. Is the bibliographic information correctly cited? Are the endnotes properly cited? Are all the citations mentioned in the endnotes listed in the bibliography, and vice versa? Note discrepancies.

Suggestions for Revision

7. Provide three focused suggestions for improvement.

CHECKLIST

Author and Title:

Reviewer:

Date:

WEAK	ADEQUATE	STRONG	CRITERIA	REVIEWER'S NOTES
			Organization Introduction/ conclusion Paragraph development	
			Analysis Historiography Argument and evidence	
			Context	
			Readability	
			Bibliography and endnotes	
			Suggestions for revision	

EXAMPLE OF COMPLETED CHECKLIST AND TWO-PAGE REVIEW

Author and Title: Jane Watson. "Women and Abolition"

Reviewer: Charles Findley

Date: August 10, 2012

WEAK	SATISFACTORY	STRONG	CRITERIA	REVIEWER'S NOTES
	X		Organization Introduction/ conclusion Paragraph development	The introduction is strong but the paper lacks a conclusion. The narrative just ends so I couldn't decide what to make of it all. Some paragraphs need smoother transitions (see notes on draft). Quotes in places need smoother integration. Too many long quotes. Title too broad.
	X		Analysis Historiography Argument and evidence	Good historiographical discussion. Partial thesis: Three driving factors compelled women into abolition movement: religious fervor, economic development, cultural transformations. Lacks "so what?" Also, these three issues are not explored. Instead Jane discusses opposition to the women. Disconnect between thesis and evidence. Need new thesis? Strong source base. Some claims about the debate on women and power unsupported by evidence (see notes on draft).

WEAK	SATISFACTORY	STRONG	CRITERIA	REVIEWER'S NOTES
		X	Context	Strong background information. I am able to understand development of ideas on abolition during the period and opposition to them.
X			Readability	Many grammatical errors, spelling mistakes, and awkward structures.
X			Bibliography and endnotes	Incomplete. Probably a time issue. Assume this will be taken care of for final paper.
			Suggestions for revision	1. Craft new thesis statement and answer the "so what?" question. 2. Add a conclusion. 3. Read your paper out loud to catch the awkward structures and seek help from the Writing Center with the grammar and spelling.

Comments:

In her paper on the emergence of the women's movement within the antislavery movement, Jane states that three key issues propelled women into the public sphere—religious fervor, economic development, and cultural tranformations. This is a statement, not an argument. Moreover, the paper emphasizes the ideas that shaped the women's movement within abolition and opposition to women's activism from the clergy, other men, and other women. Jane needs to rethink her argument and try to explain the significance of this opposition.

Jane's narrative tells the story of how women for the first time began to form their own anti-slavery societies and how, as the movement grew, two different ideologies emerged within the movement. One group thought that abolition was a woman's moral responsibility, a position that derived from women's moral authority within the home; and the other viewed abolition as an issue of rights. This second group of women fought for an end to slavery on the basis of equal rights and came to support the idea of equal rights for women too. She describes these groups and what they did to raise money and awareness for their cause.

continued on next page

continued

Jane might also want to give the reader some idea about what the women of the period were thinking. She wrote that women were "banned from having a voice in a government in which they thought they were regarded as equals." Did they really think they were regarded as equals? It seems to me that throughout the paper she presents women in the anti-slavery movement as trying to gain equality, which is a contradiction to the quote. An explanation on this might help clarify the overall understanding of the paper.

Finally, Jane delves into the debate on just how much power women should have in society, and the vicious opposition from men, the clergy, and other women. After the introduction of the "three particularly harsh" opponents of women in the movement, she focuses chiefly on the conservative clergy. Her evidence from women's opposition groups and criticisms of other male groups is weak. Also, her paper ends with a discussion of having women admitted as delegates to anti-slavery conventions. She needs to make a stronger connection between opposition and the conventions and their consequences. What did the women achieve? This question should be answered in a conclusion.

All in all, the first draft suggests the possibility of a really strong paper. The reader is presented with a solid picture of the role of women in the anti-slavery movement. With some clarifications, a little more explanation and analysis, and greater attention to grammar and syntax, the paper could be excellent.

⑥ Oral presentation

Presentation of your research gives you a chance to share your findings with a larger group of people, most likely your classmates, perhaps your department, and face questions, comments, and even challenges to your argument. Questions can be useful. They help you nuance your argument or examine an issue you had not yet considered. Always thank questioners and respond to concerns positively. Whether you address the issues they raise in your final paper depends on their relevance, the type of evidence you have found, and the time available. If the issues are relevant and you cannot address them, you should consider raising them in your paper as issues to be pursued in further research.

When presenting your research verbally you need to organize your notes just as you did for your written paper. Presentation demands additional skills, however. Personal behavior in public certainly contributes to establishing or demolishing your credibility. Follow these suggestions for a successful presentation.

Organization

- Create a one-page outline of your key points with key evidence. Include a small number of quotes to support your arguments, but do not rely on quotes to carry your presentation.
- Order your evidence in a logical sequence and be sure to explain details that your audience is unlikely to know.
- Practice your talk several times so that you feel comfortable and will not be obliged to refer to your outline after every sentence you speak.
- Keep to your time limit. If you are given ten minutes to present, practice to be sure that you can complete your delivery within ten minutes.

- If you intend to provide visual images, make sure they are appropriate to the subject matter and not simply distractions.
- If you use PowerPoint slides, do not clutter them with excessive text and never read them word for word. They should serve to provide key points for you and the audience, from which you can launch into an argument, explanation, or discussion.

Delivery

- Speak clearly, at a moderate pace, and loudly enough for everyone to hear. Modify your intonation. Do not mumble and try to avoid interjections such as "like" and "um," and "you know." Pause instead.
- Avoid slang words.
- If your presentation contains foreign personal or place names, find out how to pronounce them correctly.
- If you feel comfortable, move around the room, but not so much that your movement becomes distracting. Do not simply read from your outline with your head down.
- Express confidence and enthusiasm but not overexcitement. Stand tall and upright. Keep excessive hand gestures, facial expressions, and leg movements to a minimum.
- Interact with audience.
- Maintain eye contact.
- Respond to questions politely and as concisely as possible. Think before you answer. If you have to answer "I don't know" or "I haven't thought about it," explain why and try to engage with the questioner on the issue.
- If in doubt about dress, err on the conservative side. It is advisable to avoid supershort skirts, torn jeans or t-shirts, and large areas of exposed flesh.

⑦ A final checklist

You have drafted, redrafted, and revised. In the meantime, you have received feedback from your professor and your peers, and you have had time to reflect on your own ideas. Use the critiques and your reflections to nuance your analysis. As you prepare your final version, use your checklist to make sure you have all the elements of a good paper.

CHECKLIST

Relevant title: ❑ Does your title tell your reader what to expect, and does it actually reflect the content of your final paper?

Introduction: ❑ Does your introduction introduce your particular topic, or is it still too broad?

❑ Does your historiographical discussion show how you build on previous scholarship?

continued on next page

continued

❏ Have you made a clear thesis statement, and does it have explanatory potential?

❏ Are your paragraphs well structured?
- Strong topic sentences
- Clearly identified actors
- Claims with supporting evidence
- Smooth transitions
- Appropriate quotations, well integrated

❏ Does your conclusion explain the significance of your findings?

❏ Is your bibliography complete and correct?

❏ Are your endnote citations complete and correct?

Citation Conventions According to *The Chicago Manual of Style*

Secondary Sources

WORK	BIBLIOGRAPHY	ENDNOTE/FOOTNOTE
One author	Hall, Catherine. *Civilising Subjects: Metropole and Colony in the English Imagination, 1830–1867*. Chicago: University of Chicago Press, 2002.	Catherine Hall, *Civilising Subjects: Metropole and Colony in the English Imagination, 1830–1867* (Chicago: University of Chicago Press, 2002), 191. Repeat: Hall, *Civilising Subjects*. Hall, *Civilising Subjects*, 191.
Several books by same author	Hanioğlu, M. Şükrü. *A Brief History of the Late Ottoman Empire*. Princeton, NJ: Princeton University Press, 2008. ———. *Preparation for a Revolution: The Young Turks, 1902–1908* (New York: Oxford University Press, 2001).	Şükrü M. Hanioğlu, *A Brief History of the Late Ottoman Empire* (Princeton, NY: Princeton University Press, 2008) and *Preparation for a Revolution: The Young Turks, 1902–1908* (New York: Oxford University Press, 2001).
One book by two authors	Hardt, Michael, and Antonio Negri. *Multitude: War and Democracy in the Age of Empire*. New York: Penguin Press, 2004.	Michael Hardt and Antonio Negri, *Multitude: War and Democracy in the Age of Empire* (New York: Penguin Press, 2004).
One book by four or more authors	List all authors	List first author, followed by *et al.*
Edited volume of articles by one author	Clarke, James F. *The Pen and the Sword: Studies in Bulgarian History*. Edited by Dennis Hupchick (Boulder, CO: East European Monographs, 1988).	James F. Clarke, *The Pen and the Sword: Studies in Bulgarian History*, ed. Dennis Hupchick (Boulder, CO: East European Monographs, 1988).

WORK	BIBLIOGRAPHY	ENDNOTE/FOOTNOTE
Edited volume of articles by several authors	Cooper, Frederick, and Ann Laura Stoler, eds., *Tensions of Empire: Colonial Cultures in a Bourgeois World*. Berkeley: University of California Press, 1997.	Frederick Cooper and Ann Laura Stoler, eds., *Tensions of Empire: Colonial Cultures in a Bourgeois World* (Berkeley: University of California Press, 1997).
Translation and edited translation	Fournier, Marcel. *Émile Durkheim: A Biography*. Translated by David Macey. Cambridge, U.K.: Polity Press, 2013. Negri, Antonio. *Books for Burning: Between Civil War and Democracy in 1970s Italy*. Edited by Timothy S. Murphy. Translated by Arianna Bove. London: Verso, 2005.	Marcel Fournier, *Émile Durkheim: A Biography*, trans. David Macey (Cambridge, U.K.: Polity Press, 2013). Antonio Negri, *Books for Burning: Between Civil War and Democracy in 1970s Italy*, ed. Timothy S. Murphy, trans. Arianna Bove (London: Verso, 2005).
Second or subsequent editions	LaFeber, Walter. *The New Empire: An Interpretation of American Expansion, 1860–1898*, 2nd ed. Ithaca: Cornell University Press, 1988.	Walter LaFeber, *The New Empire: An Interpretation of American Expansion, 1860-1898*, 2nd ed. (Ithaca, NY: Cornell University Press, 1988).
Multivolume work	Comaroff, John, and Jean Comaroff. *Of Revelation and Revolution*. Vol. 1, *Christianity, Colonialism, and Consciousness in South Africa*. Chicago: University of Chicago Press, 1991.	John Comaroff and Jean Comaroff, *Of Revelation and Revolution*, vol. 1, *Christianity, Colonialism, and Consciousness in South Africa* (Chicago: University of Chicago Press, 1991.)
Electronic edition	Sexton, Jay. *The Monroe Doctrine: Empire and Nation in Nineteenth-Century America*. New York: Hill and Wang, 2011. Kindle edition.	Jay Sexton, *The Monroe Doctrine: Empire and Nation in Nineteenth-Century America* (New York: Hill and Wang, 2011), Kindle edition, chap. 2.
Chapter in edited volume	Angol, Padma. "Indian Christian Women and Indigenous Feminism, C. 1850–1920." In *Gender and Imperialism*, edited by Clare Midgely, 79-103. Manchester: Manchester University Press, 1998.	Padma Angol, "Indian Christian Women and Indigenous Feminism, C. 1850–1920," in *Gender and Imperialism*, ed. Clare Midgeley (Manchester: Manchester University Press, 1998), 79–103.

WORK	BIBLIOGRAPHY	ENDNOTE/FOOTNOTE
Reprint	Mardin, Şerif. *The Genesis of Young Ottoman Thought: A Study in the Modernization of Turkish Political Ideas* Princeton: Princeton University Press, 1962. Reprint, Syracuse: Syracuse University Press, 2000.	Şerif Mardin, *The Genesis of Young Ottoman Thought: A Study in the Modernization of Turkish Political Ideas* (Princeton: Princeton University Press, 1962. Reprint, Syracuse: Syracuse University Press, 2000).
Journal article with one author	Bossler, Beverley. "Gender and Empire: A View from Yuan China," *Journal of Medieval and Early Modern Studies* 34, no. 1 (2004): 197–223.	Bossler, Beverley. "Gender and Empire: A View from Yuan China," *Journal of Medieval and Early Modern Studies* 34, no. 1 (2004): 197–223.
Journal article with more than one author	Dayton, Cornelia H., and Lisa Levenstein. "The Big Tent of U.S. Women's and Gender History: A State of the Field." *The Journal of American History* 99, no. 3 (2012): 793–817.	Cornelia H. Dayton and Lisa Levenstein, "The Big Tent of U.S. Women's and Gender History: A State of the Field," *The Journal of American History* 99, no. 3 (2012): 793–817.
Journal article in online database	Carole Faulkner. "How Did an International Agenda Shape the American Women's Rights Movement, 1840–1869?" In *Women and Social Movements in the United States, 1600–2000*, edited by Kathryn Kish Sklar and Thomas Dublin. Accessed through Siena College at http://ezproxy.siena.edu:2398/wam2/wam2.help.aspx?dorpID=1001114227#cite/ on May 14, 2014.	Carole Faulkner. "How Did an International Agenda Shape the American Women's Rights Movement, 1840–1869?" in *Women and Social Movements in the United States, 1600–2000*, eds. Kathryn Kish Sklar and Thomas Dublin, accessed through Siena College at http://ezproxy.siena.edu:2398/wam2/wam2.help.aspx?dorpID=1001114227#cite/ on May 14, 2014.
Book review in journal	Carey, Elaine. Review of *Braceros: Migrant Citizens and Transnational Subjects in the Postwar United States and Mexico*, by Deborah Cohen. *Diplomatic History* 37, no. 3 (2013): 619–21.	Elaine Carey, review of *Braceros: Migrant Citizens and Transnational Subjects in the Postwar United States and Mexico*, by Deborah Cohen, *Diplomatic History* 37, no. 3 (2013): 619–21.

WORK	BIBLIOGRAPHY	ENDNOTE/FOOTNOTE
Authored encyclopedic article	Sharkey, Heather J. "Women, Gender, and Missionary Education: Sudan." In *The Encyclopedia of Women and Islamic Cultures*, Vol. 4, *Economics, Education, Mobility and Space*, edited by Suad Joseph, 287–88. Leiden: Brill, 2007.	Heather J. Sharkey, "Women, Gender, and Missionary Education: Sudan," in *The Encyclopedia of Women and Islamic Cultures*, Vol. 4, *Economics, Education, Mobility and Space*, ed. Suad Joseph (Leiden: Brill, 2007), 287–88.
Dissertation	Goffman, Carolyn, "'More Than the Conversion of Souls': Rhetoric and Ideology at the American College for Girls in Istanbul, 1871–1923." Ph.D. diss., Ball State University, 2002.	Carolyn Goffman, "'More Than the Conversion of Souls': Rhetoric and Ideology at the American College for Girls in Istanbul, 1871–1923" (Ph.D. diss., Ball State University, 2002).
Film	*Iron Jawed Angels*. Directed by Katja Von Garnier. New York: Home Box Office, 2004. DVD, 124 minutes.	*Iron Jawed Angels*, directed by Katja Von Garnier (New York: Home Box Office, 2004), DVD.

Primary Sources

WORK	BIBLIOGRAPHY	ENDNOTE /FOOTNOTE
Book	Barton, Clara. *Red Cross: A History of this Remarkable International Movement in the Interest of Humanity*. Washington, D.C.: American National Red Cross, 1898.	Clara Barton, *Red Cross: A History of this Remarkable International Movement in the Interest of Humanity* (Washington, D.C.: American National Red Cross, 1898).
Signed newspaper article	*The Guardian* (U.K.) (List only title in bibliography)	Mark Brown, "Death on the Nile: Mummy Secrets on Show," *The Guardian*, April 10, 2014.
Unsigned newspaper article	*New York Times* (List only title in bibliography)	"Educate Near East, Morgenthau Urges," *New York Times*, January 7, 1922.

WORK	BIBLIOGRAPHY	ENDNOTE /FOOTNOTE
Signed journal article	Telford, Emma Paddock. "The American College for Girls at Constantinople." *The New England Magazine* 24, no. 1 (1898): 10–20.	Emma Paddock Telford, "The American College for Girls at Constantinople." *The New England Magazine* 24, no. 1 (1898): 10–20, quotation on 17.
Document in print collection	Shewmaker, Kenneth E., and Kenneth R. Stevens, eds. *The Papers of Daniel Webster, Diplomatic Papers.* Vol. 2, *1850–1852.* Hanover, NH: University Press of New England, 1987.	Letter, Daniel Webster to Friedrich Carl Joseph Von Gerolt, January 16, 1852, in *The Papers of Daniel Webster, Diplomatic Papers, vol. 2., 1850–1852,* eds. Kenneth E. Shewmaker and Kenneth R. Stevens (Hanover, NH: University Press of New England, 1987), 193.
Document in archival collection	Mount Holyoke College Special Collections, Locke Family Papers.	Diary of Zoe Noyes Locke, 1886–1924, Locke Family Papers, box 1, folder 1, Mount Holyoke College Special Collections, South Hadley, MA.
Document in digitalized collection	Yale University Avalon Project, World War II Papers.	"Atlantic Charter," *The Avalon Project,* Lillian Goldman Law Library, Yale University, New Haven, CT, accessed May 20, 20014, http://avalon.law.yale.edu/wwii/atlantic.asp/.
Document on microfilm	United States Department of State. *Foreign Relations of the United States, Despatches from United States Ministers to Turkey, 1818–1906.* Microfilm edition.	Letter, Henry Elliot to Edward Joy Morris, December 2, 1867, U.S. Department of State, *Despatches from United States Ministers to Turkey, 1818–1906,* microfilm ed. no. 757, reel 21.

WORK	BIBLIOGRAPHY	ENDNOTE /FOOTNOTE
Visual image online	"Mao as God." In Pickowicz, Paul, "Images of the Chinese Cultural Revolution." *University of California San Diego Magazine* 4, no. 2 (May 2007). Accessed June 10, 2012. http://ucsdmag.ucsd.edu/vol4no2/features/posters.htm/.	"Mao as God," in Paul Pickowicz, "Images of the Chinese Cultural Revolution," *University of California San Diego Magazine* 4, no. 2 (May 2007), accessed June 10, 2012, http://ucsdmag.ucsd.edu/vol4no2/features/posters.htm/.
Online news report	"How Addictive Is Sugar?" *BBC News Health*, January 20, 2013. http://www.bbc.co.uk/news/health-21082629/.	"How Addictive Is Sugar?" *BBC News Health*, January 20, 2013, http://www.bbc.co.uk/news/health-21082629.
Interview	Not applicable.	Senator Kirsten Gillibrand, interview with author, 23 April 2013.
E-mail	Not applicable	Senator Kirsten Gillibrand, email to author, 23 April 2013.

Academy: Refers to an institution of higher learning, such as a college or university. It may also mean a research institution or an organization into which members are elected. Academe and academia are related words denoting a community of scholars.

Ahistoricism: Means without history and thus refers to a lack of attention to historical relevance or accuracy. Ahistoricism sometimes stems from ignorance, that is, not knowing the facts, but may also derive from the idea that history is not worth examining because it cannot really tell us anything about the present.

Annotated bibliography: Adds to the bibliographic citation a paragraph (150–200 words) of assessment for each source listed. Different materials require different assessments, but in general a good annotation includes the scope of the book (what the book is about), a brief indication of the author's credentials, the author's thesis, an assessment of the author's evidence, use of sources, and impact of argument, as well as an assessment of the book for the purpose of research.

Bibliography: A list of secondary sources (books and journal articles) gathered for a research paper on a specific topic. The list is presented in alphabetical order of authors' last names and offers identifying information about the book: author's name, full title of book, place of publication, name of publisher, and date of publication. We call this a citation. There are many different possibilities for citations of different materials. In history, the Chicago style is prevalent.

Cause and effect, or causality: Establishing a relationship between actions and events and demonstrating through evidence that a given action led to a specific reaction or event. Just because an action precedes an event does not necessarily mean that it caused it.

Chronological trajectory: Following the order of time from the earliest to the latest. Historians may use dates to establish a sequence of events and organize a narrative based on the passage of time rather than on other criteria.

Collective memory: The shared memory or memories of a group that are recounted and establish an identity for that group, however large or small. Historians are especially interested in how the experiences of individuals come together to establish the stories of larger communities. Some connection between present and past is often used by groups to create a sense of belonging that becomes a shared history.

Cyclical: A cyclical view of history postulates that certain forces recur in cycles to provoke change.

Dialectical: The idea of a dialectic of history is based on the work of theorists Friedrich Engels and Karl Marx who saw historical advancement in terms of struggles between opposing forces based on material conditions. According to them, progress came not in a linear form but through a series of disruptive moments. They viewed class struggle as the principal driving force of history and analyzed the many times in history when an oppressed class had overthrown the dominant class and then become dominant itself, such as in the case of the middle-class revolution against the aristocracy during the French Revolution (1789–1799).

Edited book volume: A book on a particular topic that contains articles or chapters by different authors who have differing perspectives to offer on the topic. The articles are brought together in one volume by one or more editors.

Enlightenment philosophes: French thinkers of the eighteenth century who ushered in a new era of thought based especially on reason. They generally believed in man's capacity to solve problems and improve the political and social conditions around them. Among the most famous of the philosophes were Denis Diderot (1713–1784), who compiled the first large-scale encyclopedia, Voltaire (1694–1778), known for his sharp wit and challenges to organized religion, and Jean-Jacques Rousseau

(1712–1778), who theorized modern concepts of property and political structures.

Historical context: The broader situation in which events unfold. Multiple factors, both directly related and not, shape historical movement and change. Context provides the background information, or setting, for the individuals, events, and ideas you analyze so that the reader can understand the significance of your argument in its time and place.

Historiography: The history of the writing of history. Historical interpretations of the past are themselves historical. They change over time and as historians engage with new evidence from the past and ask new questions that derive from circumstances in the present.

History from below: Focuses on the experiences of the common people. In contrast to traditional narratives that emphasize the roles of leaders and high politics (history from above) in making history, writers of history from below look at how popular protest and culture drive events and implement change. Unlike labor history, however, history from below usually features groups such as peasants and artisans rather than industrial workers.

Humanities: The study of the human experience, especially when undertaken to understand what it means to be human. In higher education, the humanities generally refers to a number of disciplines, such as history, philosophy, literature, languages, art, music, and classics, that seek to document and understand the human world.

Linear approach: Moving forward in one direction following a set series of steps.

Mentalité: The shared mindset of a group of people. Social and cultural historians are often interested in how sets of attitudes or beliefs held by a particular community evolve over long periods of time.

Metanarrative: Grand narrative, or master narrative: a story accepted as universal truth. After the postmodernist turn, a metanarrative came to be understood as a long-standing story providing an apparently unquestionable explanation about an event. Explanations can always be questioned, however, and new interpretations offered.

Monograph: A book on a particular topic written by one author. In the study of history, we use the word monograph or book to indicate that we are talking about a work of scholarship. We do not use the word novel. A novel is a work of fiction. We do not use the word textbook. In a monograph, the author makes an argument about events in the past, presents evidence to defend the argument, and explains its significance to the reader. Because historians engage in debate about the meaning of events in the past, they offer interpretations; they do not "prove" their case. As a work of historical scholarship, a monograph usually includes endnotes, a bibliography, and an index.

Narrative: A form of writing that basically means to narrate, or tell, a story. Although narration is mostly associated with writers of fiction, good historians also need to acquire the art of storytelling. Stories are useful to engage the interest of a reader, particularly in an introduction to a book or article. Historians do not rely solely on narrative, however. Their writing must be driven by argument and interpretation.

Native advertising: Paid advertising that appears to be journalism, similar to an "advertorial" or "infomercial." A native advertisement will resemble a news article, may be published by a news organization, and may show up in results in an online search for news items. The student must look closely for the phrase "paid advertisement" and pay attention to the URL, which may reveal the true source of the piece.

Peer review: Scholarly presses send texts (books and articles) to one or more experts in a given field to evaluate their quality and decide whether they should be published. Student work can also be peer reviewed, that is, shared with other students who offer an assessment and possible suggestions for revision.

Polemic: A controversial argument. Historians may use polemics to establish the validity of their own arguments over those of others by vehemently critiquing opposing positions while offering evidence for the credibility of their own. Unlike debate, polemics does not generally allow for an exchange of ideas but seek to solidify the historian's own perspective or perceived truth.

Primary source evidence: Material gathered from records that were created during the historical moment under examination, such as a birth certificate, a letter, or a photograph, or evidence created after the event that records the experience of someone who lived through it, such as a diary, oral history, or memoir.

Revisionism: A rewriting of history offering different interpretations based on new evidence or rereadings of existing evidence. New generations of historians pose new questions and uncover new evidence or have access to evidence that previous generations could not use, perhaps because of linguistic, political, or financial obstacles.

Romanticist: A follower of the Romantic movement of the late eighteenth to nineteenth centuries. Romantics challenged the faith put in reason during the Enlightenment and called for a return to emotions and intuition. In historical study, Romantics often emphasized the importance of glorifying great heroes and the nation-state over striving for accuracy.

Scholarly journal: A peer-reviewed publication printed several times a year (periodical) to present the most recent scholarship in a given field. Most scholarly (or academic) journals include original articles and book reviews. The articles are distinguished from those in popular magazines by their length (scholarly articles range from six thousand to ten thousand words), inclusion of endnotes, and exclusion of multiple illustrations.

Secondary source evidence: Material gathered from peer-reviewed monographs, essays, and articles written by scholars and published by reputable presses.

Social science: The study of human society and relationships that utilizes methodologies borrowed from the sciences. In higher education, the disciplines of political science, economics, psychology, sociology, anthropology, economics, and sometimes history are housed within the social sciences.

Subaltern: Refers to oppressed people who exist at the margins of society. They generally have no or little access to the power structures controlled by a dominant group. The term comes from the work of Italian Marxist Antonio Gramsci (1891–1937), who used it to describe the working classes and has since been used by postcolonial theorists to discuss colonial subjects who had little voice of their own.

Tertiary sources: Sources considered of third-level significance after primary and secondary sources, such as encyclopedias and bibliographic guides.

Textbook: A book used in many school and college history courses to offer an informative overview of a given subject. A textbook provides information, or content, generally in chronological order. A history textbook usually includes many maps and photographs and illustrations to aid comprehension. It may be written by a single author or by a group of authors.

Transnational history: A concept still being defined. A transnational approach crosses boundaries, decenters the nation, and explores connections between peoples of different nations. At its best, transnational history employs archival materials from more than one national perspective and language source.

Appleby, Joyce, Lynn Hunt, and Margaret Jacob. *Telling the Truth about History.* New York: Norton, 1994.

Arnold, John H. *History: A Very Short Introduction.* New York: Oxford University Press, 2000.

Carr, Edward Hallett. *What Is History?* New York: Knopf, 1961.

Collingwood, R. G. *The Idea of History,* revised ed. New York: Oxford University Press, 1994.

Evans, Richard J. *In Defense of History.* New York: Norton, 1999.

Gaddis, John Lewis. *The Landscape of History: How Historians Map the Past.* New York: Oxford University Press, 2002.

Gilderhaus, Mark T. *History and Historians: A Historiographical Introduction,* 6th ed. Upper Saddle River, NJ: Pearson Prentice Hall, 2007.

Iggers, George G., Q. Edward Wang, and Supriya Mukherjee. *A Global History of Modern Historiography.* New York: Pearson Longman, 2008.

Novick, Peter. *That Noble Dream: The "Objectivity Question" and the American Historical Profession.* Cambridge: University of Cambridge Press, 1988.

Rampolla, Mary Lynn. *A Pocket Guide to Writing in History,* 7th ed. Boston: Bedford/St. Martin's, 2012.

Southgate, Beverley. *History: What & Why? Ancient, Modern, and Postmodern Perspectives.* London: Routledge, 1996.

Tosh, John, with Seán Lang. *The Pursuit of History: Aims, Methods, and New Directions in the Study of Modern History,* 4th ed. New York: Pearson Longman, 2006.

Wilson, Norman J. *History in Crisis? Recent Directions in Historiography,* 3rd ed. New York: Pearson, 2013.

INDEX